Introducing Microsoft® FrontPage™

Kerry A. Lehto and W. Brett Polonsky

with a Foreword by FrontPage Co-Creator Randy Forgaard

Microsoft® Press

PUBLISHED BY
Microsoft Press
A Division of Microsoft Corporation
One Microsoft Way
Redmond, Washington 98052-6399

Library of Congress Cataloging-in-Publication Data
Lehto, Kerry A., 1966–
Introducing Microsoft FrontPage / Kerry A. Lehto, W. Brett Polonsky.
p. cm.
Includes index.
ISBN 1-57231-338-2
1. World Wide Web servers--Computer programs. 2. FrontPage (Computer file) 3. Electronic publishing. I. Polonsky, W. Brett, 1965– . II. Title.
TK5105.888.L44 1996
005.75--dc20 96-18564
CIP

Printed and bound in the United States of America.

3 4 5 6 7 8 9 QFQF 1 0 9 8 7 6

Distributed to the book trade in Canada by Macmillan of Canada, a division of Canada Publishing Corporation.

A CIP catalogue record for this book is available from the British Library.

Microsoft Press books are available through booksellers and distributors worldwide. For further information about international editions, contact your local Microsoft Corporation office. Or contact Microsoft Press International directly at fax (206) 936-7329.

Acquisitions Editor: Casey Doyle
Project Editor: Ina Chang
Technical Editor: Stuart Stuple

For Janell, Gage, and Emma

&

Dad and Mom

—WBP

To my wonderful mom, my terrific family,
the best corps of friends anyone can imagine,
and my faithful Siamese, Kaline.
Also, to the memories of my father and sister.
You all helped me get to where I am today.
Thank you.

—KAL

Contents

Chapter 4 Wizards and Templates 59

Chapter 5 Managing Your Web Site 95

PART 4 The Server End

Chapter 9 Web Servers 237

Appendix: Installing FrontPage 249

Acknowledgments

It's amazing what a huge amount of work can be done by a small group of people in a very short time. A big, hearty "thank you" goes out to all who helped put this book together.

To the great folks at Microsoft Press: Casey Doyle, for providing the spark for the project and helping to smooth out the rough spots; Ina Chang, for superb editing and helping to keep us on track; The Wonderful Bill Teel, for his time spent laboring over screen shots; and Mike Victor, for working on those humongous photos. And as always, we appreciate the help and support of Mary DeJong, Jim Fuchs, and Jack Litewka. Many thanks also to Microsoft's Randy Forgaard for his valuable input.

Tremendous thanks go to all others who helped make this project a success: To Stuart Stuple, for his wise-owl technical editing; The Lovely and Talented David Holter, for his cool illustrations (btw, David, we're only Luddite wannabes); Tami Beaumont, for her spectacular proofreading work; and Lynne Ertle, for her early-on editing help.

Also, special thanks go to Brook and Kelly at Tommy's, for not laughing at all of our buggy-eyed 9-ball shots.

Foreword

One Thursday afternoon in early April 1994, my wife took an urgent phone call from a man on a car phone. He had gotten my name from my MIT masters thesis adviser, and was calling to offer me a job. Thinking he was one of those pesky headhunters, my wife declined to give him my work phone number, but said he could phone back that evening. He was worried about the time delay, but nonetheless phoned back at 7 p.m. and we chatted. The man was Charles H. Ferguson, a renowned computer industry consultant on technology policy and corporate strategy. We met and talked several times over that weekend. His professional references spoke glowingly of him, including a contact in the White House whose only negative remark was that Charles was no longer invited as often to testify in front of Congressional subcommittees because of his impatience with the slow pace of lawmaking. Four days later I quit my job and became cofounder of a software company that within a few months was named Vermeer Technologies, Inc.—after Charles's favorite Dutch painter. As it turns out, Charles's general sense of urgency was extraordinarily justified.

In the beginning, Charles was the idea person, and I was the one charged with filling out the details and helping to refine the goals into tasks that were achievable by a small group of extremely talented engineers in a reasonable timeframe. His central thesis was at once unusually insightful and incredibly ambitious. He had noticed that many companies had spent millions building their own private computer online services—Apple's eWorld, Dow Jones News Retrieval, Bloomberg's Financial Network, etc. Not only were these efforts expensive, but they were incompatible with one another, requiring different client software to interact with each one. They were based on outmoded mainframe-based technology, requiring a computing priesthood to build and maintain them. They were centralized, making it very difficult to access distributed data. Their cost structure was sufficiently high that free services—such as providing online marketing and customer support information—were not economically viable. And finally, such centralized systems were not suitable for private, distributed, internal information dissemination within an organization.

Thus, our goal was to build a standardized, shrink-wrapped infrastructure for online services, architected for interoperability and providing standardized client software and a visual development environment that would allow nonprogrammers to create and maintain a new online service. The idea was that you could walk into a software store, buy our standard online-service server software, buy several copies of our authoring software, and resell the standard online client software to your customers. You could easily create and maintain your online service. Your customers could use the client software to dial in to your service, and then use that same client software to dial in to other online services created with our software. The standardized server software would be architected so that online services could communicate with each other easily. Everything was interoperable, the APIs and protocols would be documented as open standards, everyone would benefit from the increased convenience and functionality of standardized components, and the whole affair would be dramatically less expensive because the development cost would be spread across all customers.

This idea changed dramatically about one month after the company was formed. In May 1994, we got wind that the Internet was starting to be adopted by businesses, and that there was a new infrastructure called the World Wide Web that provided a type of online service functionality on top of the Internet protocols. Mosaic, from the National Center for Supercomputing Applications, had been released five months earlier, and it provided the first graphical user interface for the Web. Netscape Communications Corp. (then called Mosaic Communications) had just been formed in April (the same time as Vermeer), and would release their famous commercial web browser toward the end of the year.

It occurred to us that the Web provided much of what we were trying to achieve: standardized protocols (HTTP) and APIs (CGI), server software that supported those protocols (various web server incarnations from various organizations), client software that supported those protocols (various web browsers), and even a communications infrastructure (the Internet) that was more robust and convenient than we were planning (dial-up to each online service). The big missing piece: a powerful, visual authoring tool for creating, maintaining, and administering whole web sites, including the individual pages that comprise such sites. This became the focus of Vermeer.

We were extraordinarily fortunate to be able to hire the most talented collective group of individuals I have ever met, despite the fact that we yet had no funding (except for direct expenses, covered by Charles) and had asked everyone to take no salary for many months. Andy Schulert and Peter Amstein, both seasoned professionals, were our first two engineering hires and became our two technical team leaders. We were joined by many other engineers, plus excellent marketing, sales, administrative, and executive personnel. Every one of them a consummate professional, every one driven and focused on the task at hand. It was—and is—a remarkable experience for us all.

While Vermeer was driving to ship its first product, the Web became an unprecedented success. Whereas there were only an estimated 10,000 web sites in existence when Vermeer was formed, there were approximately 500,000 such sites one year later, both external sites on the Internet and intranet sites within organizations. By just about any measure—communications traffic, new web sites going up, downloads of web browsers and servers, new Internet subscriptions—the web was growing 20 percent per month, the fastest-growing phenomenon in economic history. It became imperative that any forward-thinking organization have a high-quality public Web site, and internal IS organizations were behooved to seriously explore the use of Web technologies for intranet information transfer and applications.

Vermeer shipped version 1.0 of its product in October 1995, just one week behind schedule. The name of the product, FrontPage, was suggested by Mitch Kapor, the founder of Lotus and On Technology. On the one hand, FrontPage was a great success, winning many industry awards, and praises from customers. On the other hand, during the brief life of Vermeer, web authoring had advanced from a curious backwater to a major focus of some of the largest players in the software industry. Tiny Vermeer, with fewer than 40 employees, suddenly found itself in the hot seat.

At around this time, Chris Peters, a vice president and 15-year veteran of Microsoft, called us up. They really liked the product. They felt we had just the right idea, to focus on building a whole web site in addition to creating individual pages. They liked the fact that FrontPage looked just like a Microsoft Office application. They were impressed that we seemed to be 9 to 12 months ahead of the industry. They wanted to know if we were interested in some sort of relationship, anywhere from co-marketing to technology licensing to the "full meal deal," as he called it—being acquired.

We took a hard look at Microsoft, and were extremely impressed. Microsoft had recently transformed itself into a highly Internet-focused company. They were extraordinarily good at shipping products. And we realized that our efforts would be multiplied a thousand fold by joining Microsoft. So we did.

Almost all of the Vermeer folk joined Microsoft with virtually the entire engineering team moving to Microsoft headquarters in Redmond, Washington. We have just shipped Microsoft FrontPage 1.1. It has been a heady experience, and with the backing of Microsoft's extensive resources, we hope to be even more effective and customer-driven with future versions of FrontPage. Vermeer was formed just two years ago, and the adventure has just begun.

Our mission with FrontPage has remained the same and, if anything, has become even more so as part of Microsoft: web authoring for everyone. Microsoft has Internet Studio and other products for advanced web development, but if you are a nontechnical professional charged with creating or updating Internet or intranet content, FrontPage was designed for you. We hope you will find it productive, instructive, and enjoyable.

Kerry Lehto and W. Brett Polonsky, the authors of this book, share that same mission, to make FrontPage and web authoring accessible to everybody. I spoke and consulted extensively with Kerry and Brett during the writing of this book. We gave them access to some of the earliest builds of FrontPage 1.1, and it shows in the depth and insight of their coverage here. I found this book a very enjoyable and instructive read, and I believe you will too.

This book exemplifies the attitude of most web-site creators: Half the fun is getting there. Enjoy yourself, and may you have great effectiveness and success.

Randy Forgaard
Senior Program Manager, Web Authoring Product Unit
Microsoft Corporation
May 1996

Introduction

Welcome to FrontPage

It's hard to turn around these days without hearing the words "Internet" or "World Wide Web," isn't it? The news media are saturated with stories about the information superhighway, even though the Net and the Web are still in the early stages of development. The 1990s might one day be described as the Decade of the Internet, but in mid-1996 it's estimated that less than 1 percent of the world's population has an Internet connection.

Thus, the Internet has amazing growth potential. Similar to other booms the computing world has witnessed, thousands of companies have formed to search for a piece of the Internet pie. Scores of good Internet-related products are available, but often they are not compatible with each other, or they require programming skills to use or develop applications in. Most of us don't have the time or the expertise required to sort through all the Internet products, learn their pros and cons, and use them in our everyday lives, whether at work or at home.

Microsoft FrontPage aims to make it easy for you to establish a presence on the World Wide Web or create a web site for your organization to use internally. Designed to fit seamlessly into the Microsoft Office suite of applications, FrontPage is the first easy-to-use Internet client *and* server product that allows you to develop an entire web site and connect it to many kinds of servers. All of the programming goes on behind the scenes in FrontPage, so you don't have to worry about it. That means you don't have to be an HTML whiz to set up your own web site. But FrontPage is also robust enough for professional developers who want to toy with the code.

Talk About Easy!

Introducing Microsoft FrontPage is your in-depth, one-stop shop for learning the ins and outs of FrontPage. You'll find out how to develop and maintain a web site with the FrontPage Explorer, develop high-quality web pages with the FrontPage Editor, and run your web site with the FrontPage Personal Web Server or another server of your choice. You'll also learn how to use templates and wizards to create web pages—and even entire web sites—with just a few mouse clicks. And chances are you haven't heard of WebBots, right? WebBots (also called *bots*) are easy-to-use drop-in programs that automatically add functions such as searching to your site, without your having to worry about programming them in.

If every web-site developer were the same, the world would be as boring as a week-long seminar on toenail transplants. Because some of you like to lift the hood and tinker with the code, this book also includes information about more advanced topics, such as adding audio, video, and animation to your sites, and FrontPage's server administration tools and Server Extensions.

A Look at the Book

Part 1, "The Beginning Stages," introduces you to FrontPage; talks about the birth of the Internet, World Wide Web, and intranets; and explains how FrontPage fits into all three scenes. You'll learn some great tips on producing sites for the Web and for your organization's intranet, and you'll learn how FrontPage works in conjunction with Microsoft Office.

Part 2, "Creating and Managing Your Site," tells you everything you need to know about creating and administering web sites in the FrontPage Explorer. In the Explorer you'll see your site in three different ways—in Outline view, Link view, and Summary view. In this part you'll also learn how to use the FrontPage templates and wizards, as well as the To Do List, an inventory of elements that need to be completed in your site.

You can add items to this list, and FrontPage can add items depending on the state of your site. Web-site management, including changing passwords, access privileges, and much more, is also explained in detail in this part.

Part 3, "Page Construction," looks into the FrontPage Editor, which you'll use to create and edit your web pages. Here you'll find in-depth descriptions and procedures describing the elements you can use in the Editor to make terrific-looking web pages, including colored text, tables, frames, character formatting, and much more. You'll find that the Editor is as easy to use as a word processor. You'll also see some hearty content on web-site graphics, how FrontPage uses them, and ways to make them appear faster in a browser. An easy way to add audio and animation to your web sites is explained in this part as well. A detailed look at FrontPage's bots and forms rounds out Part 3.

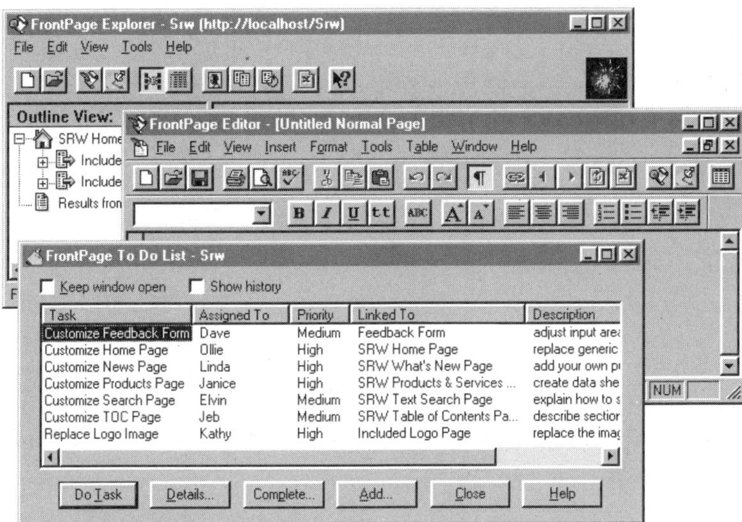

The FrontPage client: You create and manage web sites in the Explorer, craft web pages in the Editor, and keep track of tasks with the To Do List.

Part 4, "The Server End," introduces you to using servers with FrontPage. Here you'll find solid information about the Personal Web Server, which allows you to test web pages and run an intranet on your local computer or network. You'll also learn about the FrontPage Server Extensions, which enable you to link your site to a wide variety of servers that use platforms such as Microsoft Windows 95, Microsoft Windows NT, and various flavors of UNIX.

The Appendix shows you how to install FrontPage on Windows 95 or Windows NT.

A Hands-On Approach

You'll find this book as easy to use as the product itself. In the back is a glossary of Internet and FrontPage-related terms; a similar glossary is provided in FrontPage's online help. Glossary terms in this book appear in boldface—when you come across a boldface term in the text, just look to the glossary in the back to find its definition.

The book also includes Shortcut, Tip, and Warning boxes that provide more detail about the subject at hand. Shortcuts show you ways to save time, such as clicking a toolbar button or using a keyboard shortcut instead of using a menu command. Just as there's often more than one way to bridge a canyon, Tips offer alternative ways to carry out tasks, and they give you additional information on a topic. Warnings caution you against performing actions that can lead to trouble.

By now you've undoubtedly noticed the full-color insert in this book; those pages include tables and graphics that list the keyboard shortcuts and toolbar buttons. You can use those pages as a quick-reference guide whenever you're wondering whether there's a faster way to get things done than using a menu command.

Who Should Read This Book?

Introducing Microsoft FrontPage is designed for both beginning and advanced FrontPage users. Just as FrontPage is designed for nonprogrammers, so is this book. It's ideal for those who want to learn how to use FrontPage to create a site for an intranet, and it's also a great resource for those creating personal or business sites for the World Wide Web.

This book picks up where the product's online help leaves off; within these pages you'll find in-depth descriptions and scenarios about possible uses of FrontPage that draw on the authors' experience in Internet production, writing, and design. We hope this book will help you fill in the holes and answer your questions as you make your FrontPage sites "sights to see."

The Beginning Stages

Chapter 1
FrontPage and the Internet

Sis-Boom-Bah—The Internet Expands

The **Internet** boom of the early 1990s shows few signs of waning as we edge toward the millennium. Millions of individuals are using the Internet to tap information sources worldwide, communicate via e-mail, and "surf" the **World Wide Web.** Businesses are sensing the power of the Internet as well; hundreds of thousands have set up informational web sites, and some have been successful at selling goods and services. The Internet is still a long way from becoming the commercial superhighway it's billed to be. But as Internet-related products get leaner, faster, and more powerful, just like most other products in the computing world, the Internet will continue to expand.

This chapter provides some background on the Internet, the World Wide Web, and **intranets.** It describes how FrontPage fits into the Internet scene, explains how easily it integrates with Microsoft Office, and shows you where *you* might fit into the latest wave of Internet technology.

The Net, the Web: What's the Difference?

The Internet is older than you might think—it's been around for almost 30 years. Considering that the first electrical computer was built just over half a century ago, the Internet is quite the veteran in the computing world. It started out in the late 1960s as a U.S. government communications network, and was used mainly by the government, universities, and other research institutions until the mid-1980s, when it expanded and took on the name "Internet."

So how does it work? When computers interoperate with others within a group, they constitute a network. The Internet is one huge network of computers consisting of thousands of smaller networks worldwide. You might think of a computer as a cell in your body—many similar cells make up your heart, your liver, and so on; each of these organs can be considered networks of cells. All of these networks together make up your entire body, which would be the Internet in computing terms.

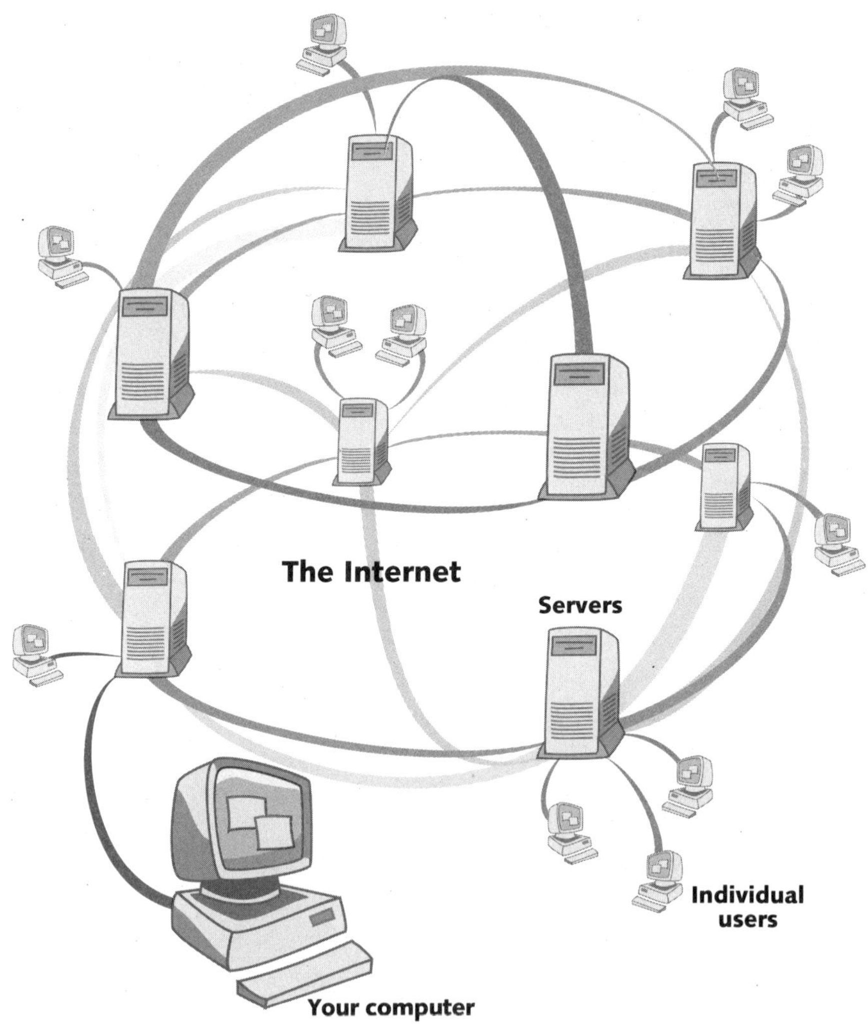

And just as cells must communicate in order to live side by side, so must the computers of the Internet. They must use a common language, and that language is stated in **protocols**—a set of agreed-upon rules governing how they interact. The standard protocols used for exchanging data on the Internet are Transmission Control Protocol and Internet Protocol; the combination of the two is known as TCP/IP. TCP/IP organizes information into tidy little packages before shipping it across the network. Each package contains a portion of the information being sent, along with a description of what the information is, where it's coming from, and where it's heading. Sending data across the Internet is like disassembling a jigsaw puzzle in one room and reassembling it in another room. To put it together again quickly, you have to identify the pieces in relation to each other and put them back together in sequence.

How about the Web? In the late 1980s, when the Internet was growing gradually with the addition of a few major networks here and there, a scientist named Tim Berners-Lee began seeking a better way for his colleagues at the European Laboratory for Particle Physics (known by its French acronym, CERN) to communicate by computer. At the time, the only information that could be transmitted across the Internet appeared as simple text on computer screens. Berners-Lee and his associates created an interface for linking information from various sources. The eventual result was the defining of the **URL**, **HTTP**, and **HTML** specifications on which the World Wide Web depends. Today, Web technology allows creation of a formatted page of information that can be linked to other pages of information and accessed across a network.

In simple terms, the Web is a collection of information that is accessible via **Web browsers**. The first Web browser was Mosaic, developed by the National Center for Supercomputing Applications (NCSA) at the University of Illinois at Urbana-Champaign. The market currently sports more than two dozen browsers, and the number is growing at a fast rate. Currently, several Netscape browsers and Microsoft's Internet Explorer hold the lion's share of the market. A browser consists of a window that displays web pages, and possibly some toolbars and menu commands that allow users to navigate among pages and sites and adjust the browser's settings. Because of the proliferation of browsers and the way that each can be configured to display information in different ways, a web page viewed in one browser can look very different in another browser.

So, Web technology provides a way of displaying formatted pages in a browser; these pages can include graphics, sounds, animation, and other special effects in addition to text. Individual pages can be linked to other pages to provide access to additional information. All of this is transmitted using the physical medium and the protocols of the Internet. That's why many people see the Web as a part of the Internet rather than as a separate technology.

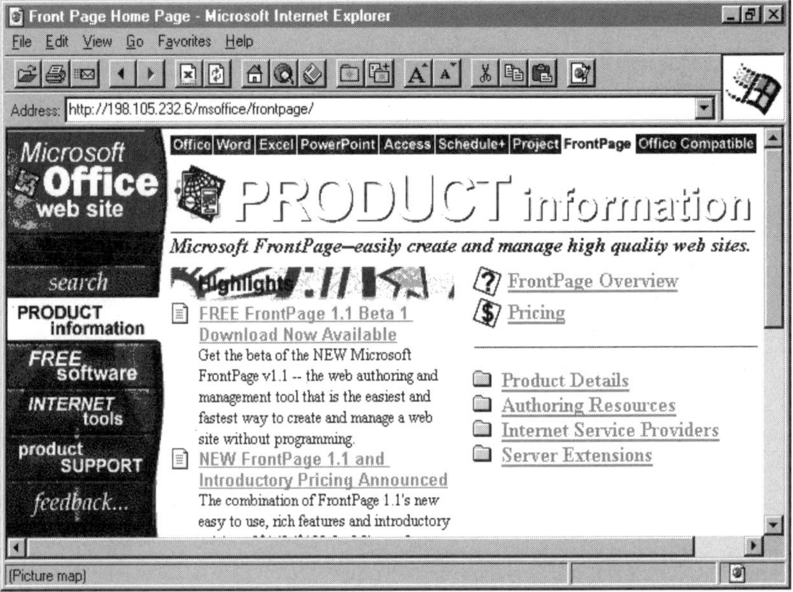

The FrontPage area in Microsoft's World Wide Web site, an example of a page on the Web.

The Web has grown at an incredible rate. Thousands of people have their own web sites, and numerous businesses have put their names up in Web lights. (The term **home page** is often used to refer to a web site; actually, a home page is the opening page of a web site, and it usually has links to other pages.) The Internet and the Web have dramatically changed people's business habits in the last few years; have you noticed that it's now standard procedure to include your e-mail or Web address on your business card?

However, the Internet is criticized for being an ineffective way of conducting business; compared with early hopeful estimates, very little commerce is actually transacted there. One reason for this lies with security issues. Many people are wary of hackers and others who can intercept credit card numbers and other personal information that is sent over the Internet, and they'd rather see more secure encryption methods in place before they send their own information.

Another reason that so little commerce is carried out over the Internet is that most sites are poorly designed. Many sites are too slow, too unorganized, too difficult to read, and so on, and it's easy for a potential customer to move to another site with the click of a mouse. Part of the reason access on the Web can be so slow is that technology is playing catch-up with demand. The Internet infrastructure was not built to handle the amount of information traveling on it now. The solution is to convert the Internet to a network medium that can transmit more information at one time (called a high-bandwidth connection). Unfortunately, such connections are costly.

Until the market dictates that costs come down and that more information travel for less money, we'll have to design web sites for the existing infrastructure. Those sites will need to be streamlined to download into a browser quickly, yet they'll still need to be professionally designed and frequently updated—all of which is easy to do with FrontPage. In the next chapter you'll get some pointers on how to create a successful web site *now*. With the help of FrontPage, yours can be a success.

Where do intranets fit in? Now that you know what the Internet and the World Wide Web are, you might be wondering what an **intranet** is. The key lies in the prefixes: *inter* (between or among) and *intra* (within). The Internet connects computers from a variety of different organizations; an intranet (sometimes called an *internal web site*) connects computers networked within a single organization. The term *intranet* also implies that the network supports Web technology. Intranets can be linked to the Internet, but they don't have to be.

Intranets are still relatively young; you'll be hearing much more about them in the next few years as businesses realize their communications potential. They're a fascinating and efficient way of communicating within an organization. In terms of communication effectiveness, intranets might do for businesses in the next few years what e-mail has done in the past few years.

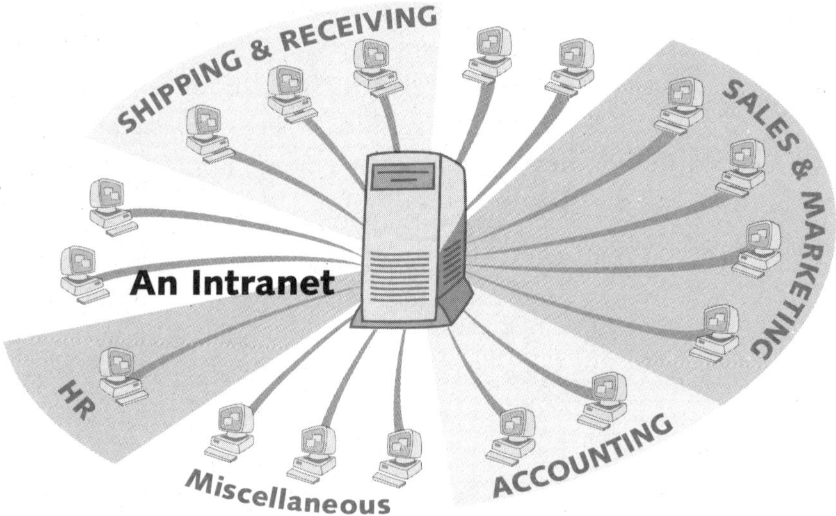

Typically, the networked computers on an intranet are at one location (e.g., in one office setting), and they can span several departments within an organization. But an intranet can involve remote locations as well. Suppose Cascade Coffee Roasters has branches in Washington, Wyoming, and Wisconsin, and all the company's computers are networked. The company can set up an intranet so that its employees can communicate and share information via computer. This sounds just like a typical network, but what makes it an intranet is that its communication is graphically based, using Web technology.

FrontPage on Center Stage

Web-site developers will find a "cast of thousands" when it comes to choosing a web authoring tool, and competition between products is driving their improving quality. The choices include HTML editors that require HTML mastery; graphical web authoring applications that require some HTML expertise; and the star performer, FrontPage, which requires very little or no HTML knowledge. FrontPage has entered the scene by offering a powerful product that makes it extraordinarily easy to develop professional-looking web sites for the Internet or intranets. FrontPage is unique in that it exploits the current wave in computing—client-server computing—which makes it easy to integrate into many computing systems. Let's dig into that a little deeper.

Client-server computing: It's hip, it's hot. Client-server computing is the latest buzzword in business computing. In a client-server system, a **server** is a machine that provides programs or data that can be used across the network. A **client** is a machine that takes advantage of these resources. In many cases, the server is a more powerful computer and the client is a more typical desktop system. For example, suppose the invoices received at Cascade Coffee Roasters are all stored in a database on the server. In a client-server invoice system, you input the information on a client computer and store the information centrally on the server when you complete the invoice. This way, an unlimited number of client workstations can be hooked up to the server, and each can have access to the same data.

FrontPage works in a similar way; in fact, it contains both a client and a server. Its client software consists of the FrontPage Explorer, Editor, and To Do List. The Explorer allows you to view and administer your site in several different ways. You create new pages and edit existing pages in the Editor. The To Do List displays an inventory of work that is yet to be completed in your site. As you build your site, you can add items to the To Do List, and FrontPage can also add items. Later chapters will describe these features in more detail, along with other client-side features such as **wizards** and **templates**.

The server side of FrontPage is the Personal Web Server. You can house the server on a computer on a **local area network** (LAN) or a **wide area network** (WAN) running TCP/IP and instantly make that network into an intranet. You can even house the Personal Web Server on the same computer you're using for the client software, but it's a little slower that way and therefore not recommended. If you need to create or edit new pages in your site, you can do that on any client computer that's linked to the server—even if your client-server setup spans half-way around the world.

All intranets require a server to store central data and perform central operations. Because FrontPage is packaged with its own server software, you might be able to avoid spending hundreds or even thousands of dollars on a server for your organization. The Personal Web Server is best used as a low-volume server, and it's ideal for developing and testing your sites internally. It's not recommended for use as a World Wide Web server, however—if you're expecting high volume for an intranet or Internet server, you'll probably want a more powerful solution, such as any of the leading web servers on the market today. For more information on the Personal Web Server, see Chapter 9.

FrontPage also provides Server Extensions to enable any of the leading web servers on the market today to communicate with FrontPage. If your organization already uses a high-end web server, the Server Extensions can be dropped in to provide seamless communication between FrontPage and the server. You'll find more details on the Server Extensions in Chapter 9.

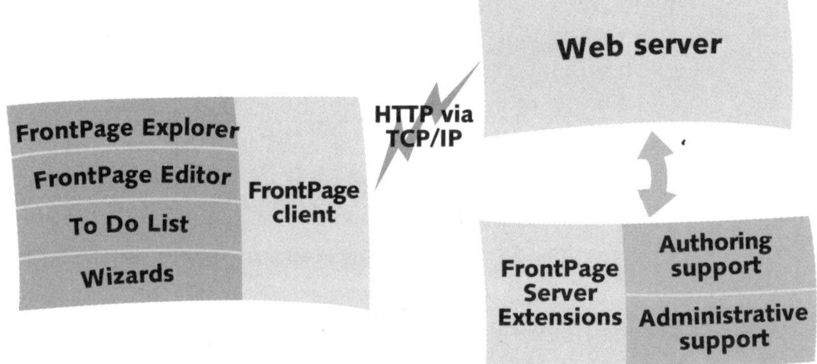

Seamless Integration with Microsoft Office

Microsoft has grown immensely in the 1990s primarily because of its success in the operating systems and business applications arenas. Now its goal is to make all of its products Internet-compatible, since the Internet is becoming the road of choice for worldwide electronic communication. The Microsoft Office suite of applications, which includes Microsoft Word, Excel, PowerPoint, and Access, is the best-selling suite of office applications on the market. The content creation capabilities of Office combined with the web-site management and web-page creation features of FrontPage provide an ideal way to create web sites. Imagine the possibilities:

- You can include a link on your web page to a self-running animated presentation created in PowerPoint. With a click of the mouse, users can launch a PowerPoint viewer to see the presentation from their computers.

- With the Word viewer, users can view a beautifully formatted Word document from a link on your site. They don't have to view it in standard HTML fonts and text sizes.
- You can store an Excel spreadsheet on your server and display it as part of your web site. To show any numbers or tables on your pages that you don't feel like recreating, you can simply link to them and use an Excel viewer.

No longer is the viewing of these files dependent on the user's browser settings. So often a site will include a nicely formatted document in HTML for viewers to read, but if a user's browser settings are different than what the document was intended to be viewed in, the document might look different. However, if a site includes an Office document, that document can look the same (or very similar) to every user who views it. How? With Office viewers.

As inexpensive as it gets Office viewers are separate applications that users can download for free from Microsoft's web site. As of this writing, viewers are available for Word, Excel, and PowerPoint. If you have a viewer installed, you can click on a link to a Word, Excel, or PowerPoint document in any web site, and the document appears as a read-only file in the viewer. You can configure a viewer to show and hide various toolbars, annotations, bookmarks, format marks, and so on. You can also print the file that appears in a viewer. More specific information on using the viewers is included in the file README.DOC, which you receive when you download and set up the viewer from Microsoft.

To download the viewers, connect to Microsoft's web site at http://www.microsoft.com. From the Select A Product drop-down list at the bottom of the page, select Internet Products, and then click the Go! button. You'll find directories for the viewers on the Internet Products page; follow the instructions to download the files.

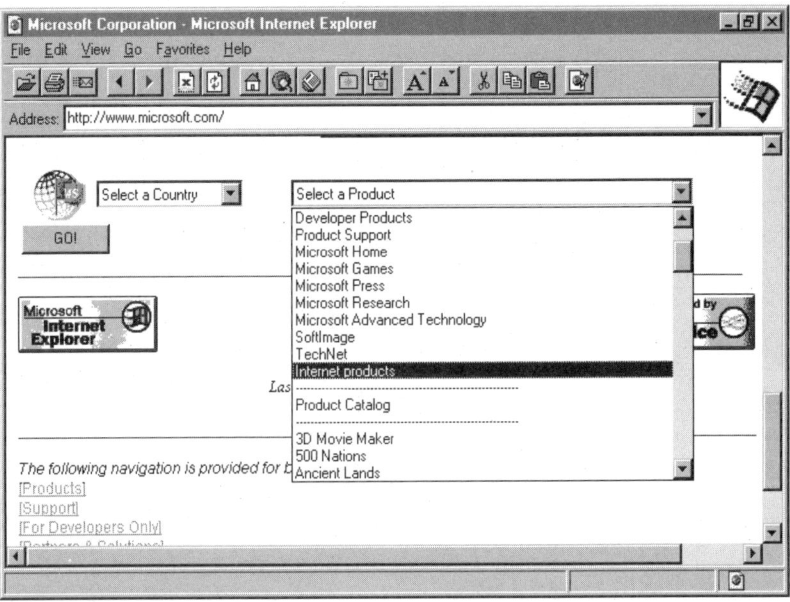

To reach the Internet Products page in Microsoft's Web site, select Internet Products from the Select A Product drop-down list and click the Go! button.

Of course, if you're viewing a site in a browser and you already have Office installed on your machine or network, the appropriate application will start when you click on a link to a Word, Excel, or PowerPoint file if your browser is configured to do so. Just as in a viewer, the file will open in read-only format, and you cannot edit it.

Ready for launch! When you're building or updating your web site, you can edit Office files from within the FrontPage Explorer so you don't have to concern yourself with opening the Office application separately. When you open a document created in Word, Excel, or PowerPoint from the Explorer, FrontPage automatically launches the appropriate application so you can edit the document in its native environment. If you update the document using the Office application, you can import the modified document back into the site with the click of a button—the Import Now button in the Import File To Web dialog box, which you open by choosing the Import command from the File menu in the Explorer.

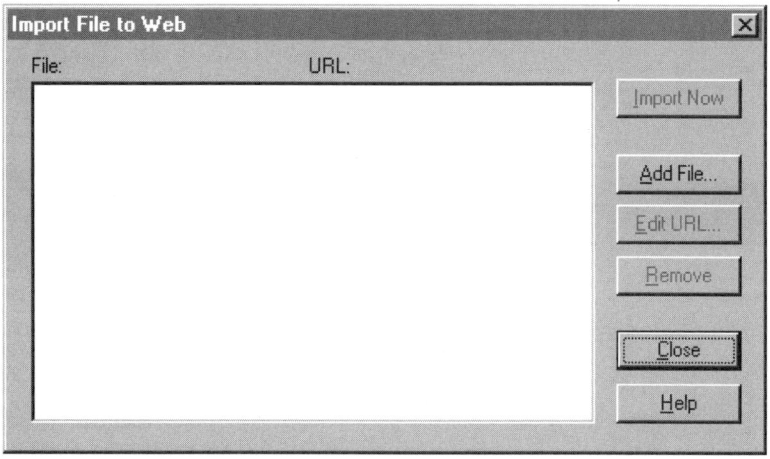

You can add or update an Office document in your FrontPage web site by using the Import File To Web dialog box, which you reach by choosing Import from the Explorer's File menu.

If you forget to import the modified document, FrontPage automatically prompts you to do so when you exit FrontPage.

Let's turn this puppy around: What if you're in Word, Excel, or PowerPoint and you want to work on a document that's in your web site? FrontPage takes care of that by offering add-ins that provide Open From Web and Save To Web commands on the Tools menus of these three applications. For example, suppose you keep your inventory on an Excel spreadsheet in your web site. You can open the spreadsheet from Excel using the Open From Web command, update the document, and then save the document back to the web site using the Save To Web command. Pretty nifty, huh, Toto?

You can obtain these add-in features for Word, Excel, and PowerPoint free from Microsoft's web site. They're located at http://www.microsoft.com/frontpage.

Office look and feel FrontPage sports the look and feel of Office. Toolbar buttons, menu commands, dialog boxes, and keyboard shortcuts are designed to be instantly recognizable by Office users.

Office spell-checker None of us has ever won a national spelling contest. (If you have, you can leave the room.) But have you ever noticed the number of misspellings on web pages? It can be thigh-slapping funny to see, but it's also a very sad sight considering that the information on the Web is there for all the world to see. A misspelling in an intranet can be even more embarrassing. Suppose you misspell your boss's name or title in a corporate bio. That could get you fired—or worse, your boss could force you to make the next two weeks' worth of bagel runs.

FrontPage might save you a bunch of bagel bucks by including the dictionary and suggestion routines available in Word. No spell-checker can substitute for good spelling knowledge, of course, but you might as well use the best if you're going to rely on one!

Coming Up

Now that you've got a better idea of how FrontPage fits into the Internet and intranet scenes, it's time to plan your first web site. You'll learn how to do this in Chapter 2, and you'll also learn how to make your sites ones that viewers won't want to leave.

Chapter 2
Web-Site Development

Planning a Stunning Site

Now it's time to move all those creative thoughts out of your brain and into a plan for your web site. Planning a web site can involve a substantial amount of work, but it certainly doesn't have to be *all* work—if you have fun in the planning stages, you'll probably end up with a better site. With FrontPage, you don't have to be a **webmaster** to create a site that visitors will return to time and again. The kind of site you create, and the kinds of information you include in it, depend on your target audience. This chapter will discuss sites targeted toward an Internet audience, and then it will look at planning a site for an intranet within your business or organization.

Surf on the World Wide Web today, and you'll find some very good sites—ones that download quickly, are pleasing to the eye, organize information into well-defined compartments, allow for easy navigation, and are easy to read. These sites simply *invite* you to come in, take off your shoes, stay a while, have some fun, and learn something new. If you stay a long time at a site without realizing it, it's probably one of the better designed sites on the Web.

Unfortunately, such sites are rare. Even though many sites proudly boast that they receive many more hits than their competitors, the number of visitors really isn't a good indication of how good a site is. How long a viewer stays at a site is a much better indicator. In the coming years, when the Internet is used more for commercial purposes, the only factor that will really matter is how much the site helps in generating sales of goods or services.

Guidelines for a Good Site

The best web sites are ones that look appealing, get the message across succinctly, and don't make users wait too long for information to appear on their screens. The following are some guidelines for creating a successful site:

- **Have a clear purpose.** What are your goals? Just to get on the Web? If so, you're like many others, and you shouldn't be surprised if your site ends up like most others. Make your goals as specific as possible. Perhaps you want your site to show off your company's products. That's all fine and dandy, but consider *how* you want to show off those products. How do you want your products positioned in the Web market? Asking these deeper-level questions will result in a clearly defined goal. Without a well-defined goal, your site is doomed for a trip to the Internet graveyard.
- **Always keep your audience in mind.** Who is the primary (and secondary) audience for your site? How old are they? What do they do for a living? How much time do they have to look at your site? For every piece of information, every graphic, and every content decision you make in your site, ask yourself, "How will the audience react to this?"
- **Use items that download quickly.** The number-one reason that people leave a site quickly—or don't visit a site at all—is that it takes too long for the information to appear on their screens. Large, cumbersome graphics cause users to twiddle their thumbs, and it's all too easy for them to click a Stop button in their browser to stop downloading your site. Use small graphics in your site, and give your users the option of downloading larger ones. For more ideas on how to streamline graphics in your site, see Chapter 7.

- **Make your site visually appealing.** You've undoubtedly seen some plain, boring sites on the Web. What makes them plain? Lack of color and lack of variation in text and heading sizes, for starters. You've probably seen some cluttered and chaotic sites as well, ones that use too many fonts in too many sizes and colors.

  Try to strike a balance: Make your text large enough that viewers don't have to squint to read it. Don't clutter your pages with too much information. Organize your information or your images in a table, or use frames for similar purposes. For information on the mechanics of formatting text, tables and frames, see Chapter 6.

> **TIP**
>
> We often think our sites are right on target with our intended audiences, but it's easy to miss the mark. To avoid this, be humble and try to have your site plan and content reviewed by as many people as possible, especially potential members of your audience. This step is critical but often overlooked.

- **Organize your content in intelligent ways.** Maybe by now you've heard the saying that "content is king." It's true. How many times have you visited a site and thought, "There's nothing here"? Perhaps some good content is buried deep within the site, but the only viewers who will "dig it up" are those who randomly come across it. If you have some information you feel your viewers *must* see, include it on the first page of your site. Don't bury it in hidden pages. The information should stare them in the face as it appears on their screens.

  Organize secondary material into groups of related information. For example, suppose you're setting up an online catalog for a music store. Would you list your jazz CDs and rock CDs in the same section? Of course not. This is a glaringly simple example, but if you look at all your information in terms of

> **TIP**
>
> Including a map or overview of your site can save your audience the frustration of searching your pages for specific information. Describe the sections of your site, and provide links to those sections. And make this overview available everywhere in your site.

appropriate categories, you'll have a much better organized site than most of the ones out there.

- **Include appropriate navigation buttons.** On every page of your site, allow your viewers to click a button to return to the **home page.** If your viewers are buried five levels deep into a site, they should be able to click a button to get back to the first page so they can start over if they need to. If they're stuck using the Back button on their browser, chances are they'll get frustrated and leave your site.

  The bottom line is: Make it easy for viewers to move through your site. When designing your site, ask yourself whether you'd want to move between certain points. Ask that question, and you'll come up with good ways to make your viewers happy little surfers.

> **TIP**
>
> Another good way to treat your audience kindly is to provide a searching mechanism so they can find information in your site quickly. With FrontPage's Search bot, you can add a complete search engine to your site in just a few seconds. To find out how, see Chapter 8.

- **Consider charting the flow of information on paper *before* you build your site.** This is particularly helpful if you have a difficult time visualizing information. Start with your home page and work down. This visual representation can help you "see" your content, organize it more clearly, and avoid major reorganizations as you build your site. Once you begin to build your site, you can see a graphical representation of it on your computer screen in the Explorer. This helps you see your site's structure more clearly, and might lead to new ideas for improving the structure and flow. For more information on the Explorer, see Chapter 3.

- **Test your site thoroughly.** The Web audience uses a colossal number of different browsers, each of which can present your site quite differently. Test your site using as many different browsers as you can, on different platforms (such as Windows 95, Windows NT, and Macintosh), and at different modem speeds. It's not unusual to find a navigation button properly appearing in a corner of a page in one browser but in the middle of a page in another browser. We're not kidding, either; this happens all the time. Wise owls test every page and every link in their sites using several different browsers.

Planning a Site for an Intranet

If you're in charge of developing a site for an intranet at a business or other organization, you've got no small task ahead of you. It can be a major undertaking that involves deciding what the site will be used for, what kind of content it will show, how it will look, who will use it, and who will have access privileges to change it. Up-front planning is the key to developing a successful site.

Depending on the size of your company, the site can be large and can involve many people in charge of different sections. FrontPage makes managing sites on an intranet easy; see Chapter 5 for details.

Does your organization need an intranet? Perhaps your business or organization already has a network in place, and it's easy to route files and view others' documents and presentations. But the process really is cumbersome; you have to connect to a network location, move the files to your computer or open them on another computer, launch the appropriate application to help you view and manipulate the files, and so on. Plus, when you're looking at a network location, all you see is a list of files. There's little presentation involved. And unless you know where to look for a specific file, it can be difficult to find a file on a network, especially if you don't know the exact filename.

Intranets allow this sharing of information in a visual forum. Suppose you want to find out your company's sales information for the previous quarter, which is contained in a Microsoft Excel file. In a typical network setting, you have to find the appropriate file, open it, and then view the information in Excel on your own computer.

With an intranet, company personnel can access information without having to memorize a network location. All they have to do is find the company sales information page on the intranet and then click on a link to open the file from the network. If they can't find the sales information page easily (which would be indicative of a bad design), they can search for it in a few seconds using a web search engine.

Servers

If you're setting up a site on an intranet, you'll need a web server to run it on. Just as with traditional network servers, it's often necessary to dedicate a single computer for use as a web server. The faster and more powerful the computer, the better your site will run. Fortunately, the web server market is wide open and getting more competitive all the time.

The web server you use will depend on the amount of traffic you expect to see. If you have a relatively small company, you might be able to use FrontPage's Personal Web Server as your sole web server. The Personal Web Server can't handle a high amount of traffic, however, so in most cases you'll want to choose from the growing market of servers. Microsoft recently released its Internet Information Server (IIS), which has received excellent reviews from several trade publications. IIS runs on Microsoft Windows NT Server; if your company is running Windows NT Server, you might want to try it out. You can download IIS from Microsoft's web site (http://www.microsoft.com) for free.

Security

You can use your network security features to protect many of the files used by your intranet. After all, these files are stored on the actual network. For example, if you want only certain personnel to be able to change information in files used on an intranet, you can restrict access at the network level.

In addition to any network security, FrontPage allows three levels of access to a web site. The web server you use for your intranet also might interact with these security features.

- End-user access (browsing).
- Author access (accessing, updating, and maintaining the site using FrontPage).
- Administrative access (updating security permissions). Administrators also have all author access rights.

With FrontPage, you can limit access to only those people who have permission to edit the site or to update other access privileges. For more information, see Chapter 5.

Content

A company or organization can harness the power of an intranet in many ways:

- **Make documents and other corporate information widely available.** Companies can use an intranet to house policy manuals, training manuals, company schedules, product data, and the like. This can save tremendous amounts of time, effort, and money.

  For example, suppose Linda works in the Bed & Bath department at a department store, and she needs specifics on what kind of perfume the store sells so she can propose a bundling of towels and perfume for a holiday promotion. Instead of calling the head of the Perfume department, who would pass the request to an assistant, who would then direct Linda to a file on the network containing pricing, availability, and sales information, Linda can simply go to the store's intranet and access that information herself.

- **Update your employees on company news.** An intranet is an ideal place to put news about your company. If you want to provide employees with information about the annual picnic, you can put it in one place for all to see. An intranet is also an ideal place for gathering your company's press releases for employees to read.

- **Use the intranet for in-house promotions.** Even though an intranet's primary purpose is to streamline information flow within a company or organization, that doesn't mean it can't be fun to use. Combining serious work information on an intranet with something fun, such as an in-house contest, can lighten up the workplace and might make employees want to use the intranet more.

- **Connect your intranet with the Internet.** Through the use of security measures such as **firewalls** and **proxy servers**, you can link your intranet to the Internet and still keep the intranet secure. You can provide links to your competitors' web sites to keep your employees up-to-date on their goings-on, or to other useful and timely information your employees might need to know. If information about your company appears on others' web sites, you can link to those locations so your company's personnel can see what the hoopla is about.

Questions to Ask

When creating a site for an intranet, you should pay attention to the same issues of design, organization, and navigation that you need to address when building a site intended for the World Wide Web. In addition, if you can address the following intranet-specific issues up front, you can save a great deal of trouble.

- **Audience** What members of the company or organization will have access to the site? What kinds of information will the site include? Will all of the information in the site be accessible to everyone?
- **Work in progress** Who will update the site? Who will be in charge of which sections and which tasks? Spell this out as clearly as possible before creating the site, because as you go along you'll probably discover more tasks that need to be performed regularly by *someone*. FrontPage makes assigning tasks easy with the To Do List, which is explained in detail in Chapter 5.
- **Keeping it under control** How will you keep the site from getting out of control? The key to controlling the size of a site is controlling who can add material to it. If everyone in your company can add pages, change information, add links, and so on, your site will seem like a runaway freight train bound for the bottom of Whiskey Gulch. You can control these privileges by setting author, end-user, and administrative permissions. You'll find more details on this in Chapter 5.

Coming Up

Now that you have an idea of what you can do with a web site, it's time to learn some specifics about how to use FrontPage to create your site. Chapter 3 starts you out on that journey with a detailed look at the FrontPage Explorer.

PART 2

Creating and Managing Your Site

Chapter 3
Inside the Explorer

A New Way of Viewing a Site

Okay, web-site designers, it's time to 'fess up. How many of you have posted sticky notes on the wall or laid note cards on the floor in an attempt to map out a site? How many times have people dropped by your office and said, "Look at that wall now, Pete! You oughtta buy stock in 3M!" How many times have you penciled out your site on paper, drawing squares, links, arrows, and small letters that you can't even read with a magnifying glass?

And as for you beginning web-site developers, do you wonder whether you've gotten in over your heads with all this web stuff? When you put your ideas down on paper and chart out a few pages, it seems pretty straightforward. But when you begin drawing **links** between all your pages, it can seem as though you're climbing Mt. Everest with a day pack, one bandage, and a bag of chips.

Several good software flowchart programs are available that allow you to build a map of your site and manipulate it as you wish. However, if you use one of those programs, you still need to create your site with a web authoring tool, which means you have to input the data in two separate programs. Wouldn't it be easier if you had to input the data only once?

If you want to organize and create your web site in a single program, you've come to the right place, because that's what the

TIP

The Explorer is the place to start when you're first using FrontPage. If you're creating your first FrontPage site, or importing non-FrontPage sites into FrontPage, this is the place to begin.

FrontPage Explorer does *for* you. The Explorer gives you graphical, outline, and summary views of your web site, allowing you to view your site and manipulate it as a whole. And there's no need to worry about making separate, manual changes to these views—the Explorer updates each view as you make changes to your site, so you can see the changes instantly in any view you like. This greatly simplifies web-site creation and maintenance, and it'll no doubt save you hours and hours of time for every site you work on. If you work with large sites, this could save your sanity.

This chapter presents the Explorer in detail. The Explorer forms the framework of the FrontPage client software, giving you direct or indirect access to the Editor, the To Do List, **templates**, **wizards**, and **bots**. Most of these tools will be explained in greater detail in later chapters; this chapter simply focuses on how to access them through the Explorer itself.

The FrontPage Explorer should not be confused with the Windows 95 Explorer, although it was designed to have the same look and feel and similar operations. Nor should you confuse the FrontPage Explorer with Microsoft Internet Explorer. Internet Explorer is Microsoft's Web browser; FrontPage Explorer gives you an overview of your web site. In this chapter, and indeed in the entire book, the term "Explorer" will refer to the FrontPage Explorer; the Windows 95 Explorer will be referred to as the "Windows 95 Explorer."

Also note that FrontPage uses the term *web* to mean a web site. To avoid confusion with the **World Wide Web** and other Web-related terminology, this book uses the term *web site* or *site* throughout. And if Web is capitalized, it refers to the World Wide Web.

Setting Explorer Options

The Explorer is the tool you use to create new web sites and open existing sites. Before you do this, however, you can set the following options so the Explorer displays the elements you want to work with.

Links To Images You can use the Links To Images command to display or hide all links to image files in a web site. If you have numerous image files in your site, it's a good idea to simplify the Explorer's view of your site by turning off Links To Images. You can turn it back on whenever you need to see these links. You turn it on and off by choosing the Links To Images command from the View menu or by clicking the Links To Images toolbar button.

Repeated Links You can use the Repeated Links command to display or hide multiple links between pages. By default, FrontPage displays only one link for pages with multiple links to another page. Turning on Repeated Links is useful for getting an overall view of all the possible paths throughout your site, and for determining how many links a page has to another page. To turn it on and off, choose the Repeated Links command from the View menu or click the Repeated Links toolbar button.

Links Inside Page The Links Inside Page command lets you view any links that a page has to itself—for instance, a link at the bottom of a page that returns the user to the top of the page. To turn this feature on and off, choose the Links Inside Page command from the View menu or click the Links Inside Page toolbar button.

Toolbar At times, you might want to hide the toolbar at the top of the FrontPage window so that you can use the extra space to view more of your site. To hide and show the toolbar, choose the Toolbar command from the View menu. A check mark beside the command indicates that the toolbar in the Explorer is visible.

Status bar The status bar at the bottom of the FrontPage window shows any activity between FrontPage and a server, as well as a brief definition of a selected command or button. To show or hide the status bar, choose the Status Bar command from the View menu. A check mark beside the command indicates that the status bar is visible.

Creating a Site

If you're creating a FrontPage web site from scratch, it's wise to first construct the framework for it in the Explorer. The framework can consist of simply a name and some preconstructed pages for you to work on later. FrontPage saves this framework on your web server, and from that point you can work on it in the Explorer or the Editor, depending on what tasks you're completing.

But suppose you have some HTML pages you'd like to use from another web site. Can you use them in a FrontPage site? You sure can—you can import each of those pages into the FrontPage Editor, make any necessary changes, and then link them to other pages in your site. (See Chapter 6 for details on how to do this.) Your previous work won't be wasted when you move over to FrontPage. Alternatively, you can recycle HTML and graphics files by importing them into the Explorer. For more on this, see "Importing a File into a Site" later in this chapter.

So let's go through the motions of creating a web site. Here's what you do:

1. In the Explorer, choose New Web from the File menu, or click the New Web toolbar button. The New Web dialog box appears, presenting you with a list of several frameworks you can use to build your site. These frameworks are FrontPage's **wizards** and **templates**.

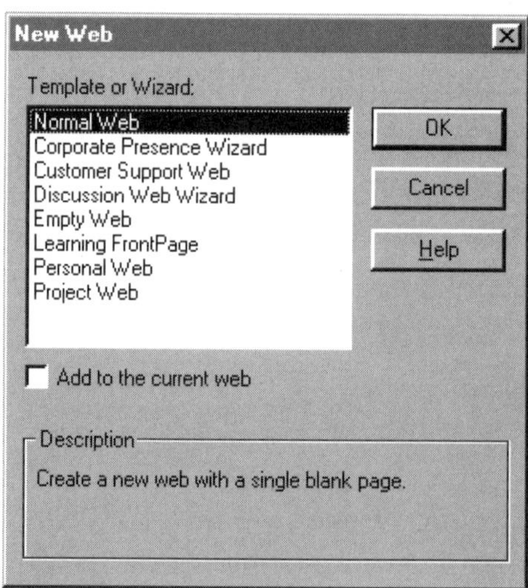

The New Web dialog box.

The easiest way to create a site is to use one of these wizards or templates, which can eliminate many preliminary design hassles. Wizards and templates are explained in detail in the next chapter, but for now, if you're creating your first site, here's a brief outline of what each can do for you.

SHORTCUT

You can also press Ctrl+N in the Explorer to create a new site.

Normal Web This template creates a new site with one blank page, so you can start with the absolute minimum. If you want to start without even a single blank page, you can use the Empty Web template.

Corporate Presence Wizard This wizard is an excellent place to start if you're creating a business site. It asks you a series of questions and offers numerous kinds of pages to highlight your business.

Customer Support Web This template sets up a customer support site for a business.

Discussion Web Wizard This wizard creates a discussion group with threads, a table of contents, and full-text searching.

Empty Web This template creates a new site with nothing in it. Generally, you'll start with the Normal Web template.

Learning FrontPage This is a template you can use with the FrontPage tutorial in online help.

Personal Web This template creates a personal web site that you can fill in with information such as employee data, favorite web sites, your interests, biographical information, and more.

Project Web This template creates a new site to help you manage a project. It includes a list of participants, project status, project schedule, and more.

2. Select one of these options and click OK. If you select a template, you'll be greeted by the New Web From Template dialog box, shown on the next page.

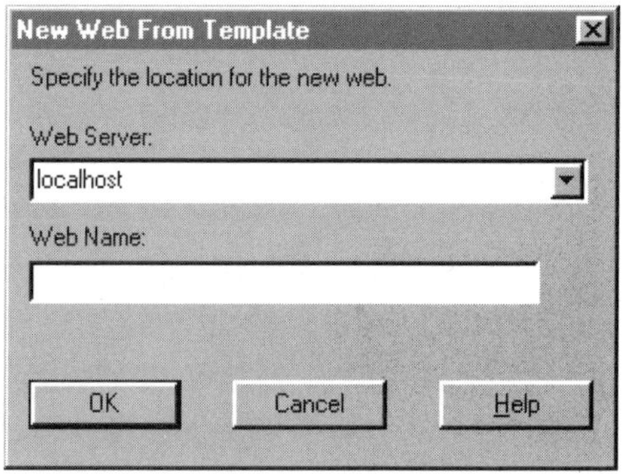

New Web From Template

Specify the location for the new web.

Web Server:

localhost

Web Name:

OK Cancel Help

The New Web From Template dialog box.

If you select a wizard to start, the only difference is that the dialog box you see is called New Web From Wizard.

3. Enter the host name of the **server** on which you want to house your site, or select it from the drop-down list. If your web server is mounted on a particular port number (for example, port 1234) rather than on the standard web server port number (80), you can include the port number as part of the web server host name; for example, internal.acme.com:1234.

4. Enter a name for your site in the Web Name text box, and click OK.

   This name stays "behind the scenes"; you can give your site a different title if you like, which shows up in the title bar whenever your site is open in the Explorer. By default, the name and title are the same; to change the title later on, see "Changing Site Settings" later in this chapter.

5. Next you'll probably see the Name And Password Required dialog box, which is presented for security purposes. FrontPage requires an author or administrator name and password to set up a new site; you must supply this information before the site can be created.

   If you have already created another site during the current session, FrontPage checks the name and password that you used previously. If they are acceptable, the dialog box does not appear. If the name and password do not work for the selected server, the dialog box appears.

The Name and Password text boxes are case-sensitive, so be sure to type in these items exactly as you've set them up. FrontPage will prompt you with the same dialog box until you supply the correct password.

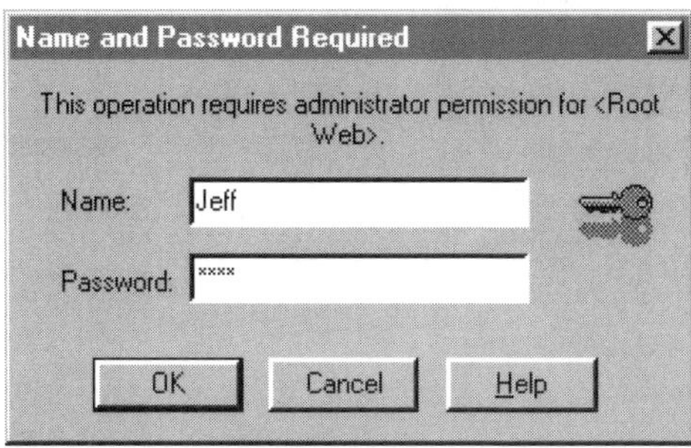

Once FrontPage has OK'd your name and password, it sets up your new site behind the scenes. This might take a few minutes, depending on the speed of your computer and the type of site you've chosen to create. FrontPage creates a directory for the site on the server you've designated. If you use a template to create your site, FrontPage adds files to this directory for each of the pages in the template. If you use a wizard, you see screens where you can customize your site before the pages are created. The directory has the same name that you just gave to your site.

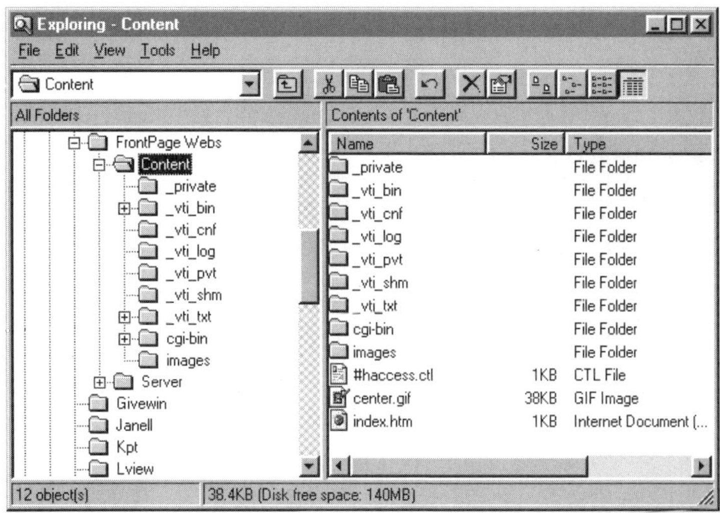

A view of the Windows 95 Explorer showing the Content directory, which holds the files for web sites created in the FrontPage Explorer.

When the process is complete, FrontPage displays the site in the Explorer.

Opening an Existing Site

You can open any web site in FrontPage, regardless of the web authoring application it was created with.

A Site Authored in FrontPage

If you've already created a site in FrontPage and want to open it in the Explorer, here's how to do it:

1. Choose Open Web from the File menu.

   You'll see the Open Web dialog box, which presents you with several options:

   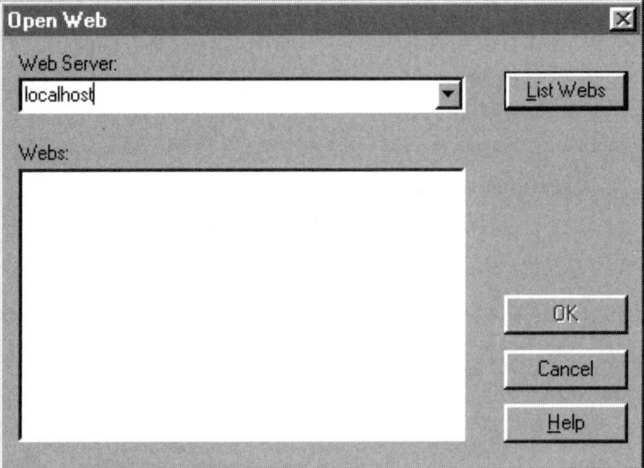

2. A default server name will appear in the Web Server text box; if necessary, type in the name of the server on which your site is located, or use the drop-down list.
3. Click the List Webs button. FrontPage will search the server you specify and display a list of sites in the Webs list box. For FrontPage-authored sites, the site titles will appear and, if a site name is different than its title, the name will appear in parentheses after the title.
4. Double-click on a title or select the title, and click OK.

   Opening a site requires author or administrative access in FrontPage. Anytime you start FrontPage and create a new site or open an existing one, the Name And Password Required dialog box appears, asking for your name and password.

5. If the dialog box appears, type in your name and password, and click OK. The name and password are case-sensitive. The site will open in the Explorer.

SHORTCUT

To quickly open a site, you can click the Open Web toolbar button, which is the standard Open button that you find in many Windows 95 applications.

A Site Authored in Another Application

If you want to open a site authored in another application, the best-case scenario happens when the site is on a web server that has the appropriate FrontPage Server Extensions installed. The Server Extensions gather the additional information needed by FrontPage and make the site's content available for editing. In this way, you might not need to change a site's format in order to work with the site in the Explorer.

To open such a site, follow the procedure outlined above. For more information on the FrontPage Server Extensions, see Chapter 9.

However, if you want to open a site from a server that does not have the FrontPage Server Extensions installed, it's a little more complicated, but it can be done. Here's how:

1. Create a subdirectory for the site underneath the Content directory on the web server. FrontPage stores its web site files in subdirectories of the Content directory.

2. Copy the entire directory of the web site into the new directory you just created.

3. In the Explorer, create a new site using the Empty Web template. Give the site the same name you gave the directory.

FrontPage will automatically notice the new web site inside the directory, and will process the site so it can be used with FrontPage.

Your Site from Different Angles

When you think of a web site, what's the first thing that comes to mind? There are several different ways of looking at a site. You might think of it as a map—icons representing pages with lines linking them. Or, you can think of it as a list of elements (files) that make up those pages. Even further, you can think of it in a hierarchical sense, starting with the main page of your site, your home page. Perhaps the most powerful feature of the Explorer is the way it presents your site in these different ways, which are called Link view, Summary view, and Outline view.

The Explorer Views, One by One

It's a well-known fact that people approach work in many different ways, and they learn in different ways. That's because people *think* differently. Some think analytically, some think linearly, and some think in more creative, flowing ways. One Explorer view might be a more effective tool for you than another simply because of the way you think. The choice of three Explorer views also provides an added bonus: It gives you a great excuse when you're staring blankly at the screen at the end of a long day, and your boss happens by. Just tell your boss you're lost in thought, trying to determine which view works best for you.

First we'll look at each of the three views to see their unique ways of presenting a web site. Then we'll explore the features that are common to the three views.

Outline View

Just like an outline for those term papers you used to write (you *did* create the outline as you were instructed to, didn't you?), Outline view presents information hierarchically. One terrific aspect of being in the real world is you don't have to create outlines if you don't want to. The FrontPage developers know you'd rather run among a herd of stampeding yaks in a desert wasteland than create another outline, so they created Outline view to help simplify the process. FrontPage takes the links within your site and creates the outline for you. The Explorer opens up with Outline view on the left side of the screen:

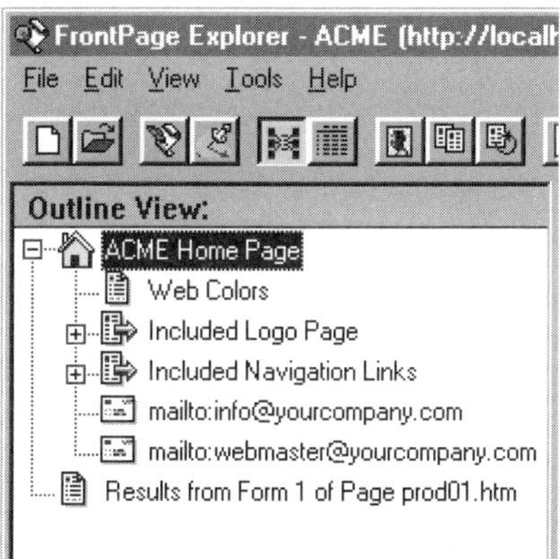

The home page of the site appears at the top of Outline view, and is represented by a cute house—in this case, it's called *ACME Home Page*. All of the material that appears in the site shows up below this icon in Outline view at first.

If you are using Outline view along with Link view, click on the ACME Home Page icon in Outline view to have the home page show up in Link view to the right. The next section will describe Link view, but for now just keep in mind that what you do in Outline view affects what appears in Link view. This works in much the same way as the folder views in the Windows 95 Explorer.

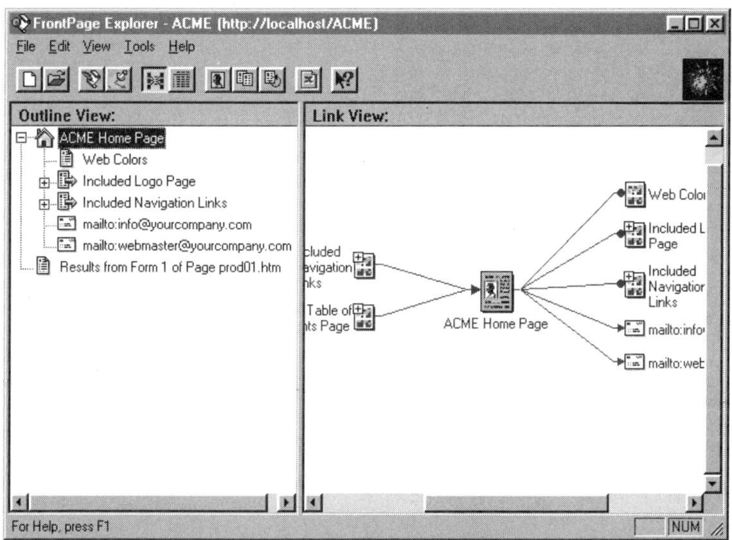

Notice the plus and minus signs next to some of the pages. If you click on a plus sign, you'll see the links and pages involved with that page. When a page is expanded so you can see its links, the plus sign changes to a minus sign. You can also expand and collapse items in Outline view by double-clicking them.

Notice the envelope icons accompanied by the "mailto:" protocol (at the bottom of the items linked to the ACME Home Page). These icons represent hotspots on pages that allow users to send e-mail from the page, such as feedback to a web administrator. In this case, the ACME Home Page has two hotspots that users can send e-mail from. The relationship to the page where the hotspot appears is shown in the same way as a link (with a line connecting the icon to the page).

Arrows are used in Outline view to indicate whether links from a page are already shown in the view. A gray arrow indicates that the page has links to other pages that are shown somewhere else in Outline view; a red arrow indicates that the page has links to pages that are not yet displayed. Notice that the Included Navigation Links page is shown near the top of Outline view. If you locate links to this page elsewhere in the site, they are represented with a gray arrow (indicating that the page is fully displayed elsewhere—in this case, at the top of Outline view). A page without either color arrow has no links leaving from that page.

If you turn on the Links To Images option (described previously in "Setting Explorer Options"), you'll see Outline view expand to include all the images on the pages that have links. The figure below shows four images on the home page:

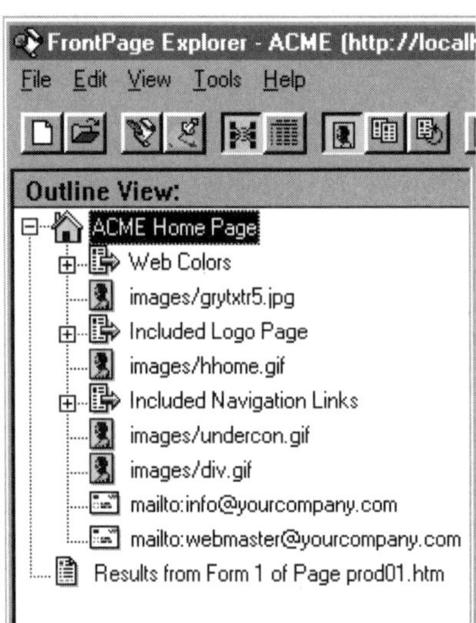

A link to the World Wide Web is indicated by a small globe icon. The following example shows a link to microsoft.com:

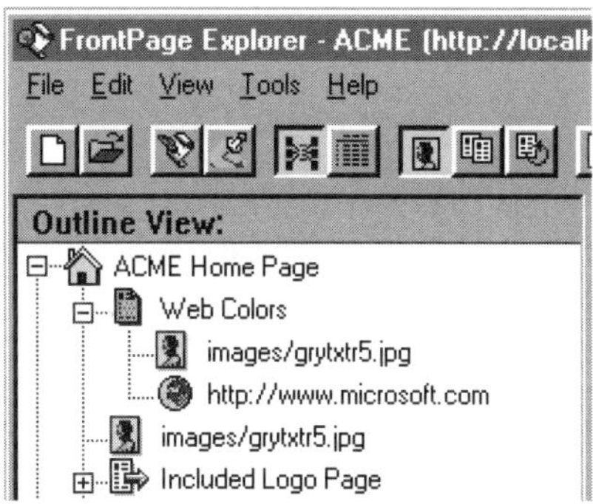

There are a couple other icons you should know about but that you won't want to see on your page: the icons for broken links and for errors on your pages.

The broken-link icon and the error icon.

The broken-link icon indicates that a link, whether internal to the current web site or external, is configured incorrectly. You can fix a broken link by opening the page containing the link in the Editor. See the section on links in Chapter 6 for more details. If you see an error icon, that means a FrontPage **bot** is configured incorrectly. For more information on bots, see Chapter 8.

Link View

Those crafty FrontPage developers didn't stop with Outline view. They figured out something that few others have even thought of. Many web-site designers today are graphically minded folks who would rather look at a Monet than read about one. Since they think in terms of pictures, why not display a site in the same way?

You've already seen how changing Outline view affects how Link view appears. Link view is the graphical representation of the links within a segment of your web site. It's the reason you can start using those sticky notes for other purposes.

To see your site in Link view, choose Link View from the View menu. Link view appears on the right side of the Explorer.

> **SHORTCUT**
>
> A quick way to see your site in Link view is to click the Link View toolbar button.

Here's a basic look at a site in Link view. Pages are shown as large icons, and their names appear directly underneath the icon. Links are shown in a left-to-right fashion; links *to the page* come in from the left, and links *to other pages and addresses* go to the right.

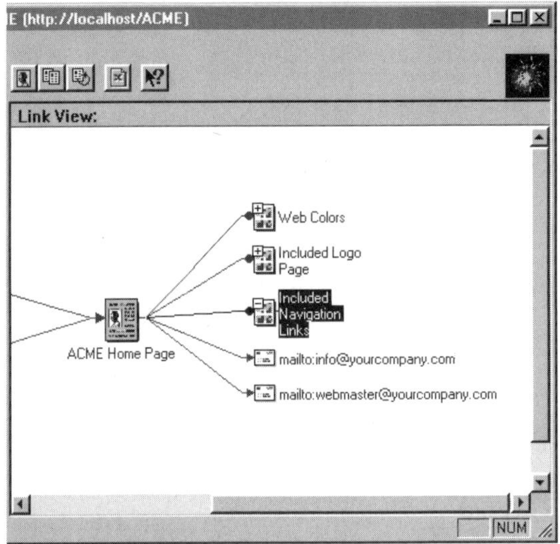

In the figure above, the links that appear on the ACME Home Page are bundled together in the Included Navigation Links item. Clicking the plus sign next to Included Navigation Links displays a graphical representation of those links, as in the following figure:

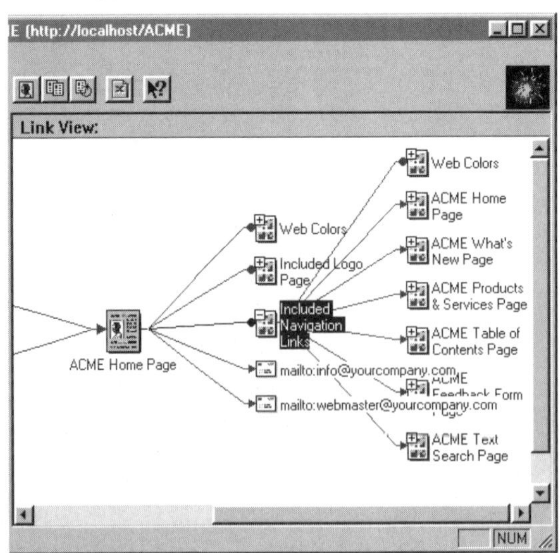

By default, all Included Navigation Links groupings are collapsed; you can see how crowded the screen would get if they were all expanded.

As in Outline view, an envelope icon indicates a hyperlink that sends e-mail, the painting icon indicates an image file, a globe icon indicates a link to the World Wide Web, a broken-link icon indicates a broken link, and the plus and minus signs indicate that something can be expanded or collapsed, respectively.

You might have noticed that some of the links end with an arrow, while others end with a bullet mark. An arrow indicates a link; in other words, that the item jumps to another item. A bullet indicates that the item to the right is included as a part of the item to the left. In the example below, image files are shown as bulleted links, meaning they appear on the pages they're linked to. Bullets can also indicate that the page contains an Include bot. For more information on Include bots, see Chapter 8.

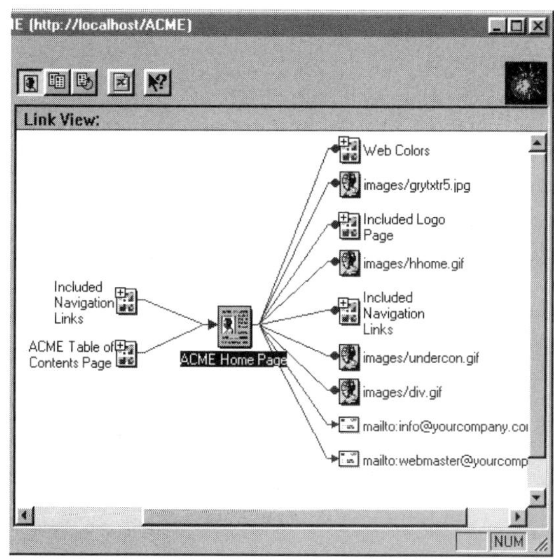

Uses for Link view Link view is especially useful for determining just how many links you've got going and coming from each page, and also for seeing what other pages link to your page. Say you went live with a new page on your intranet a week ago, and you want to know how many others in your organization have linked to your page. You can simply look at your page in Link view to find out.

Link view is also useful for verifying that you've included all the links you think you have on a particular page. Suppose you promised several departments in your organization that you'd link to their home page from your "For More Information" page, and those links are embedded in the paragraphs on your page. Instead of looking at the page in an editor, finding the links, and then checking them against a master list, you can view all the links on your page in one place—Link view—and check *that* against your list.

Modifying the view The size of the Link view window and the size of your monitor dictate how much of your site appears in Link view. You'll notice as you expand the site that links go off the screen. You can view the off-the-screen material in two ways: by using the scroll bar at the bottom of the Link view window, or by clicking on any open area in Link view and dragging the material wherever you want it. When dragging a blank area, the mouse pointer changes to a hand to indicate that you can move the material around.

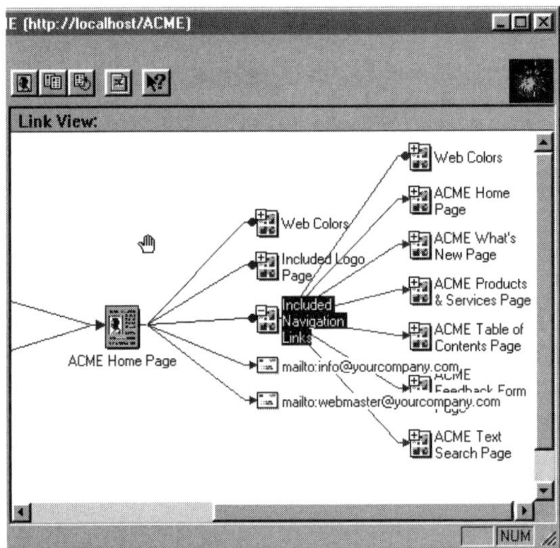

When you click the mouse on a blank area, the cursor changes to a hand. Then you can reposition the material on the page by dragging the mouse.

There's also a way to center any item on your screen in Link view: Right-click on the item and choose Move To Center from the pop-up menu, as in the figure on the facing page.

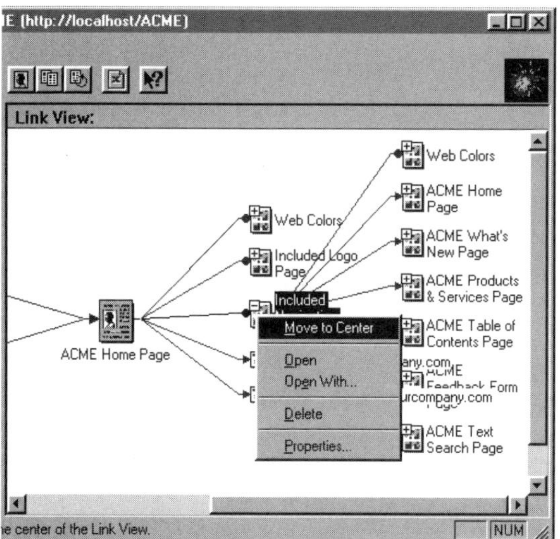

You'll also notice that because Link view is a representation of links, it can seem to go on forever. Again, think spatially, and you'll see that if page A is linked to page B, which is linked to page C, which is linked back to page A, you're already going around in circles. And that's only a tiny example. It's best to use Link view for viewing small portions of your site. You can get a good overall view of your site by collapsing everything; when you need to see specifics, it's time to expand those icons.

Summary View

Somewhere along the FrontPage development line, someone must have created a huge site to test in the Explorer. The higher-ups probably wanted to know all the specifics: How many hundreds of image files and page files were there, what were their names, how big were they, and where did they appear in the site? What other kinds of files did the site contain? Instead of panicking and heading down the turnpike to become a full-time New York Mets bleacher bum, the developer created Summary view.

SHORTCUT

You can also see your site in Summary view by clicking the Summary View toolbar button.

Summary view organizes the properties of all the site's files in a view that you can manipulate as you wish. Summary view lives on the right side of the Explorer, using the same space as Link view, paying half the rent, doing half the dishes, and yes—doing half the Windows. To see your site in Summary view, choose Summary View from the View menu.

Summary view provides the following information about the file: title, name, size, type, date it was last modified, who modified it, its **URL**, and any comments added to the file. This information is taken from the property settings for that item. To sort the columns, click on the column heading. Files are sorted in ascending order, except for files in the Modified Date column, which are sorted in chronological order starting with the most recent date and time.

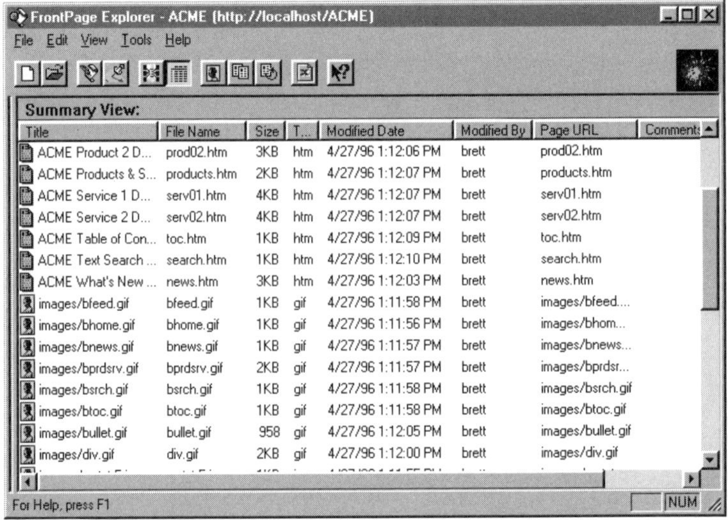

A site in Summary view. Notice that the Summary View toolbar button is depressed.

Only three icons are used in Summary view; the same painting icon that is used for image files in Outline and Link views, an icon indicating HTML files, and an icon indicating a file other than an image file or HTML file.

Summary view icons: Image file, HTML file, and "other" file.

Uses for Summary view Summary view is especially useful for quickly locating summary information about files whose location in the site you're unsure of. For example, suppose you're in the Explorer and you need to find out the URL for a certain page in your site. Instead of searching for the page in Outline view or Link view, you can go to Summary view, sort the list by title if necessary, locate your file alphabetically, and look across the columns for the file's URL.

Here are some other good uses for Summary view:

- Finding images that might take a long time to download into a browser. Sort the files by size, and then look for larger image files at the bottom of the list.
- Finding all pages that you authored. Sort the Modified By column and then look for your name.
- Finding all the pages that haven't been updated in a long time. Sort the list by the Modified Date, and then look at the bottom of the column for older dates.
- Finding all files of a specific file type in your site. Group the list by type of file by clicking on the Type column, and then look for the specific file type.

Adjusting the column widths Besides sorting the items in Summary view, there's another way to change the view: You can change column widths. Place your mouse in the column heading area, near a border between the columns. When the cursor changes to a crosshair, click and drag to adjust the width.

What's Common to All Three Views

All three views of the Explorer share some features that can be accessed within any of the views. Here's the rundown:

Opening files from a view The three views are not just a compilation of pages and links; they are also avenues for opening their associated files in the Editor or whatever application you want to work in to manipulate those files. For example, if you want to manipulate a Graphics Interchange Format (**GIF**) file that appears in any view, you can launch the application and edit the file with a few clicks of the mouse.

You can open pages or image files from any view. To open a file, right-click on the title or the icon. You'll get a short list of options, as in the figure on the following page.

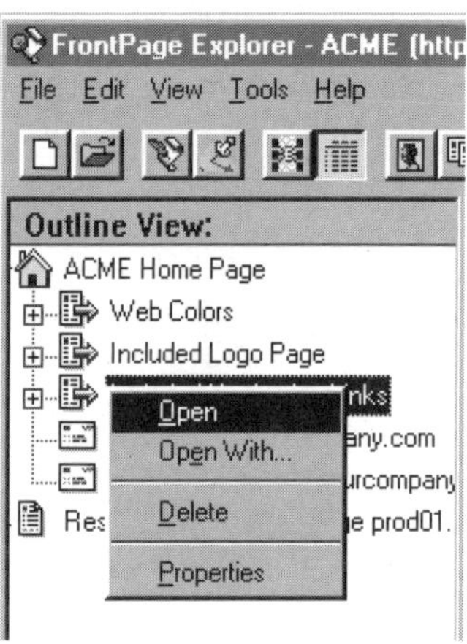

If you right-click on a page and choose Open from the pop-up menu, the page appears in the Editor, ready for you to edit. If you choose the Open With command, you can open the page with any other editor. After choosing Open With, you get a list of editors in the Open With Editor dialog box; you can select an editor and click OK.

SHORTCUT

You can also double-click on a file in Link view and Summary view to open it. The file opens with its associated editor.

But what if you want a different editor to open when you choose the Open command for a particular type of file, or what if your editor doesn't show up at all in the Open With Editor dialog box? You can change the editor type by choosing the Configure Editors command from the Tools menu. This process is described in "Configuring Editors" later in this chapter.

SHORTCUT

You can access the properties for an item by right-clicking the item and choosing Properties from the pop-up menu.

Viewing file properties To view properties for a file, click on the file and then choose the Properties command from the Edit menu. In the Properties dialog box, you'll find summary information, such as when the file was created, who created it, when it was modified, and who modified it. There's also a text box to add comments to the file.

You'll also find general information on the file, such as its title, name, type, size, and **URL** (Uniform Resource Locator). A URL indicates the address of a resource on a network and the method by which it can be accessed. URLs can use various **protocols**; the most common one on the World Wide Web today is HTTP. The terms *URL* and *HTTP address* refer to the same thing.

Refreshing a view To update the views in the Explorer, choose Refresh from the View menu. The command refreshes all views for the current site in the Explorer. If more than one person is working on a site at one time, refreshing the site allows you to see all of the changes up to the second you refresh.

Changing names of files and pages You can change the names of files from any view. Here's how:

1. Right-click on the file in any view, and then choose Properties from the pop-up menu.
2. Enter the new filename in the Page URL text box on the General tab of the Properties dialog box. Do not change the directory portion of the name unless you want to move the file.

> **WARNING**
>
> When changing the name of a file in the Explorer, do not have the file open in any other application, such as the Editor.

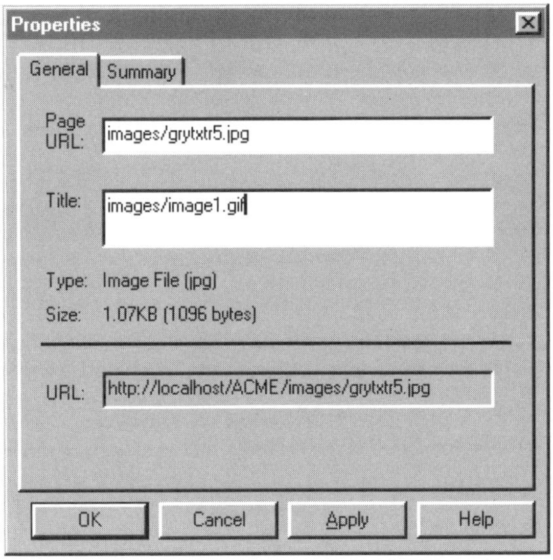

Properties
General | Summary
Page URL: images/grytxtr5.jpg
Title: images/image1.gif
Type: Image File (jpg)
Size: 1.07KB (1096 bytes)
URL: http://localhost/ACME/images/grytxtr5.jpg
OK | Cancel | Apply | Help

FrontPage displays a dialog box telling you that it will update all links in the site to the file whose name you changed. Click OK to allow FrontPage to perform this operation.

Changing the size of a view A split bar separates Outline view from Link view and Summary view. To move the bar and change the amount of the window devoted to each of the views, place your cursor directly over the bar until it changes to a double-line cursor, and then click and drag the bar. You can also use the Split command on the View menu.

It's important to remember that the three views in the Explorer display your site according to its links, and not in a sequential order. Our increasing use of **hypertext** is causing us to think about documents differently than we used to. Before hypertext, we thought of documents in terms of their classic book form—one page stacked on another, perhaps indexed or referenced so you could manually find a cross-referenced term elsewhere in the book. Hypertext allows you to automatically jump to anywhere in a document. It's as if all the pages of a book are drifting in space, with links between any or all of them. If you think of your site in these spatial terms instead of in the standard book form, you'll fare much better in designing and manipulating your site.

Other Functions of the Explorer

So far in this chapter, you've learned that the Explorer can be used to create and open sites, as well as to view them in several different ways. The Explorer also sports a host of other functions you can use in your everyday site management.

Closing a Site

Because FrontPage can display only one site at a time (which is true of most browsers), any time you open another site or create a new one, the current site is closed. To close the current site without opening another, choose Close Web from the File menu in the Explorer.

Copying a Site

You can use the Copy Web command on the File menu to copy a site that is currently open in the Explorer to a server. This command is handy if you want to develop web sites locally on the Personal Web Server and then promote them onto a higher-volume web server for live use. Assuming that the appropriate FrontPage Server Extensions are installed for the server you're copying to, and you've got administrative access, it's an easy task. Here's how to do it:

1. With the site you want to copy currently open in the Explorer, choose Copy Web from the File menu. You'll see the Copy Web dialog box.

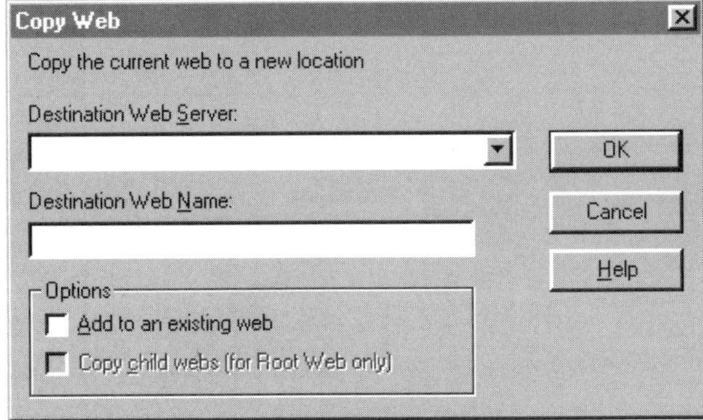

2. In the Destination Web Server text box, enter the name of the server you're copying to, or use the drop-down list to select a server.

3. In the Destination Web Name text box, enter a name for the copy of the site. These names are subject to the naming conventions used by the destination server, so you might have to consider length as well as case-sensitivity conventions as you name the site.

   You can select the Add To An Existing Web check box if you're combining the copy with another site; otherwise, don't worry about this check box. If you're copying a **root web** site, select the Copy Child Webs check box if you also want to copy all child web sites (web sites that have a link from the root web site).

4. When you're ready to copy the site, click OK. FrontPage copies the site to the destination server and then notifies you that the copy is on the new server.

You can also copy a site to a web server that does not have the FrontPage Server Extensions installed by using the new Microsoft FrontPage Publishing Wizard. Keep in mind, however, that it's best to use FrontPage web sites on web servers that have the Server Extensions installed. Without the Server Extensions, you lose some FrontPage functionality; for example, FrontPage's bots won't perform at all. For details, see Chapter 9.

Deleting a Site

> **WARNING**
>
> Be sure to delete sites by using the Delete Web command, not by manually removing their files from a server. If you remove the files manually, FrontPage might not recognize that they've been deleted.

You must have administrative access to FrontPage to delete a site, and the site must be open in the Explorer before you can delete it. To delete the site that is currently open, choose Delete Web from the File menu in the Explorer.

Consider this before you delete: Once you delete a site, even if you've removed it properly with the Delete Web command, it cannot be recovered—not even from the Recycle Bin in the Windows 95 Explorer.

Deleting Files

You must have at least author-level access to delete files in the Explorer. You can delete files by selecting them in any view and then choosing Delete from the Edit menu.

Adding a New Page to a Site

You can add two kinds of pages to your web sites: pages that you start from scratch, and preexisting pages. To add a new page to your site that you'll work on from scratch, you use the Editor. See Chapter 6 for more details. To add a completed page to your site, you use the Import command on the File menu in the Explorer. For more information, see the next section.

Importing a File into a Site

An application's ability to incorporate documents created by earlier versions of the program or from competing programs is one way of determining its value: "utility" versus "futility." You shouldn't have to lose the work you've already done in another web authoring application if you're moving over to FrontPage. If you've already created pages or files (for example, RTF or HTML files) that you'd like to include in your current site, FrontPage allows you to do it, and quite easily:

1. With the destination web site open in the Explorer, choose Import from the File menu. The Import File To Web dialog box appears:

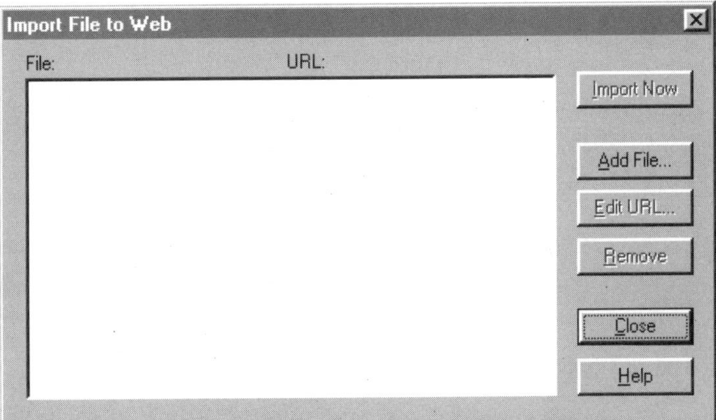

2. Click the Add File button. This brings up the Add File To Import List dialog box (shown on the next page), where you specify the file or files you want to import. Locate the directory containing the file by using the directory controls at the top of the dialog box. Be sure to select the type of files to be listed by using the Files Of Type drop-down list box. (If you're not sure of the extension of the file you're looking for, select All Files from the drop-down list.)

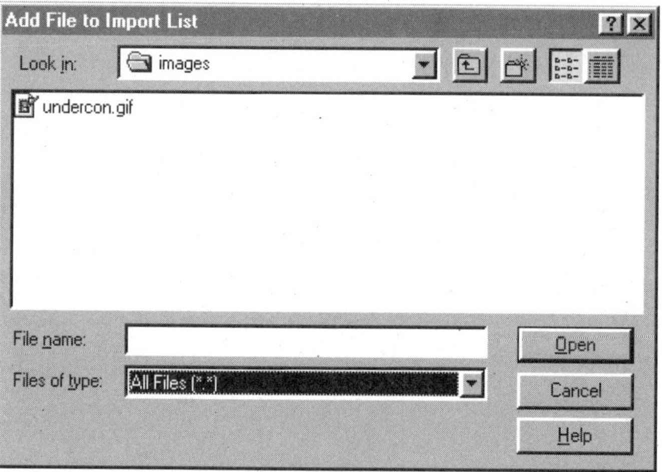

3. Select the file or files you want to import. You select files in the same way that you do in the Windows 95 Explorer. To select a group of contiguous files, click on the first file in the group, press the Shift key, and then click on the last file in the group. To select multiple noncontiguous files, press the Ctrl key while clicking on the files you want to select. To remove a file from a selection, press the Ctrl key while clicking on the file.
4. Click the Open button. This adds the files to a list in the Import File To Web dialog box and closes the Add File To Import List dialog box.
5. If you need to add more files to the list, repeat steps 2, 3, and 4. To remove files from the list before you add them to your site, select them and click the Remove button.
6. If you want to change the URL of any file, select the file in the Import File To Web dialog box and click the Edit URL button. This is handy if you want to save the file separately from the other material in the web site; you enter the new URL (pointing the file to the directory of your choice) in the Edit URL dialog box that appears, and then click OK.
7. Click the Import Now button to add the files to your site. When you click the button, it changes to a Stop button so you can halt the process at any time.
8. Click the Close button after you finish importing files.

The files you import are added to the bottom of Outline view and are not linked to any pages in the site.

You can also add image files to your site by using the Import command. As described in Chapter 7, you can also do this in several different ways in the Editor, but if you know you're going to use certain files in your site, the Import command allows you to add them all at once.

If you try to close the Explorer while items are still in the Import list, the Explorer will warn you. Also, if you open a FrontPage file such as a GIF file (to edit it or to make sure it's the correct image), the file is automatically added to the Import list. If you make changes to the file outside of FrontPage, this ensures that your site includes the latest version of the file.

Exporting a File from a Site

Suppose you want to copy an item from your site, such as a page or an image, to another location. You can save any file to your hard disk, a network location, or a floppy disk by choosing the Export Selected command from the File menu in the Explorer. First, select the file in any view, and then choose Export Selected. In the Export Selected As dialog box that appears, you can specify the location you want the file to be copied to.

The command copies a file to another location; it does not remove it from your site. To remove a file from your site, you must delete it.

Changing Site Settings

Nightmare from Hell, version 1: You've just completed a site for your company, which includes the company's phone and fax numbers on nearly every one of its 175 pages. After you come up for air, you discover that your area code is about to change. You're faced with editing every one of those 175 pages. You could use a utility program to search for the old area code and replace it with the new one, and there are other ways to get the job done. But how about a one-stop-shop way?

FrontPage uses placeholders, also called *parameters* or *configuration variables,* so that it can track where this information is used in the current site. The wizards and templates in FrontPage add some parameters automatically, and you can define your own and insert them using the Substitution bot discussed in Chapter 8. By using the Web Settings command on the Tools menu in the Explorer, you can update the information wherever it occurs in your site. Choose the command, and you'll be greeted with the Web Settings dialog box, which has three tabs.

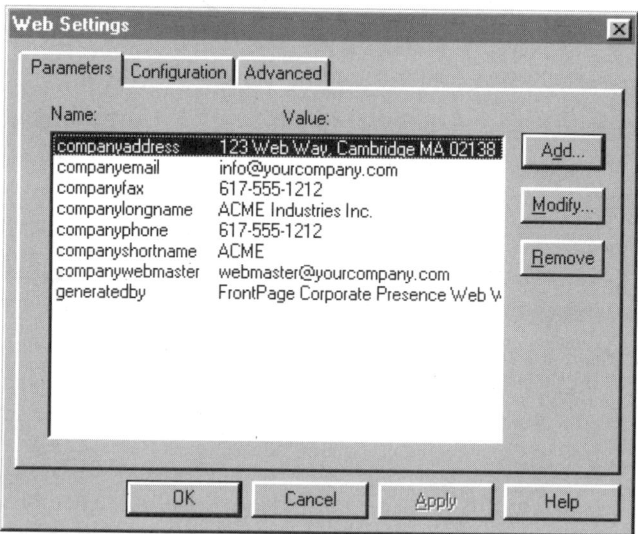

Parameters tab If your site was constructed using a template or wizard that contained parameters for later authors to fill in, or if you've defined your own, those parameters will show up here.

- You can add parameters by clicking the Add button. The Add Name And Value dialog box appears, asking you for the name of the parameter and the value of the parameter (whatever information you wish to enter). Click OK to exit the dialog box and add the new parameter to your list. Use the Substitution bot in the Editor to add the information to your pages.
- To change the parameter information, such as in the scenario described above, select the parameter you want to change and click the Modify button. In the Modify Name And Value dialog box that appears, you can enter the new information. Click OK to save the information

and exit the dialog box. This automatically updates the parameter in all pages of your web site where the parameter appears.

- Clicking the Remove button removes the selected parameter from the list.

Configuration tab To change the name and title of your site, click on the Configuration tab of the Web Settings dialog box, replace the information, and click OK. The name should not contain spaces, because the name will be used as part of the site's **URL**, and URLs normally do not contain spaces. The site title, however, can contain spaces.

It's important to give your site a name that you'll easily recognize among a list of sites. Each time you open a site to work on it in the Explorer or the Editor, you'll select the site from a list; if you create numerous sites on your server, the list can get long and confusing. If you give your site an intuitive and distinctive name at the outset, you'll save yourself headaches later on.

Advanced tab The Advanced tab allows you to set or modify advanced settings, including the following:

- You can configure how FrontPage supports **clickable image** maps in the Image Maps section. In the Style drop-down list box, select the server type for the images and set an optional prefix if the Prefix text box is enabled. Select the Generate Client-Side Image Maps check box if you want FrontPage to generate image maps from the client and not the server. It's a good idea to select this check box. FrontPage generates client-side image maps in such a way that if a browser does not support client-side image maps, it will simply ignore the client-side image map information in the FrontPage HTML file. So, no harm can be done if you select this check box. (In fact, you can often gain more speed—see Chapter 7 for more details.)
- In the Options section, select the Show Documents In Hidden Directories check box to display documents in **hidden directories**— directories preceded by an underscore (_). By default, you can't view pages and files in hidden directories when you are in the Explorer. This feature allows you to act as a moderator for a

discussion group; individual messages in a discussion are kept in a hidden directory.

Changing a Password

Your officemate, Mark Shmirkwrinkle, looked over your shoulder and memorized your FrontPage administrator password as you were typing it in. What to do? Change your password when Mark isn't looking over your shoulder. Here's how: First, tell Mark there's a three-alarm fire in the dumpster next to where his car is parked. After he leaves the office, choose the Change Password command from the Tools menu in the Explorer. You'll see a dialog box like the one shown below, asking you for your old password, which Mark knows, your new password, which he'll never have a clue about because you'll be watching over your shoulder from now on, and a confirmation of that password. Enter the passwords, and then click OK to exit the dialog box and save your new password. Then put a sea bass fillet in the lining of Mark's trenchcoat.

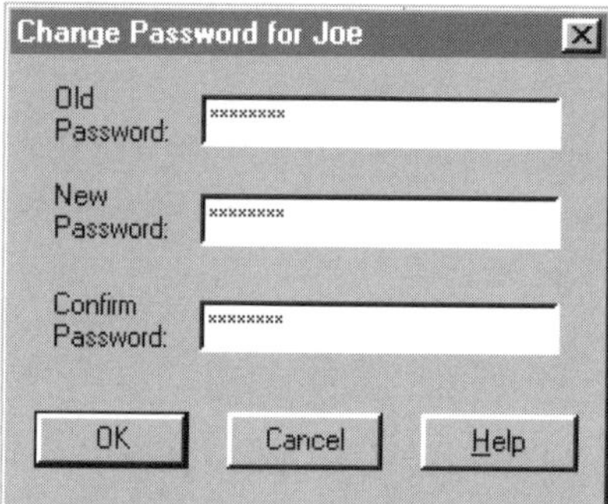

Configuring Editors

Have you ever opened a file from the Windows 95 Explorer? If you have, you know that the file opens in an application that it can be viewed and/or edited in. The FrontPage Explorer offers the same feature. When you double-click a file in your web site, such as a **GIF** or **JPEG** file or any Office file, you can have the Explorer open the file in whatever application you choose.

Here's how to tell FrontPage which application to open for specific file types. First, choose Configure Editors from the Tools menu. The Configure Editors dialog box appears:

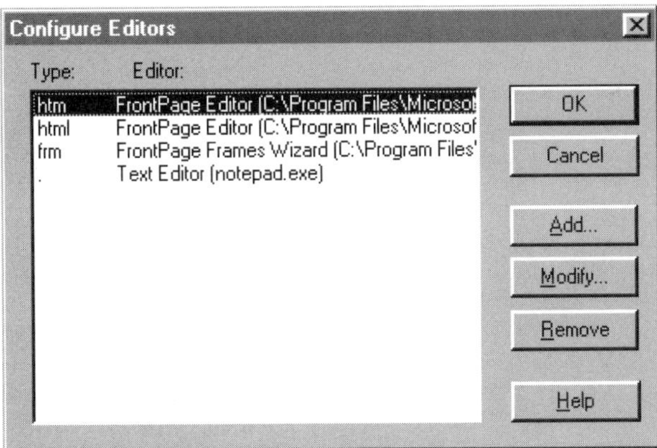

The dialog box has two columns, one for the extension of the type of file to edit and the other for the application that's used to edit the file. As you can see, the dialog box includes default settings for some common file types and their editors.

To add a file type, click the Add button. In the Add Editor Association dialog box, add the extension that identifies the file type and the name you want to use for the editor. Then, enter the name and location of the executable file in the Command text box. If you don't know the exact location, click the Browse button to search your directories for the executable file. When you finish, click OK.

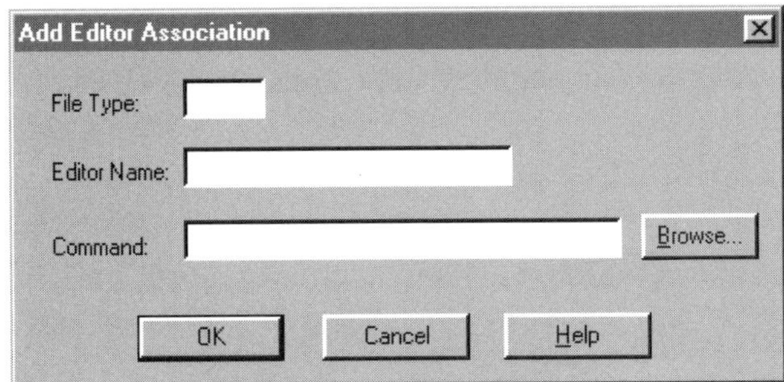

To modify settings in the Configure Editors dialog box, select an entry and click the Modify button. This takes you to the Modify Editor Association dialog box, where you can change the name of the editor or where the editor is located.

FrontPage allows you to designate only one editor application per file type. Each of the editors listed in the Configure Editors dialog box appears in the Open With Editor dialog box. If you don't specify an editor for a particular file type in the Explorer, FrontPage uses the default Windows 95 editor for that file type.

Verifying Internal and External Links

> **TIP**
>
> Verifying links in FrontPage ensures that the targets of your links exist, and that they will work in a browser. It does *not* confirm that your links jump where you want them to. You confirm this yourself.

The testing of links is a vital component of any site-testing plan. Simply stated, you've got to be sure the links work. Broken links not only make your site look bad, they make *you* look bad. But even for small sites, this phase of testing can take a long time. FrontPage includes a tool to verify your links, which can save you bunches of time when you're in a crunch.

To verify the links, do the following:

1. With the site open in the Explorer, choose Verify Links from the Tools menu. The Verify Links dialog box appears, listing all broken internal links along with all external links in your site (whether broken or not).

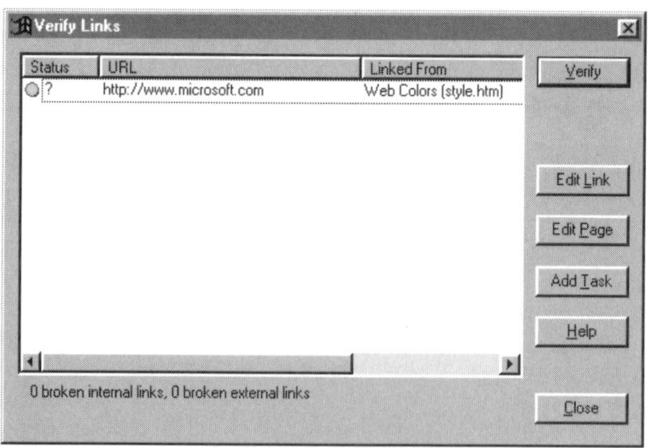

Each link is preceded by a colored circle, which is yellow at first but changes as you verify it:

Green—indicates that the link is good.

Yellow—indicates that the link has not been verified or has changed since the last verification.

Red—indicates that the link is broken.

2. To start the process, click the Verify button. FrontPage checks all links, and then tells you their status in the Status column. To verify external links, such as links to the World Wide Web, FrontPage must be able to reach those links; in other words, to verify Web links, you must be connected live to the Web. Verifying external links can take a long time.

> **TIP**
>
> The Verify button changes to a Stop button while FrontPage verifies the links. Click the Stop button to stop the process at any time.

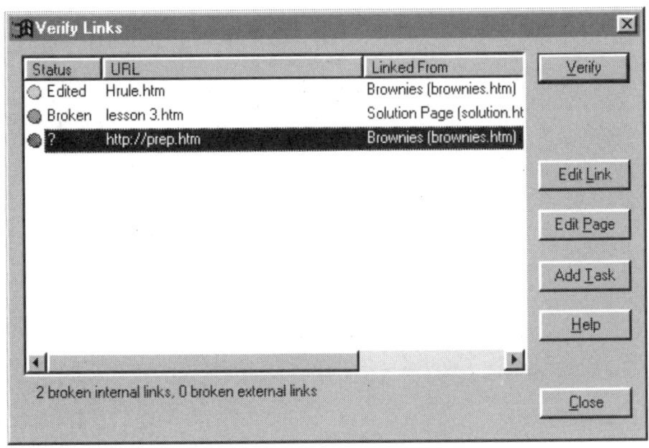

3. If you want to fix a broken link right away, select that link and click the Edit Link button. Change the URL in the Edit Link dialog box, and then click OK to return to the Verify Links dialog box.

4. To move to a page that contains a link, select the link and then click the Edit Page button. The page opens in the Editor and scrolls to the link, allowing you to edit the link or remove it. To edit a link in the Editor, see Chapter 6. The Verify Links dialog box remains open in the Explorer so that you can switch between the two programs.

5. If you don't have time to fix the link right away, or you need some time to find the correct address, you can add the task to the To Do List by selecting the link and clicking the Add Task button.

6. When you finish editing the links or adding them to the To Do List, click Close to exit the Verify Links dialog box.

Recalculating Links

Recalculating links updates or "refreshes" your site. If you've made significant changes to your site, such as removing entire pages, it's wise to go through the recalculating links operation. This is especially true if you've added, deleted, or modified documents in your site without using FrontPage. All you need to do is choose Recalculate Links from the Tools menu. FrontPage warns you that the process might take a long time, and asks you to confirm that you want to go through with it.

When you use this command, FrontPage performs the following tasks:

- Updates the display for the current site for all three Explorer views.
- Updates the text index that's created by a Search bot. When you implement searching on a page using a Search bot, FrontPage creates a text index for the bot to use. When you add a page or save a modified page in your site, entries are added to the text index, but no entries are deleted. Thus, if you delete material from a page and then save the modified page, the text index still contains entries for the deleted material. Whenever you delete material, including entire pages, from your site, you need to use the Recalculate Links command to update the text index. For more information on the Search bot, see Chapter 8.

Coming Up

As you can see, you can use the Explorer, the engine of FrontPage's client software, not only to view a web site but to administer it. Other key parts of the FrontPage client are wizards and templates, which are detailed in the next chapter.

Chapter 4
Wizards and Templates

Tick, Tick, Tick

Have you ever had this kind of thought cross your mind: "I've got so much to do today, I don't even *remotely* have enough time to get it done. So I'm goin' fishin' instead." Of course you have. But that kind of attitude will get most people fired—unless, of course, you're the owner of your company, in which case you can go fishin' anytime you darn well please.

The fact is, the amount of information we are forced to consume increases at an ever-greater rate. It also seems that there's less and less time to get things done. Consequently, people are always looking for ways to get more things done in less time.

Everyone's looking for a shortcut, and you've got a huge one in FrontPage by not having to know a lick of HTML to create professional-looking web sites. FrontPage also provides a couple of other pretty cool shortcuts in its **templates** and **wizards**. A template, as you might know, is a document that you use as the basis for a new document. A wizard is a software module of one or more screens that asks you questions, offers you choices, and then generates a customized document as a result. Templates are not customizable up front, as wizards are. The result of both templates and wizards is a document that serves as a framework for your finished product—a framework that you can modify if you like, and add information to.

This chapter explores the FrontPage templates and wizards. It shows you how to work with them and gives you plenty of examples along the way. You'll find that using wizards and templates is a terrific way to get started on your web site, and a sensational time-saver as well.

Templates

Templates are examples of sites or pages that FrontPage provides to fill a particular need. Like wizards, they give you a framework, or a great place to start, for a site or a page. Wizards, however, offer you choices in creating the new document; when you select a template, you get an exact copy of the original template.

Web Templates

Web templates in FrontPage are very similar to web wizards, except they don't ask you a series of questions in order to generate a customized site. That's because most of the sites the templates are based on are small; they have few items that need customizing. You can do all of the finishing work on these pages—including adding images, text, links, and so forth—in the Editor.

The web templates can be accessed via the New Web command on the Explorer's File menu. In the New Web dialog box that appears, you can select one of the following templates to use as the basis for your site or page:

Empty Web When you want to create an entire site from scratch, you can use this "template." It creates an empty site with no pages, and you do all the rest by adding content in the Editor.

Normal Web This template creates a new site with one blank page. Besides the Empty Web template, this is the least-complicated template in FrontPage.

Customer Support Web This template creates a place where your customers can go to report bugs, find solutions to previously reported problems, and suggest improvements for your products and services. This is an ideal site for software companies, but it is applicable to many kinds of businesses.

Learning FrontPage This is the template you use with the Learning FrontPage Tutorial, which you'll find in online help.

Personal Web This template creates a very simple site with a single personal home page. For a more in-depth and customized home page, you can do the following:

- Use the Editor to customize the page.
- Use the Personal Home Page Wizard instead of the Personal Web template. For details on using wizards, see "Wizards" later in this chapter.

Project Web Use this template to create a site that will serve as a central informational forum for a project. It creates a home page, a page that lists members of the project team, a schedule page, a status page, a search page, and a page that links to all public discussions about the project.

Page Templates

FrontPage offers you a wide variety of page templates to choose from, ranging from a bare-bones Normal page to a fairly complex "frequently asked questions" (FAQ) page. Adding pages to an existing site with a page template is a fast and easy way to customize a site.

Using page templates You create a page using a template in the Editor. The process is very simple:

1. In the Explorer, open the site that the new page will belong to. (You can skip this step if you want to; after you save the page, you can import it to any web site.)
2. In the Editor, choose New from the File menu.
3. In the New Page dialog box that appears, select a template from the Template Or Wizard list, and then click OK.

FrontPage creates the page using the template you selected, and presents it in the Editor for you to work on. Whenever you create a new page from a page template, it includes advice at the top about how to customize the page, as in the example on the next page:

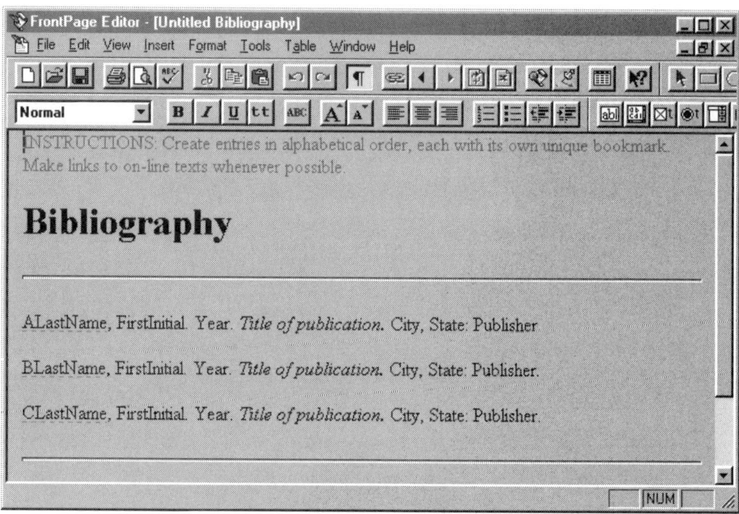

A page created with the Bibliography template, with advice at the top on how best to proceed.

You can use 25 different templates to create new pages in your site. The following are brief descriptions of the templates, starting with Normal Page, the most general template. The rest are listed alphabetically. You'll find that the templates have a wide variety of uses, and that some of them are designed to be used together in the same site.

Normal Page This template simply creates a blank page. If you want to create a new page from scratch, this is the place to start.

Bibliography If you need to compile a bibliography of sources, you can use this template to begin. It provides some examples for you to mimic, so you don't have to create each entry from scratch.

Confirmation Form Use this template to display confirmation entries to users who have submitted information to your organization. The example provided in the template consists of a letter to confirm the submission of customer feedback.

Directory of Press Releases You can use this template to produce a page on which your press releases are organized by date and title. The page includes sections for current releases and past releases. You can use the Press Release template, described on page 64, to create a release and then link to it from this directory page.

Employee Directory You can alphabetically organize your employee information using this template, which includes areas for you to enter an employee's title, project, office location, e-mail address, and more.

Employment Opportunities This is quite a complex template. It provides sections for job listings, job descriptions, and a place for users to submit general employment inquiries. Users can send you their employment history, goals, and contact information through this page.

Feedback Form This template creates a page for users to submit specific comments about your company, products, web site, and so on.

Frequently Asked Questions You can use this template to create an FAQ page, where users can get answers to frequently asked questions.

Glossary of Terms This template produces a glossary page that is separated into alphabetized sections. Glossaries can be quite useful to viewers if your pages include technical terms that they might not understand. Otherwise, glossary pages are rarely used in web sites.

Guest Book This template creates a page where your viewers can leave comments. Watch out when using this one; if your web site contains controversial information, you could get negative comments on this page for the rest of the world to see. This page is best used in an intranet setting.

Hot List If you'd like your site to include a page that lists links to other sites, you can use this template to begin. You can use this page in any kind of site, whether it's a personal or business site and whether the site is on an intranet or on the World Wide Web.

HyperDocument Page This template creates a page that is intended to be one section of a linked manual or report. You can build a document by putting several of these pages together.

Lecture Abstract This template creates a page describing an upcoming lecture. It includes space for a speaker name, organization, topics of discussion, and more. You can use this with the Seminar Schedule template, which is described on the next page.

Meeting Agenda When you want to make sure that everyone attending a meeting has an opportunity to look over the agenda, you can post the agenda on your intranet using this template. You can then build links to any documents that should be reviewed before the meeting.

Office Directory Use this template to produce a page that lists the locations of all your organization's offices. It includes placeholders for the 50 U.S. states, all of the Canadian provinces, and a collection of international listings.

Press Release This template creates a press release page, which when completed can be linked to a page created with the Directory of Press Releases template. You add these links in the Editor.

Product Description You can use this template to create a page containing descriptions of your products; the page is separated into product summary, key features, product benefits, and specifications sections.

Product or Event Registration This template produces a registration form page for users to fill out and submit. You can use it for product support, events, or other registration purposes.

Search Page Use this template to create a page where users can perform keyword searches of your entire web site. The template inserts a Search bot for you, which includes all the code needed to perform a search. This template provides a ready-made search page; all you need to do is customize it in the Editor. For more information on bots, see Chapter 8.

Seminar Schedule This template produces the main page for a collection of seminar information. The page is divided into several sections, each with placeholders where you can fill in specific information on sessions or tracks of the seminar. You can use this template in conjunction with the Lecture Abstract template, which is described on the previous page.

Software Data Sheet This template creates a page you can use to show off the benefits of your software. It contains places to list key benefits, features, system requirements, product availability, and more.

Survey Form This template creates an extremely detailed survey form with several sections. Each section includes placeholders for different types of questions, with answers ranging in style from check boxes to drop-down list boxes.

Table of Contents You can use this template to produce a Table of Contents page for your site, which will contain links to the other pages in the site.

User Registration This template creates a page where users can register for other protected web sites on a server. It contains explicit directions for the user, and it must be loaded as part of the **root web site** on your server in order to work correctly.

What's New You can use this template to create a simple What's New page that lists changes to your site by date.

Custom Templates

Because everyone has a different style, and because you might have specific needs that the templates don't address, FrontPage allows you to create and save your own page templates in the Editor. To find out how to create custom web site templates, see the next page.

Perhaps you want to create several similar pages that don't look much like any of the existing FrontPage templates. You can create your own template to use when creating these pages and minimize the number of changes you need to make to each (rather than starting with a FrontPage template and having to modify it extensively to meet your needs).

Using a custom template is a great way to streamline the gathering of employee information at a company. You can create a specific form with places for each kind of information you need from your employees, and then save that form as a template. That template can then be distributed within your organization for all to use.

Creating and saving a custom template requires only a few steps, which are listed on the next page:

1. Start with the Normal Page template in the Editor, and create the content that you want to have appear in your new template.
2. Choose the Save As command from the File menu in the Editor.
3. In the Save As dialog box that appears, click the As Template button. You do not need to supply a template name or a **URL** before you click this button.
4. In the Save As Template dialog box, give your template a name and title, and then enter a short description of the template in the Description text box. If you want to save the current template in place of another template, click the Browse button and find the template you want to replace.

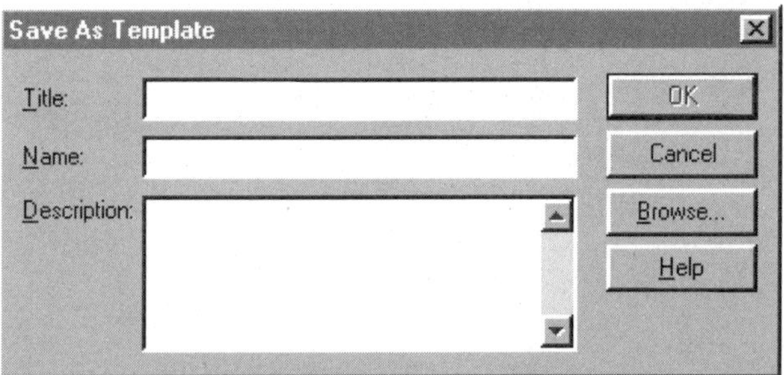

5. Click OK in the Save As Template dialog box. FrontPage saves the page as a template and returns you to the page.

After you save the template, any time you create a new page in the Editor the template will appear in the New Page dialog box along with all the page templates and wizards included with FrontPage.

Custom web site templates You can use the FrontPage Developer's Kit to create custom web site templates. For information on obtaining this free kit, see the FrontPage portion of Microsoft's Web site at http://www.microsoft.com/msoffice/frontpage.

Wizards

How long do you suppose it would take to create a web site for your business from scratch that includes all of the following?

- A home page with places for an introduction, mission statement, company profile, and/or contact information
- A What's New page that contains links for press releases, articles, reviews, and information about your site
- Numerous products and services pages, each with room for a description of the product or service, images, pricing information, and more
- A table of contents page that indexes your site and is updated automatically as your site structure changes
- A feedback form that asks users for specific information such as their name, title, address, phone number, fax number, and e-mail address

As you know by now, creating all of this from scratch and writing it in HTML would take quite a long time. You can find other web-design programs that let you create web pages without your having to know much HTML, but they still require you to put the site together piece by piece, which can also take a long time. And afterward, you have to link all those pages together. Would you believe that with FrontPage, completing all of the above can take less than two minutes? You can do it all with the Corporate Presence Wizard, which is one of several wizards included with FrontPage, and a couple dozen clicks of the mouse. And when you're done, you'll have a set of linked pages complete with elements that are ready for you to customize.

FrontPage offers two web wizards, which create the framework for entire web sites, and three page wizards, which create web pages.

Web Wizards

The two web wizards are the Corporate Presence Wizard and the Discussion Web Wizard. The Corporate Presence Wizard creates the framework for a site that includes the items described on the previous page, and the Discussion Web Wizard produces a site in which users can participate in discussions on various topics. First we'll walk through the Corporate Presence Wizard; after that, you'll find a description of the Discussion Web Wizard.

Keep in mind that you can easily change the resulting site later on if you want to, using the Editor. You can customize text and graphics to give your site a branded look and feel, add to the pages, delete items or pages, and modify the pages in any other way you like.

Creating a Corporate Presence site Using the Corporate Presence Wizard, you can create a site to highlight your business without having to do much up-front work. Let's step through the process of using this wizard, as someone might when designing a site for the Snake River Winery:

1. From the File menu in the Explorer, choose New Web. In the New Web dialog box that appears, select Corporate Presence Wizard.

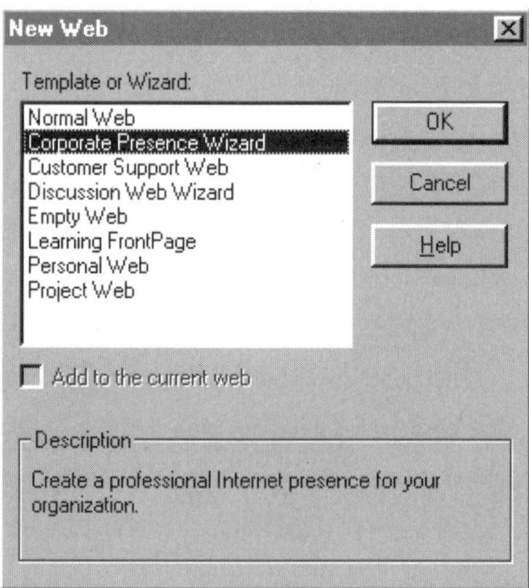

If you already have a site up and running, you can select the Add To The Current Web check box to integrate your Corporate Presence site with it. For example, you can combine a Corporate Presence site with a Customer Support site. This is a great option to experiment with once you get to know the different kinds of sites FrontPage can create for you. If you're creating just this site, do not select the Add To The Current Web check box.

When you are ready to continue, click OK.

2. Next you'll be greeted by the New Web From Wizard dialog box. In the Web Server text box, you type in the name of the server you want to house the site on, or you select a server from the drop-down list. Then, you name your site in the Web Name text box—this is the name that will appear on the server.

   The winery has a web server of its own, called Teton, so they would type that name in the Web Server text box. If you want to follow along on your own system, you should select the name of your server from the drop-down list. For more information about using the Personal Web Server, see Chapter 9.

   Next, you type the name of the site, Snake River Winery Cellar, in the Web Name text box. Because FrontPage doesn't allow spaces in the name of a site, you need to replace the spaces with underscore characters. Therefore, you should enter the name *Snake_River_Winery_Cellar.*

   When you click OK, FrontPage creates the site on the server.

3. You might be presented with the Name And Password Required dialog box for security purposes. You must have administrative access to create a site. Enter your name and password, and then click OK to continue with the procedure.

4. Next you'll see the opening screen of the Corporate Presence Wizard, as shown on the next page.

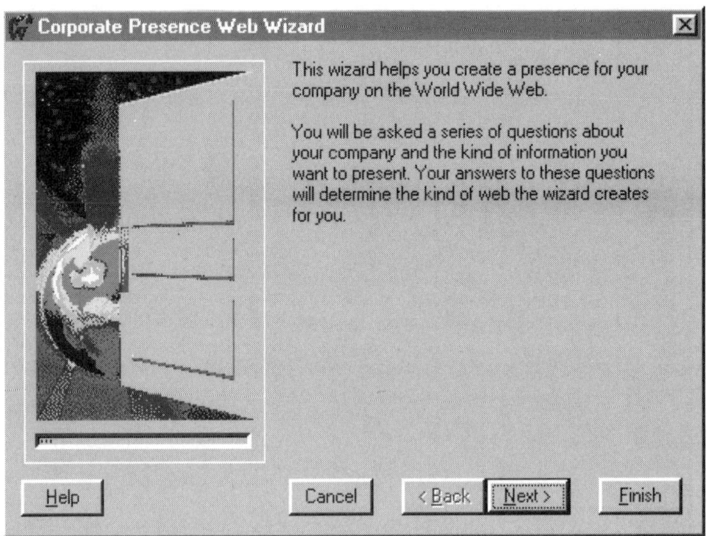

It contains a brief description of the wizard and informs you that you'll be asked a few questions about how you want your site to appear. Several buttons appear at the bottom of this screen and the ones following it:

Help At any time, you can click the Help button to open a Corporate Presence Web Wizard topic in online help.

Cancel The Cancel button stops the wizard and takes you back to the Explorer. Because some of the material for the site will have already been created, you are asked whether to delete the site.

Back When the Back button is enabled, you can click it to return to the previous page or pages and change any information you already entered.

Next Clicking the Next button takes you to the next screen in the wizard.

Finish The Finish button ends the wizard process at whatever point you click it. You can stop using the wizard anytime before the final wizard screen. When you click Finish, FrontPage immediately begins to populate the site with all the information you've supplied up to that point.

Click Next to proceed.

5. The next screen gives you several options for pages to include in your site. You'll notice that the Back button is now enabled.

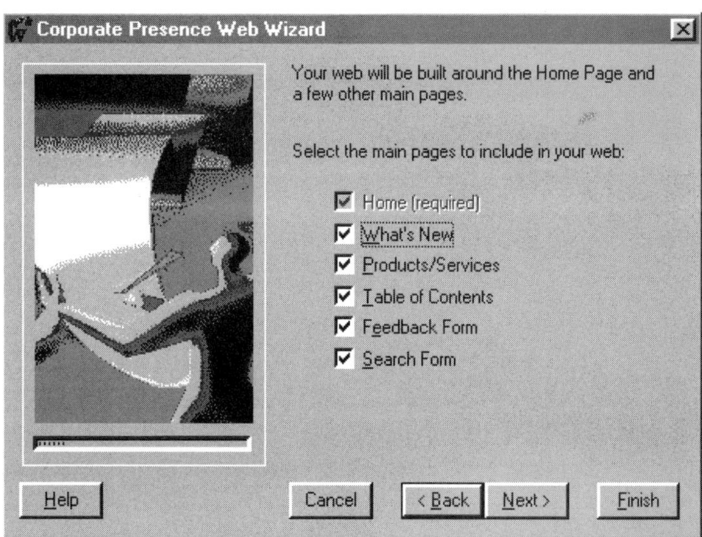

The Snake River Winery is building a very sophisticated site and will include all of the available types of pages (listed below). The site starts with a required home page, the contents of which can be customized in the next step of the wizard.

> **TIP**
>
> If at any point in the wizard you're certain that all the remaining items are filled in the way you want, or if you know you don't want to include any remaining optional pages that could be created with the wizard, you can click Finish.

What's New page This page is a must! For any users that return to the site multiple times, this page can provide information on recent updates to the site. Perhaps there's a new chardonnay being offered in the fall, or maybe there's a special group rate for tours of the winery in July. The What's New page can link to these items in your site.

Products/Services page Simply because the winery sells products, and especially because the products have mass appeal, the Products/Services page is a wise addition to the site. Here the winery can highlight all of the wines and other products it offers, and this might be a good place to tell people how to order.

Table of Contents page Those who want to see an overview of what the winery's site has to offer can go to this page, which links to all other pages in the site. As explained in Chapter 2, it's wise to include some sort of overview page in your site. These pages can help prevent users from getting "lost" in your site.

Feedback Form The winery management wants to know what users think of the products offered in the site, and what they think of the site. Users can use the feedback form to submit comments to the winery.

Search Form The winery considers a search form a "value-add" for its site. It allows users to search the site for any word that might appear on its pages. Enabling the search form is as easy as selecting the Search Form check box in the wizard. FrontPage automatically compiles a word list that the search form uses when someone searches the site.

For each page you decide to include in your web site, the wizard will present you with a subsequent screen to customize the page further. The wizard will not show screens for pages you did not select on this screen.

Click Next when you're ready to move on.

6. Next you'll see a screen with several options for the format of your home page. Your choices include creating spaces for an introduction, mission statement, company profile, and contact information for your company. You're not asked to supply the exact information, such as the text of your mission statement, at this time; you enter that later. The wizard simply creates a space for you to fill with the actual content at your leisure.

   The folks at the Snake River Winery want their site to look professional, so at the very least they'll include the introduction, company profile, and contact information. Including the contact information is vital; potential wholesalers or individual customers who view the site might want to find out more about purchasing products.

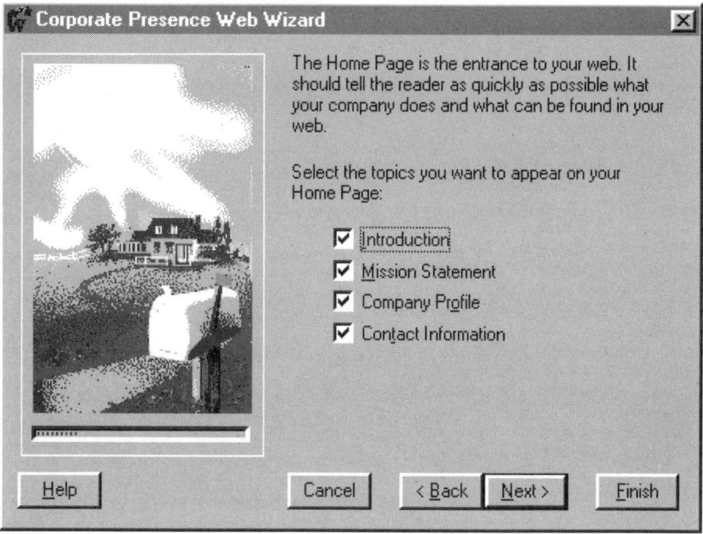

After you select the check boxes for the topics you want to include, click Next.

7. Options for the What's New page are presented on the next screen, shown below. Select any of the three check boxes if you want to include that type of information on the page. FrontPage creates subsections for any items that you want to include on the What's New page.

   If a contact phone number changes at the Snake River Winery, the winery can alert its web-site viewers to the new number on the What's New page in the Web Changes section. Any other breaking news about the company can easily be added to this page later on as well.

   The What's New page is also a great place to put information about the industry, such as a list of upcoming trade shows, positive information about stock trends, or other business news. It's great to have a place in your site where visitors can expect new, timely content. Such information can lure your customers back to your pages, where they'll be exposed to your products again and again. You can use the Press Releases section and the Articles And Reviews section for this purpose.

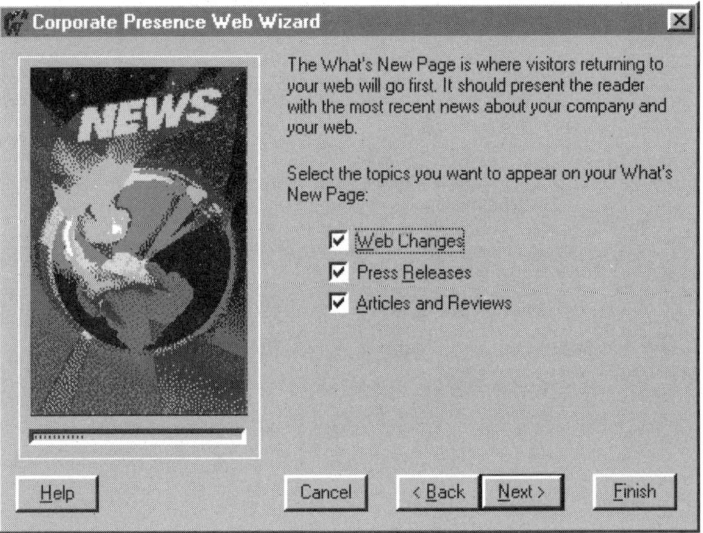

After you select the kind of information you want to include on your page to start with, click Next.

8. The next screen provides options for the Products/Services page. Enter the values for the number of products and/or services you want to highlight on this page. The wizard creates sections on the page for the number of products and services you enter on this screen.

   The Snake River Winery plans to highlight all of its 10 fine wines on the web site, so the site developers will enter 10 in the Products text box. The winery also prides itself on providing top-flight customer service, so it'll enter 1 in the Services text box to provide a section to highlight that aspect of the company.

> **TIP**
>
> You can tab through the content options on the wizard screens instead of using your mouse. To select or deselect a check box, use the Spacebar.

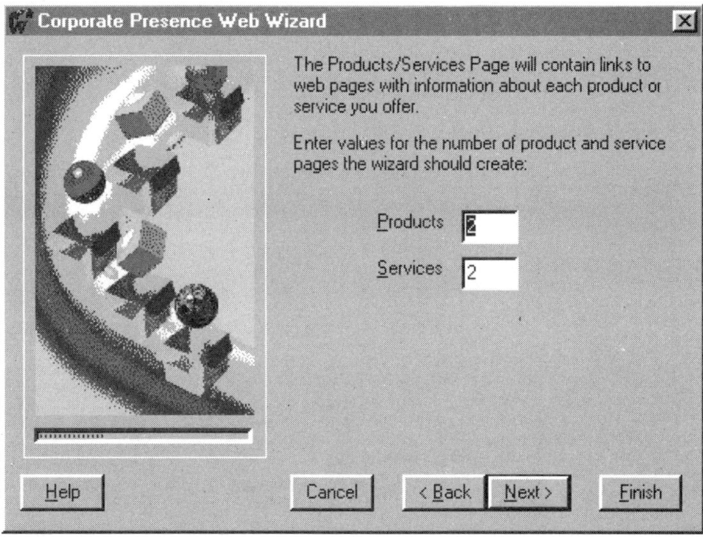

Click Next to move to the next screen.

9. Next you'll choose how you want to customize any product or service pages you have in your site. The wizard gives you choices to provide placeholders for product images, pricing information, and information request forms on the Products pages, and to provide capabilities lists, reference accounts, and information request forms on Services pages.

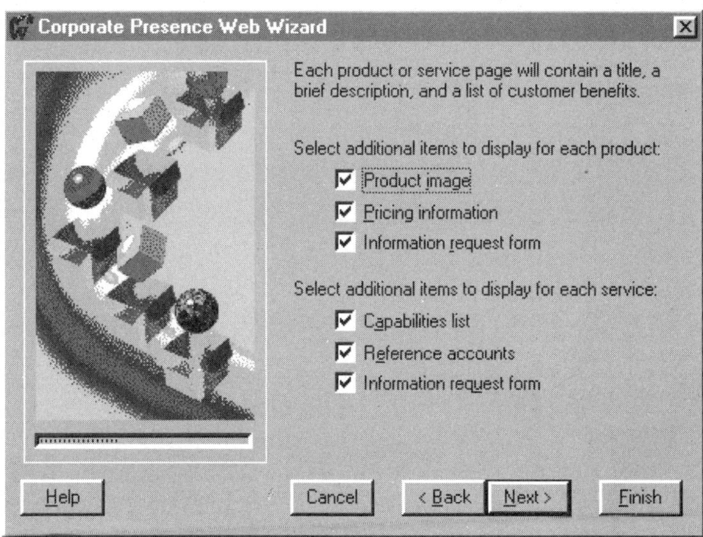

Select the options you want to include on those pages, and then click Next.

10. The next screen provides options for the feedback form, where you specify the information you want to receive from your audience. Think carefully about this, keeping in mind what kind of audience you expect to view your pages. If the audience doesn't have lots of time to fill out every item, seeing all of them at once might overwhelm them. Even though it takes only seconds to fill out a feedback form, Web surfers are keen on clicking out of a page if it looks like too much work.

    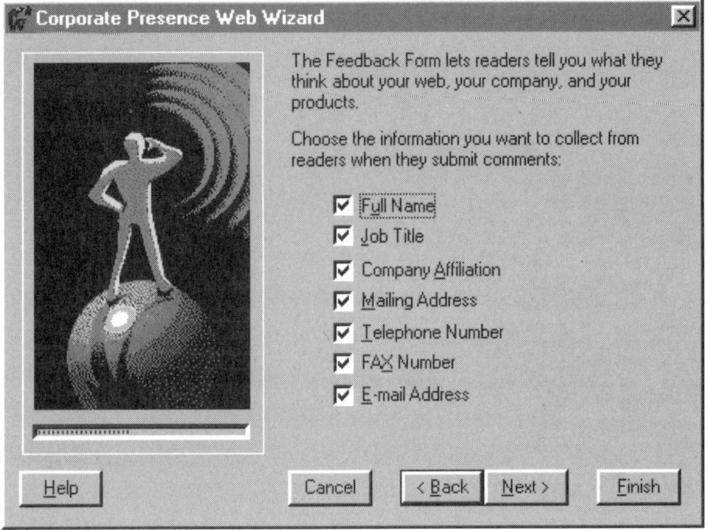

    After you select the options you want for the feedback form, click Next.

11. The next screen includes a neat feature: It allows you to specify how the feedback you receive from your viewers is stored. If you plan to manipulate the information using a database or spreadsheet application (such as Microsoft Access or Microsoft Excel), select the first option and FrontPage will store the information in tab-delimited format. If you don't plan to use such an application, select the second option and FrontPage will store the information in web-page format.

    The Snake River Winery is not a large company, but management does expect to receive heavy traffic on its web site. It's easier to manipulate feedback information in Access and Excel—this reduces the workload significantly—so management wants to save the feedback information in tab-delimited format. That means the Yes, Use Tab-Delimited Format option should be selected.

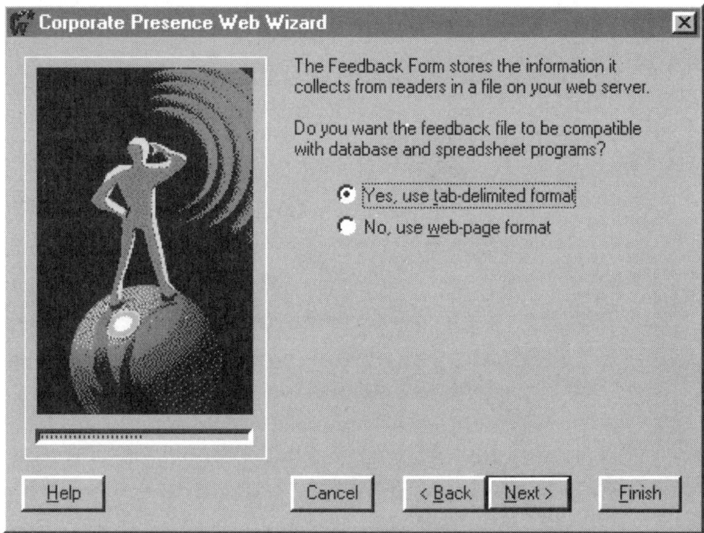

When you've made your choice, click Next to continue.

12. Next you'll see a screen with options to customize the Table of Contents (TOC) page, shown on page 78. Here you can select options to update the TOC automatically each time a page is edited, to show pages not linked to the pages that appear in the TOC, and to use bullets for top-level pages.

    If you anticipate that your site will be small or that it won't be updated often, it's a good idea to select the Keep Page List Up-To-Date Automatically check box. However, if you anticipate that your site will be large or that it will grow significantly, then you should not select this check box. Updating the page list can be time-consuming in these cases. You can update the TOC manually later on, so don't be overly concerned about this option.

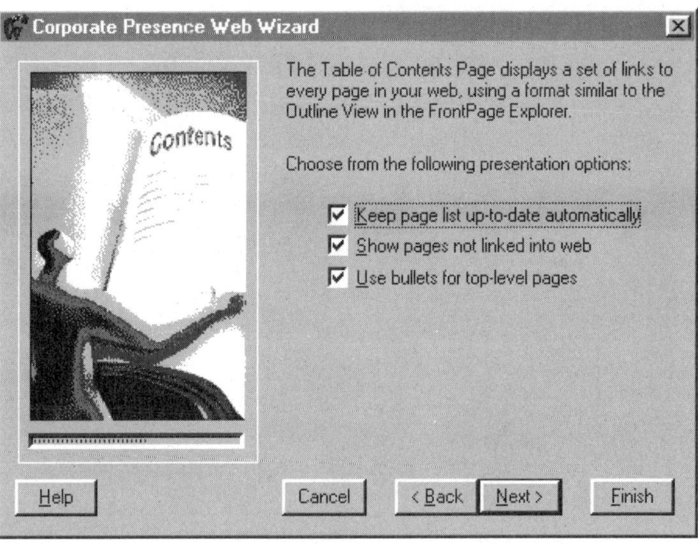

After you select the options to customize your TOC page, click Next.

13. The next screen deals with the items you want at the top and bottom of every page in your site. You can include your company's logo, a page title, and links to your main web pages at the top. You can also include links to your main web pages at the bottom, along with your **webmaster**'s e-mail address, a copyright notice, and the date the page was last modified (which is supplied automatically by FrontPage).

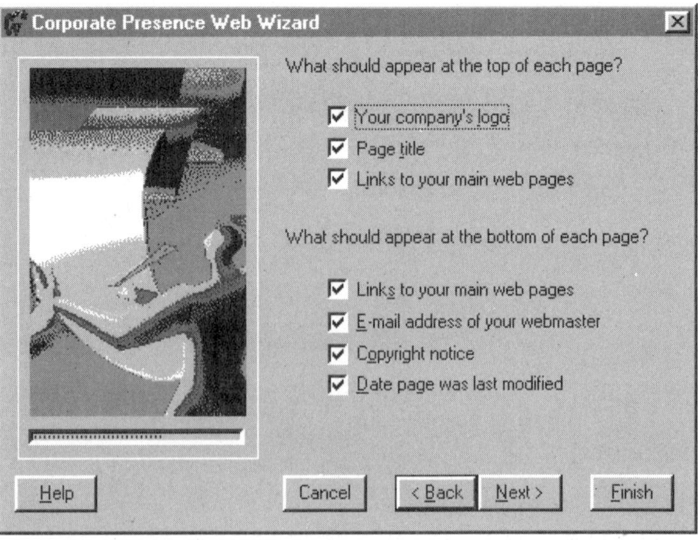

Again, these options control whether FrontPage leaves room for the item, not the actual content for each item.

Select the options you want even if you plan to use different items on different pages.

The winery web site will sport a different logo for the pages in each section, so you should select the Your Company's Logo check box to include a space for the logo. Later, in the Editor you can manually insert a different logo at the beginning of each page.

FrontPage doesn't check the contents of each space, so you can be flexible in how you use these options. For example, if the winery wants to include the e-mail address of someone other than the webmaster on the pages, the E-mail Address Of Your Webmaster check box should be selected to leave the space open. The e-mail address can be changed in the Editor later on.

Select the options you want, and then click Next.

14. On the next screen, you can control the "look and feel" of your site. This screen gives you four options for the presentation style of your site—Plain, Conservative, Flashy, or Cool. Selecting one of these options displays the corresponding style on the left side of the screen.

    As a young, energetic, up-and-coming business, the Snake River Winery does not want to present itself as conservative, so it selects the Cool option.

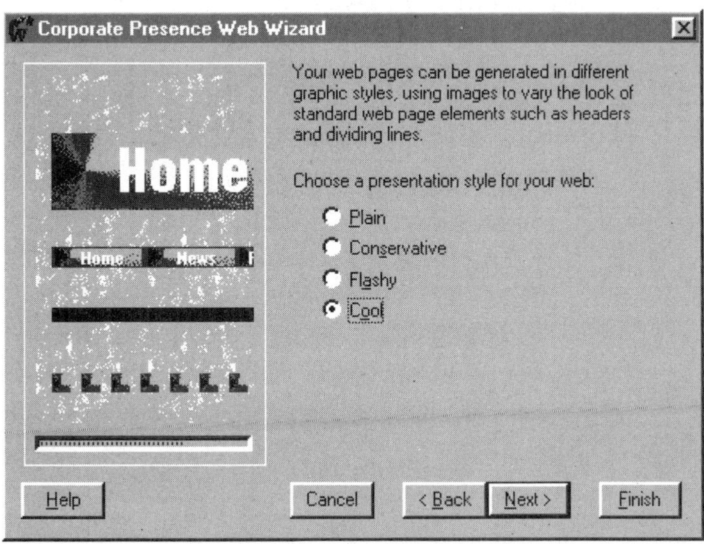

After you select a presentation style, click Next.

15. Next you'll see a screen that asks you to specify settings for the page background and text in your site.

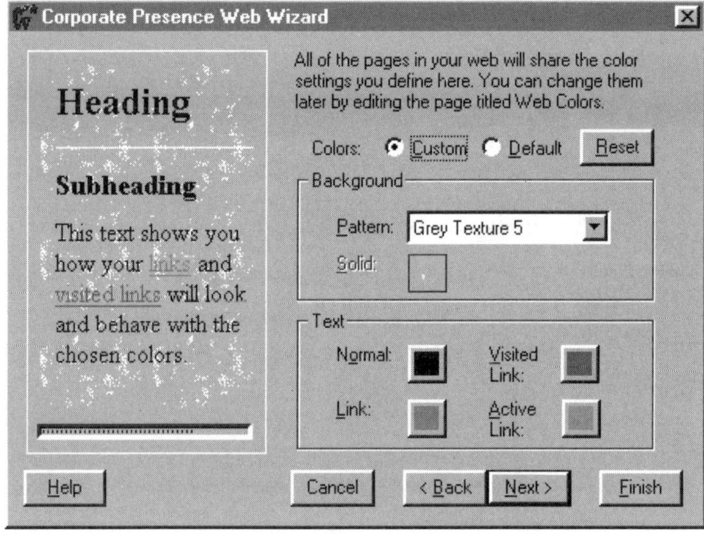

You can set your colors as follows:

- In the Colors section, select the Custom option to set your own colors and textures for the site, or select Default to use the FrontPage default settings. Clicking the Reset button refreshes the screen with the default settings. If you select Default, your only choice is to move to the next screen by clicking the Next button. If you select Custom, you can first specify settings in the Background and Text sections.
- In the Background section, select any textured option in the Pattern drop-down list box if you want a textured screen. The sample on the left changes to a preview of your selection. If you want a solid screen, select None in the drop-down list box, and then click the color button next to Solid. The Color dialog box appears, giving you 48 colors to choose from, as well as the option to set a custom color for your background. Select a color, and then click OK to return to the wizard screen.
- In the Text section, select a color for Normal text, links, visited links, and active links. Click the color button next to each item, and then select a color from the Color dialog box and click OK.

These settings are in no way permanent; you can always change them later by editing the properties of the Web Colors page that's created by this wizard as a part of the Corporate Presence site. You can locate this page easily by using Summary view.

The winery wants to mimic as much as possible the look and feel of a wine cellar, so select the Brown Texture 1 background color. Retain the default black text, which can be read easily against that background. Use the default colors for the links for the same reasons. (Default colors are blue for active links, purple for visited links, and red for active links.)

After you select all your color options, click Next.

16. The next screen gives you the option of showing an Under Construction icon on all unfinished pages of your site. It's always a good idea to label a page as "under construction" if it's not finished. This way, viewers won't think a page is final if it's not. For example, the winery wants to show its Products page, but the page is not yet complete. By using an Under Construction icon, the winery can at least expose the public to its products while the page is being completed.

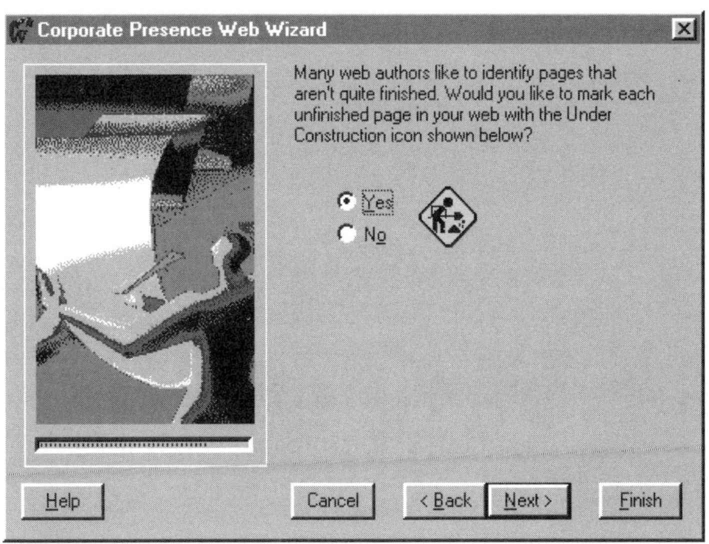

Select Yes, and then click Next.

17. The next two screens offer *huge* potential time-savers. They ask for your company information, such as the company's full name, one-word name, address, phone number, and fax number; the e-mail address of the webmaster; and a general-information e-mail address. These screens are time-savers because you enter this information once, and FrontPage inserts the information into the placeholders already in your site. For example, on an earlier screen of the wizard (step 13), if you requested that FrontPage display your webmaster's e-mail address at the bottom of every page, all you need to do is type the address here, and FrontPage will take care of the rest.

    If you need to make changes to this information later on, you only need to change it in one place. (You can change these settings later on by using the Web Settings command on the Explorer's Tools menu.)

    The Snake River Winery wants to start with all this information on its pages, even though it might decide later not to include some of it.

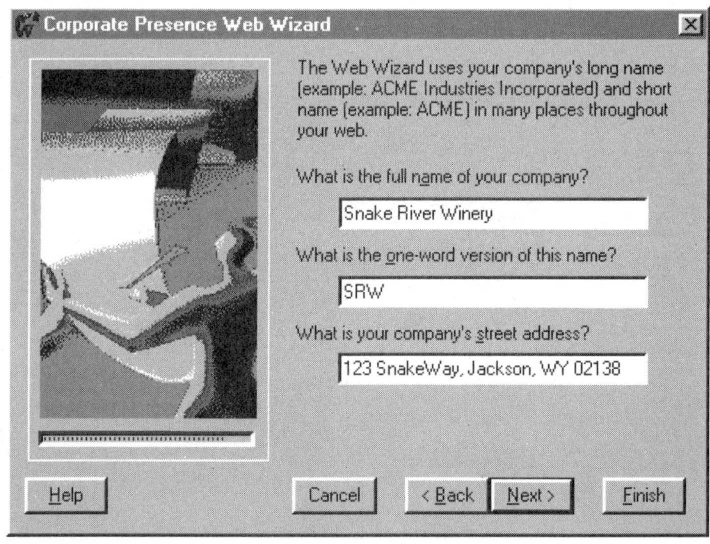

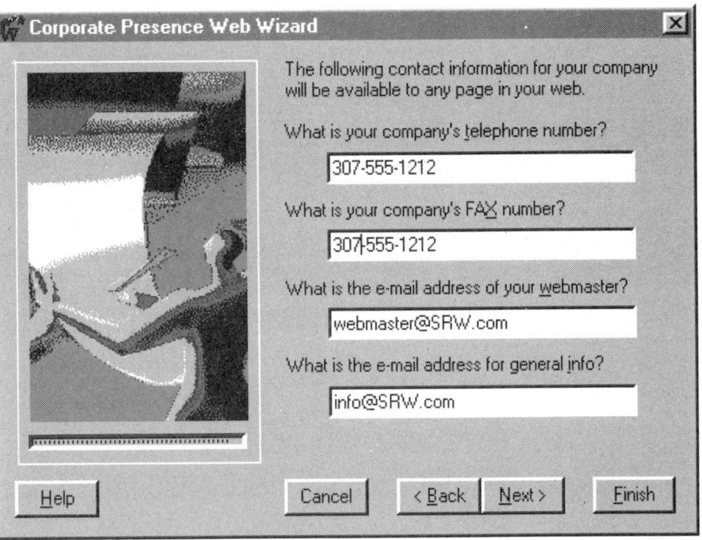

When you finish entering this information on each screen, click Next to move on.

18. The final screen tells you that FrontPage has gathered all the information it needs to create your Corporate Presence site. It includes a Show The To Do List After Web Is Uploaded check box. The To Do List is a list of tasks that need to be completed in your site. FrontPage adds several tasks to the list after it creates this site; among them are customizing various pages with specific text and other files, and replacing images. The To Do List is explained in greater detail in Chapter 5.

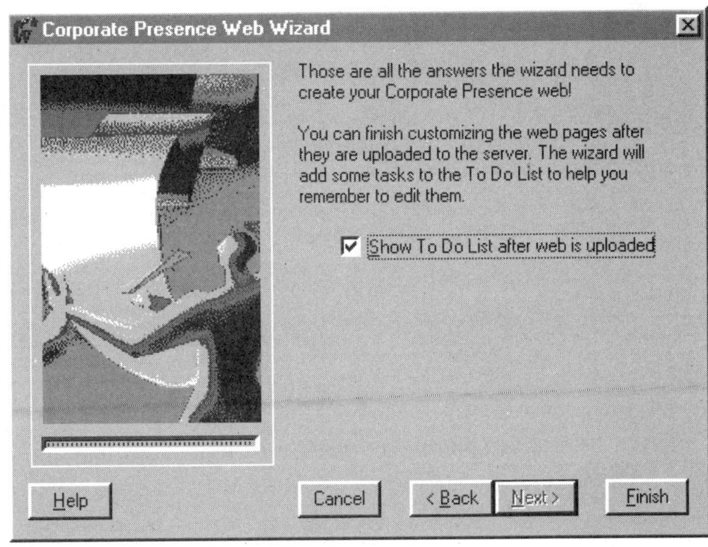

Click Finish, and FrontPage fills in the Corporate Presence site with the information you've supplied and saves the site to the server. It shows the outline for the site in the Explorer and also shows the To Do List if you've directed it to. From this point you can fill in the fine details of your site and craft it to give it your own "look and feel."

That's all there is to creating the framework for a web site using the Corporate Presence Wizard—a bunch of tiny steps, all of which add up to huge time savings.

Discussion Web Wizard The Discussion Web Wizard creates a threaded **discussion group** about a topic of your choice. Each user can contribute thoughts and associate them with a particular ongoing conversation (a **thread**). Each separate entry from a user is referred to as an **article**. The wizard asks you to decide the following:

- What kinds of pages you want to include
- The title of the discussion
- Some input fields to separate topics of discussion
- Whether the discussion will take place in a protected site (meaning that only registered users can participate)
- How the table of contents should sort the posted articles
- Whether the Table of Contents page should be the site's home page
- The information you want reported about each article found in a search of past discussions
- The colors for the background and text
- Whether you want to create the site using **frames**

As always, you can change the look and feel and add or delete features to these pages later, using the Editor.

Administering a discussion group You can administer a discussion group in FrontPage quite easily by using the Explorer the Editor. All you need is author or administrative access to the discussion site. If you're in charge of administering a discussion group, here are a few things you can do:

- Edit messages—Each page that a user completes and sends to the discussion group is called a message; it's saved as an HTML file in a hidden directory of the web site. To see a list of messages, you need to tell FrontPage to show files in hidden directories. You can do this by selecting the Show Documents In Hidden Directories check box on the Advanced tab of the Web Settings dialog box. You reach the Web Settings dialog box by choosing Web Settings from the Tools menu in the Explorer.

  You edit a message by double-clicking on it in the Explorer. The message appears in the Editor, where you can delete text such as objectionable language. The modified message can then be saved back to the web site in a directory representing a topic in the discussion.

- Delete old messages—If you can see the files that are in hidden directories, you can sort the files and delete old messages that are no longer needed. In Summary view, sort the list of files in the discussion site by date, and then delete any files you don't need by selecting them and pressing the Del key.

- Limit administrative access—As you can see, any author can view and edit any message in the discussion group if he or she has access to the site. This amounts to little administrative control if a large number of authors are members of the discussion group. To limit administrative access, put the discussion group into a separate web site (with a link from the main discussion), where the moderator(s) of the discussion group are added as the only authors allowed to modify that site.

Page Wizards

FrontPage includes three page wizards, which make it easy to create customized multisection pages. They are the Form Page Wizard, the Personal Home Page Wizard, and the Frames Wizard.

The Form Page Wizard creates a form that you can use to gather input from users and save the results to a web page or text file on the web server. This form can be very useful in situations where you need to gather contact information, account information, product information, and so on, from your viewers. The Personal Home Page Wizard produces a page that includes placeholders for you to insert information on your work, current projects, favorite web sites, biographical information, and more. The Frames Wizard allows you to divide one web page into several sections, each of which displays an individual page on your screen.

You use these page wizards in the Editor. Each resulting page can be placed in your site and linked to other pages.

Using the Form Page Wizard and the Personal Home Page Wizard To add a page to your site using the Form Page Wizard or the Personal Home Page Wizard, do the following:

1. In the Explorer, open the site that the new page will belong to. (You can skip this step if you want to; after you save the page, you can import it to any web site.)
2. From the File menu in the Editor, choose New. The New Page dialog box appears, as shown below.

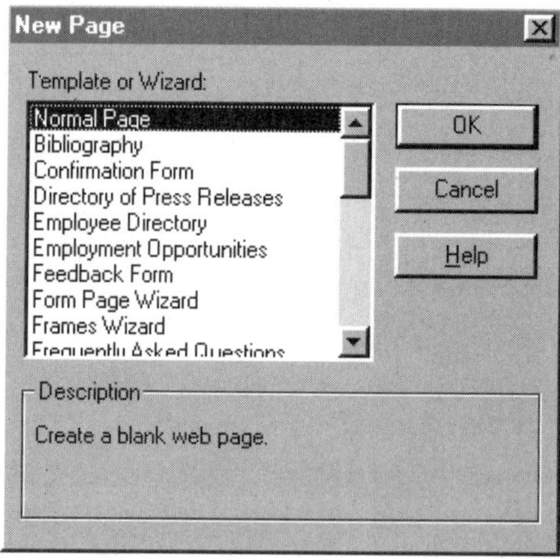

3. From the list of page wizards and templates, select either the Form Page Wizard or the Personal Home Page Wizard, and then click OK. A description of each wizard appears in the lower portion of the dialog box as you highlight it.
4. Move through the screens of the wizard and answer the questions that FrontPage asks you. The process of using these wizards is the same as for using the Corporate Web Wizard, described above, but the questions are of course different. For example, you'll be asked to name the page instead of naming a site.
5. When you reach the final screen, click Finish and FrontPage will create the page and add it to your site. You can then edit the page in the Editor, adding text and/or images, linking it to other pages, and so on.

Frames Frames are a relatively new Internet advance. They allow you to define a region of a page to display content from a different page and manage it independently. You can place one or more frames on a page (referred to as the **frameset** for that page). This lets you create a page on which different regions have different content. Changing the content of one region doesn't necessarily change the content of another, but when desired, links in one frame can cause the page that is displayed in another frame to change.

Here's a classic example of the use of frames: Imagine a web page divided vertically into two regions, each of which is a frame. The left frame is occupied by a Table of Contents page, containing a complete list of links to all pages in the site. The contents of the frame on the right side of the screen change, depending on what link is clicked in the Table of Contents on the left side. If you click on a link to a Products page in the Table of Contents, the Products page appears on the right side; if you click on the Feedback link, the Feedback page appears, and so on. This scenerio is depicted in the illustration on the next page.

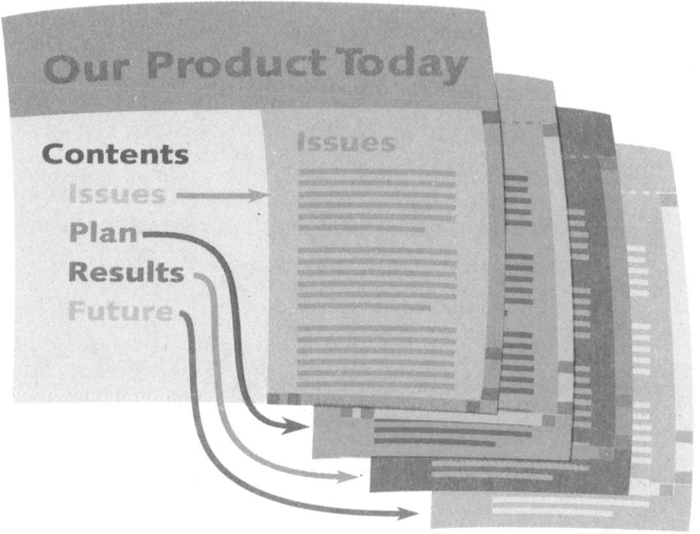

A page divided into frames. Click on a link in the TOC on the left side, and that page appears on the right side.

Frames are currently supported in Netscape Navigator version 2.0, and in the upcoming beta release of Microsoft's Internet Explorer version 3.0, scheduled for the summer of 1996. Frames undoubtedly will be supported in other browsers in the near future, and Microsoft is working to make frames in FrontPage compatible with the support provided by all the leading browsers.

You can include as many frames on a page as you want, and you can include frames on one page or on every page of your site. You designate the content of your frames using various resources in the Editor. For details on this, see Chapter 6. You also create pages containing frames in the Editor; this process is described next.

Using the Frames Wizard To create pages containing frames, follow this process:

1. Create all the pages that will be displayed within the frame(s) in your site. You'll link to these pages later in this procedure.
2. In the Explorer, open the site that the new page will belong to. (You can skip this step if you want to; after you save the page, you can import it to any web site.)

3. In the Editor, choose New from the File menu. Select Frames Wizard in the New Page dialog box that appears, and then click OK.

4. From this step forward, you'll be in the Frames Wizard. On the first screen, you're asked to choose between creating a page by using one of six templates or by making a custom grid. Using a template, you can create a page with frames already arranged in formats appropriate for Table of Contents pages, pages for documents and footnotes, and other pages with hierarchical layouts. Select the Pick A Template check box or the Make A Custom Grid check box, and then click Next.

   If you decide to use a template, follow step 4a; if you decide to create your own grid, follow steps 4b–4c.

4a. Using a template: On the Frames Wizard - Pick Template Layout screen, select a layout by clicking on an item in the Layout section. Clicking on a layout description yields a preview of the layout on the left side of the screen and a description of the layout at the bottom of the screen. After you select a layout, click OK. Then move on to step 5.

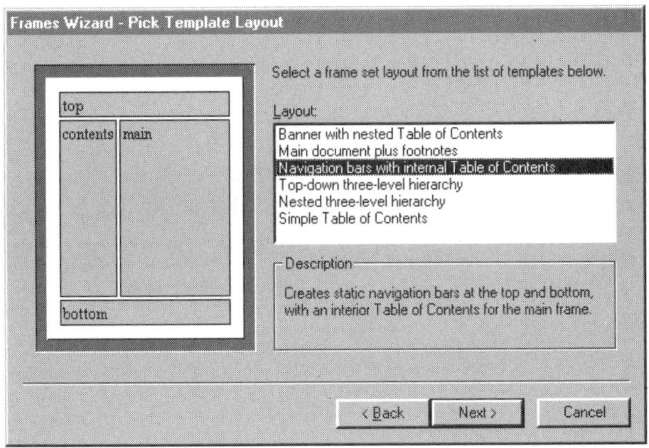

4b. Creating your own grid: On the Edit Frameset Grid screen shown on the next page, specify the number of rows and columns you want in their respective controls (thereby determining the number of frames). You can initally have up to five rows and five columns of frames on a page. The example on the left side of the screen changes to show the selected organization of frames. If you select a template and then change your mind and try to create a custom grid, the template's organization is used as the basis for the page. You can modify it, but be aware that some of the rows might have frames that have already been divided (as explained below).

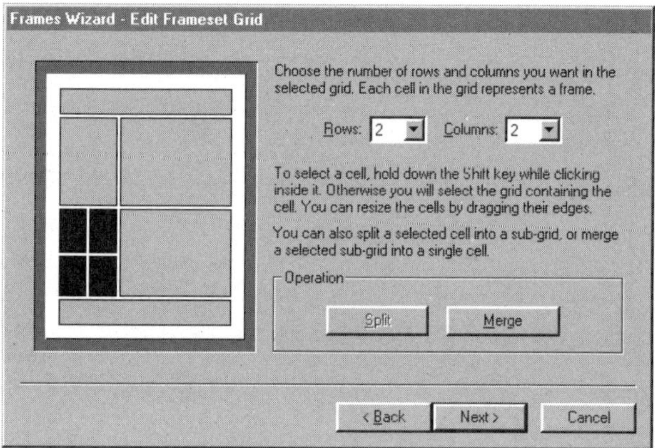

The Edit Frameset Grid screen lets you divide your page into frames.

To resize a frame, move your mouse pointer over the border of the frame in the sample on the left, and when the pointer becomes a double-headed arrow, click and drag the border.

Each frame can further be divided into additional frames. To divide a frame, hold down the Shift key while clicking on the frame. Click the Split button in the Operation section of the wizard screen, and then use the controls at the top of the form to specify the number of rows and columns you want to subdivide the frame into. To merge a divided frame back to its former state, click on any frame within the split frame (which selects all of the original frame) and click the Merge button.

The small frames that are created when you divide a row can be used for many purposes, and we'll undoubtedly see some inventive ones on the Web in the near future. In general, rows are used to represent sections within the page (each with different topics), and the columns within a row are used for related (but independent) information. You might use small frames to display an image file or other element—an item that you want to appear on that row all the time. There are other ways of accomplishing this, of course, but designating content in frames is a handy and relatively easy way.

4c. After you create your grid, click the Next button. The Frames Wizard - Edit Frame Attributes screen appears, asking you to name all of your frames on the page. Click on each frame to highlight it, and then give it a name and specify the URL of the page or other file that you want to place in it. Give your frames easy-to-remember names; you'll need to type these names in later when you create links to them.

To link the contents of one frame to another, select the frame containing the page with the links that should control the contents of the other frame, and then click the Edit button. This opens the page containing the links in the Editor. To have all of the linked pages appear in the same frame, right-click on the page, select Page Properties, enter the name of the frame where the linked pages should appear in the Default Target Frame text box, and click OK. To have a linked page appear in a specific frame, right-click on the link, select Link Properties, enter the name of the frame where that page should appear in the Target Frame text box, and click OK.

Also for each frame, specify the margin width in **pixels**, and specify whether the frame should be a scrolling frame. If you anticipate that your frame will be smaller than the pages or other content that will fill them, you should specify the frame as a scrolling frame. Here are some of the attributes you can give a frame and the values that you might use for placing a logo into an independent frame:

Name (the name you'll use to refer to this frame)—Logo Frame.

Source URL (the location of the page that should be used for the contents of the frame)—Logo.htm.

Margin Width and Margin Height (the amount of space that should be left around the border of the frame, between the edge and the contents)—2 pixels.

Scrolling (whether scroll bars appear on the frame when the contents are too large to fit within the frame)—No. (You want users to see all of the logo, and you don't want the logo to change sizes.)

Not Resizable (whether the frame can be resized within a browser)—Not checked. (It's best to allow users to do this if they want.)

After you enter all the settings for your frames, continue on to step 5.

5. Now you'll see the Frames Wizard - Choose Alternate Content screen. Because some browsers don't yet support frames, it's wise to specify a page to appear in place of the one created with frames. This way, *something* will appear on a user's screen in place of this page if he or she is using a browser that doesn't support frames. Type in the URL of the page you want to use, or click the Browse button to search for a page. Then click the Next button.
6. Now you'll see the final screen of the wizard, the Frames Wizard - Save Page screen. This one is a no-brainer; type in a name and a URL for the page, and then click the Finish button. Make the name intuitive and easy to remember, especially if you plan to have more than one page with frames on your site.

After you click the Finish button, FrontPage creates the page and saves it to the web site, if one is currently open in the Explorer. To learn about editing frames and the content that appears in them, see Chapter 6.

Custom Wizards

Anyone can create custom web wizards and page wizards for FrontPage using Microsoft Visual Basic or Microsoft Visual C++. You can learn how in the FrontPage Developer's Kit. Look on the FrontPage portion of Microsoft's Web site at http://www.microsoft.com/msoffice/frontpage for information on obtaining this free kit. Custom wizards leverage the OLE methods provided by the FrontPage client. The wizards are then stored on the client workstation, where they are automatically made available in FrontPage using OLE automation.

FrontPage wizards and templates can free up some extra time for you to get more things done in your life. Maybe they'll free up enough time that you can put up one of your favorite signs on your office door: "Gone Fishin'!!!"

Coming Up

Speaking of freeing up time, FrontPage also helps you to administer a site once it's up and running. FrontPage makes it easier for you to implement security, manage tasks, update content, do testing, and go live with your site. Chapter 5 looks at these topics.

Chapter 5
Managing Your Web Site

The Explorer Makes It Easy

You've worked hard to plan and design your web site, and you've started putting it together. You've begun to turn all those ideas into actual pages, and now—whoa there, varmint! "How am I ever going to get all this done? Who's going to make sure it's kept up-to-date? How can I be sure it works perfectly before it goes online? And how can I be sure that my officemate, Georgio Trustnomore, who makes more than I do with half the talent, doesn't get into my site and mess it up?"

Dozens of questions like these can go through your mind at all stages of developing your site, especially if your company or organization has a large web-site development team. But even one-person development teams have to consider numerous web-site administration issues. Before you get to the point where you single-handedly cause stock in ibuprofen companies to soar to an all-time high, read this chapter and find out how FrontPage simplifies web-site administration.

Whenever you think of web-site administration, think "Explorer." The Explorer is the starting point for most of your administrative tasks—it's where you can see what work needs to be done in your site, assign those tasks as necessary, deal with **proxy servers** (also known as **firewalls**), set permissions, and much more. This chapter explains how FrontPage helps you deal with all these issues, beginning with security.

Security

If Wyatt Earp were alive today, he'd probably have his own web site, titled "Sheriffing the Net Frontier." He could showcase all the ways that Internet-related companies are trying to make the global Internet more secure from hackers and from grabbers of free-traveling information. FrontPage offers several features that provide better security than many other web-site authoring applications. While it doesn't provide security in the form of a Winchester, it does give you several ways to protect your information.

Permissions

FrontPage supports three levels of access to a site through its Server Extensions: end-user (browsing), author (changing content), and administrative (site administration, including updating end-user, author, and/or administrative permissions). Web servers (such as the Personal Web Server discussed in Chapter 9) often have built-in permissions mechanisms that allow you to restrict access by using a password/user name scheme, an **IP address mask**, or a combination. The passwords, user names, and IP address mask schemes can be manipulated by an administrator in the Explorer using the Permissions command on the Tools menu.

An **IP address** contains four numbers separated by periods; each number is less than 256. An example would be *150.200.45.65*. An IP address mask uses a combination of actual values and asterisks (also known as a *wildcards*) to create a model of an acceptable IP address. Masks are used to determine whether a computer has access to a location on the Internet—for example, a FrontPage site. An example of an IP address mask that would permit connections with the IP address above would be *150.200.*.**. Computers with IP addresses beginning with *150.200* would be given access to a FrontPage site, and computers whose IP addresses did not begin with those numbers would be denied access.

Setting and changing permissions Here's how to set and change permissions for a site:

With the site open in the Explorer, choose the Permissions command from the Tools menu. You'll be greeted by the Web Permissions dialog box, which has four tabs, each dealing with a specific level of access.

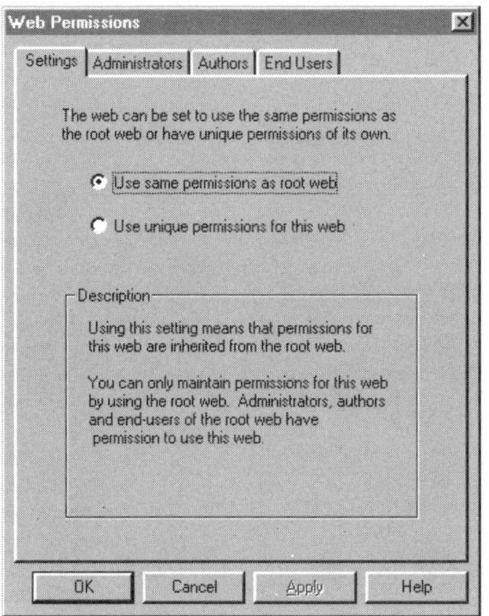

- The first tab, Settings, has two option buttons, one allowing you to use the same permissions in the current site that are used by the root web site (called the **root web** by FrontPage), and another allowing you to set unique permissions for the current site. Selecting either button yields a description of the option at the bottom of the dialog box. If you want to assign administrative, author and/or end-user permissions to certain people for this site but not for the root site, select the second option. Otherwise, the first option should be selected, and you must make any changes to permissions to the root site. After making changes on this tab, click the Apply button before working with any of the other tabs.
- The next two tabs deal with administrators and authors. Setting permissions for administrators and authors works the same way: A list of users that have access

> **TIP**
>
> The Add and Remove buttons are enabled only when you've chosen to set unique permissions for the site on the Settings tab.

at each level is displayed at the top of the dialog box. To add a user, click the Add button. A dialog box appears (the New Administrator or New Author dialog box); enter the name and password of the new user. Names and passwords can consist of letters, numbers, or both, but they cannot include spaces. Type the same password in the Confirm Password text box, and then click OK.

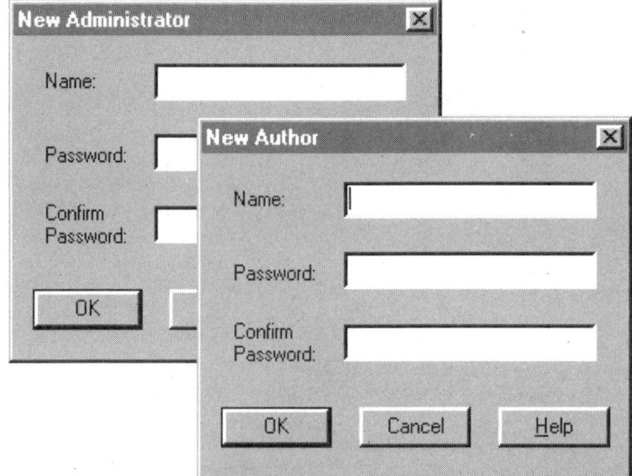

> **WARNING**
>
> When removing administrators or authors from your permissions list, make sure the users highlighted in the upper box are the ones you want to remove—FrontPage does not prompt you to confirm your action.

To remove an administrator or an author, highlight the name of the user and click the Remove button on the appropriate tab of the Web Permissions dialog box.

The text box at the bottom of the dialog box displays the IP address mask for the current site. Users whose address falls within the IP address mask are allowed administrative or author access to the site. You can add or remove address masks by using either the Add or Remove button to the right of the address list. As with removing administrators and authors, FrontPage does not prompt you to confirm your decision before it removes an IP address from the list, so be sure you've highlighted the right addresses before you click the Remove button. The *.*.*.* entry is a mask for any IP address; if you want to restrict access based on IP addresses, you must remove this entry and add in masks specific to those systems that are allowed to connect.

- The End User tab allows you to set access privileges for everyone (meaning everyone who can visit your site) or for a select group of registered users. To allow everyone access, select the Everyone Has Access option. To restrict access to registered users, select the Registered Users Only option. You can then add users to the list by clicking the Add button for the upper text box (for names and passwords). With either option, you can use the lower text box to set IP address masks and restrict access to users on certain systems. To remove entries from the lists, select the entries and click the respective Remove buttons.

When you finish updating the permissions, click OK to return to the Explorer.

Encryption

FrontPage encrypts all communications between the FrontPage client and the FrontPage Server Extensions, including any commands issued from the Explorer, the To Do List, or the Editor. This means the information is protected as it travels between the FrontPage client and the web server, wherever they're located. This security comes in handy in several situations:

- If you're on the road and you need to make changes to a site that is on a server back home, you can connect to that site via the FrontPage Server Extensions, download the site, make your changes, and upload the changes back to the server.
- If your business or organization has more than one office but has only one web server, someone at a remote office can make changes to the site.
- If you have a personal home page on an Internet access provider's server, and you access that server to make changes to your site with FrontPage, the information is encrypted as it's being sent to the server. It's much more secure that way. Even though sites on the World Wide Web are public, you don't want anyone to intercept your transmission to the server and change or delete material before it gets there.

The level of encryption meets U.S. government requirements for export outside the United States, and is proprietary to FrontPage. It does not meet the Secure HTTP specification proposed by Enterprise Integration Technologies (EIT) or the Secure Sockets Layer (SSL) support proposed by Netscape Communications Corporation. As these specifications become more universally supported by web-server vendors, future versions of FrontPage will probably support one or both of these specifications.

Proxy Servers

A **proxy server**, or **firewall**, protects a network from uninvited outside access. FrontPage makes communicating with proxy servers very easy, in either direction. For example, communication can be "inbound"—communicating from the outside through the proxy server and into your internal server, or "outbound"—communicating from your server, through a proxy, and to another server on the outside. Only communications related to the web site are permitted through the proxy, so uninvited guests are barred from your system.

If your local network uses a proxy server, you must specify that server in the Explorer in order for FrontPage to communicate with it. To specify a proxy server for your machine or to specify any server that can be used without going through the firewall, follow this procedure:

1. Choose the Proxies command from the Tools menu in the Explorer. You'll see the Proxies dialog box, which looks like this:

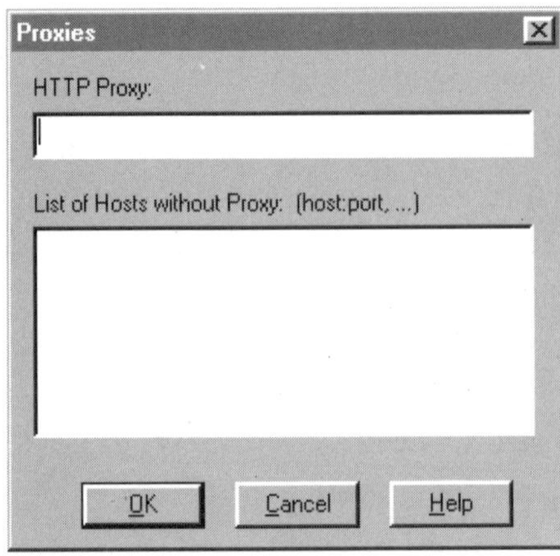

2. In the HTTP Proxy text box, enter the name of the proxy server and the port; for example, *roxy.proxy:1000.*
3. If your organization has servers that are inside the firewall, list them in the List Of Hosts Without Proxy text box. You can connect to these servers without using the proxy server. Port numbers are optional, and items in the list must be separated by commas. For example, *jeffserver:345,deborahserver:222*. To remove the proxy server or any servers in the list, select the information and press the Del key.
4. When you finish updating the information in the Proxies dialog box, click OK.

FrontPage saves the proxy server information and uses it for all future connections, so you don't have to enter the information again and again. Whenever you request a connection to a server (for example, when you are following a link), FrontPage first checks to see if the server appears in the List Of Hosts Without Proxy list. If the server is listed, FrontPage makes the connection directly. If not, FrontPage first connects to the proxy server and has the proxy server connect to the server you want to use. This means that once you supply that information for the proxy server, all proxy communication is handled automatically by FrontPage, and you don't even have to be aware that a proxy server is in use.

Managing Tasks: The To Do List

It's said that Albert Einstein chose not to memorize his phone number because he believed that memorizing such details took up too much space in his brain and too much energy. He preferred to reserve his brainpower and energy for his creative endeavors, and would simply write down any details that he could look up later. Do you wish you could do that with the small details about your site so you don't have to remember them all? If the list of tasks is long, however, writing them down and keeping track of them can be difficult.

The To Do List not only records those details, but it allows you the luxury of not having to organize them. The To Do List is a list of tasks that need to be completed for a given site; it is compiled either by FrontPage or by you, or both. It lists each task, describes it, indicates who's assigned to complete it, and more; this allows you more freedom to take care of other details. The following section describes the To Do List and explains what it can do for you.

Showing the To Do List

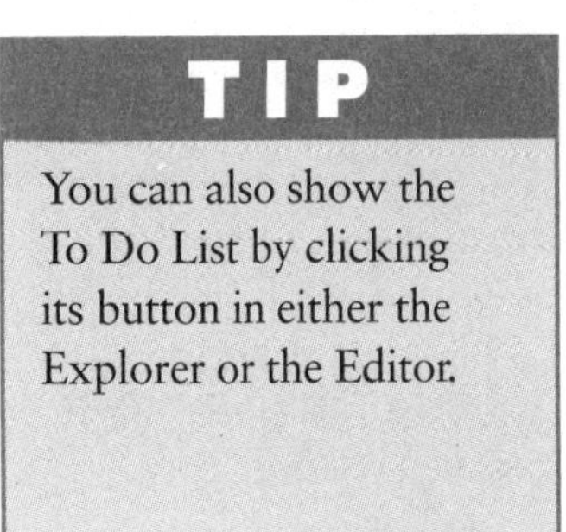

To show the To Do List for your site, choose Show To Do List from the Tools menu in the Explorer. The number of tasks on the list is indicated in parentheses following the command on the menu. If the To Do List window is already active but hidden underneath other windows on your screen, choosing the Show To Do List command brings it to the top. The following is the To Do List window, with a list of tasks to be completed after creating a new site with the Corporate Presence Wizard. FrontPage added the tasks in this list.

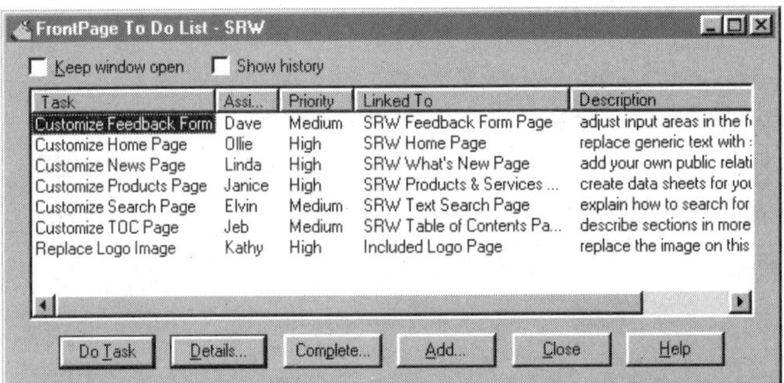

The tasks are listed in the leftmost column, the Tasks column. You can see who is responsible for completing each task in the adjacent column, the Assigned To column. A priority of high, medium, or low is assigned to each task and noted in the Priority column. The page or file that needs to be edited in order for the task to be competed is indicated in the Linked To column. Finally, a description of each task is provided in the rightmost column, the Description column.

You'll notice that the To Do List window has several buttons and two check boxes. Don't let these features confuse you; they're rather simple to use.

Keeping the To Do List open Normally, when you click the Do Task button to begin working on the selected task, the To Do List window is closed. If you want to keep the To Do List window open, select the Keep Window Open check box at the top of the To Do List.

Showing all completed tasks Select the Show History check box if you want to see a list of all tasks, including those that have been marked as completed. When this check box is selected, a new column is added that lists the date the task was marked as completed. When this check box is not selected, the To Do List shows only tasks that still need to be completed.

Sorting the columns Sorting the columns can be useful for large lists, and it's easy—simply click on a column heading. Suppose you want to find out how many tasks are assigned to you. Just click on the Assigned To column heading, and then find your name in the column. All of your tasks will be grouped together. The To Do List sorts text in ascending alphabetic order; dates are sorted from earliest to most recent.

Changing the view It's often quite useful to maximize the To Do List window so it takes up the entire screen. Click the standard Maximize button in the upper-right portion of the window—this will give you a much larger area to work in, allowing you to see many more details at once.

You can also adjust the column widths by moving your mouse pointer between the column headings until it changes to a resizing pointer, and then clicking and dragging. This lets you expand a column to see detail descriptions that are too long to fit into a column.

In addition, there are many ways to update the information in the To Do List, either by completing a task or by changing a task's details, as explained below.

Completing Tasks and Changing Details

Completing a task on the spot This is one of the most helpful features of the To Do List. If you see a task on the list that's assigned to you or someone else and you want to complete the task right then and there, you can do so. For instance, in the example above, suppose you want to complete the "Customize

Feedback Form" task. All you need to do is select the task and click the Do Task button at the bottom of the To Do List window. The Editor opens to the page on which the task needs to be completed. Even better, the page opens to the very spot where the task needs to be completed, so you don't have to search for it.

When you complete the task, FrontPage asks you whether you want to mark the task as completed in the To Do List. For administrative purposes, it's best to click the Yes button.

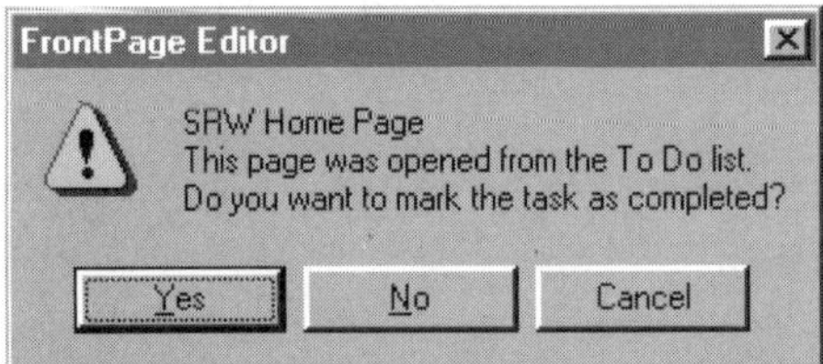

Changing the details for a task You can reassign a task, change the priority of a task, and change the description of a task by selecting the task and then clicking the Details button. You'll see the Task Details dialog box:

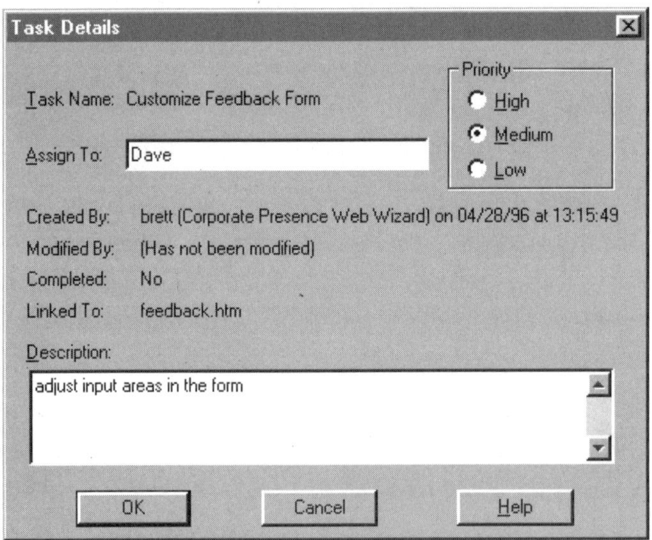

To assign the task to a different person, or to change the description of the task, simply replace the existing text. To change the priority, select the appropriate option button. You'll notice that not all details can be changed—only the three mentioned here. When you finish entering the new information, click OK to return to the To Do List.

Deleting a task or marking a task as completed To delete a task from the list or to mark a task as completed, click the Complete button. You'll see the Complete Task dialog box, which gives you the two options. If someone worked on a task but wasn't certain whether the task was completed, he or she might not have marked the task as completed at that point. The Mark this Task As Completed option is useful at those times, for confirming that a task has indeed been completed. The Delete this Task option is useful when you no longer want a task to appear in the To Do List history.

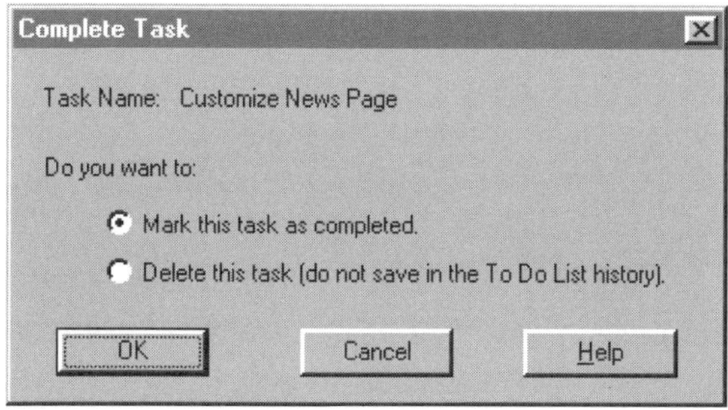

Adding a task If a task does not need to be linked to a particular page, click the Add button in the To Do List window to add the task. If you want to link a new task to a page in your site, start in the Explorer, select the page, and then choose Add To Do Task from the Edit menu. With either method, you'll see the Add To Do Task dialog box, which looks like this:

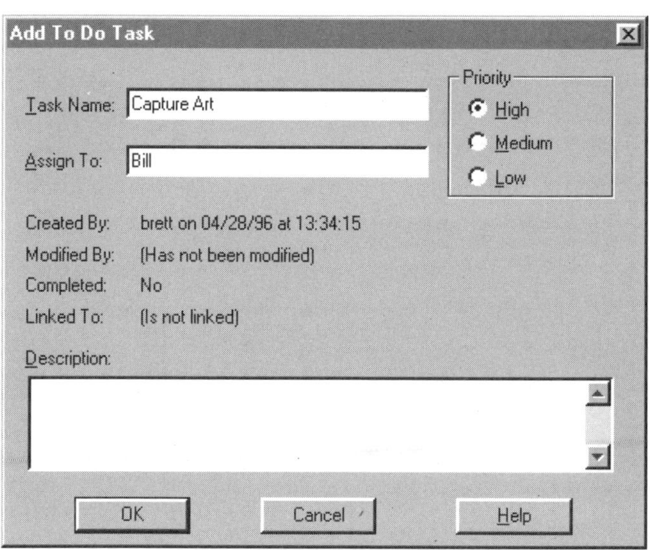

Enter the task name in the Task Name text box, and assign it to someone in the Assign To text box. Mark the priority as High, Medium, or Low in the upper right portion of the dialog box. Finally, add a description of the task in the text box at the bottom, and click OK. Be sure to use a short but specific description, because the column widths in the To Do List are often narrow. For information on changing column widths, see page 103.

Managing with the To Do List

The To Do List can be a powerful management tool. It gives you the ability to assign or reassign tasks, observe what work has been completed in a site, and determine what work still needs to be done. You can perform the following team management tasks using the To Do List:

Evening up the workload If someone on your team has a great deal more work to perform on a site than others, you can even up the workload by reassigning some of that person's tasks to others.

Seeing whether a task is completed I. M. Asleep, your team's resident procrastinator, often takes a long time to get things done. To check on her progress, you can look at the To Do List and sort the Task column to find a task. If the task doesn't appear on the list, I. M. gets a reprieve; if it's still there, it's time for I. M. to write on her whiteboard 50 times, "I will get my To Do List tasks done on time."

Determining the state of your site You can determine a site's condition in many ways using the To Do List. One way is to simply look at the number of tasks to be completed. Another way is to sort the tasks by priority—if you see many high- and medium-priority tasks remaining, you have more work to do than if most of the remaining tasks are weighted toward the low-priority level.

Determining what pages or files need the most work Sorting the Linked To column can give you an indication of which pages and/or files in your site need the most work. If you have many tasks associated with a few pages, you can assign more resources to those areas.

Testing Your Site

Once your site is all nice and spiffy, and you think it'll run just fine, it's always a good idea to test it. Testing can prevent the following from happening: It's the morning that you are scheduled to present your finished, working site to the CEO for final approval. It's a small site, but you're mighty proud of it. Your officemate, Barry Clueless, who is jealous over your recent raise and subsequent purchase of a red sports car, drops by the office around 11:30 the night before. He gets into your site and makes a teensy-weensy change in one of your links. So instead of linking to a profile of the CEO from the See Profile button as you've set it up, the button links to a picture of Kansas City feedlot sludge on an environmental activist's web site.

But you're craftier than Mr. Clueless, and you show up a little early the next morning to make sure your site runs fine. Here are three techniques you should use to check those links:

- You can check them individually in the FrontPage Editor. It's a slow way to check links, but if you're ever in the Editor and want to make sure a link works, you can put your cursor on the link, press Ctrl, and click on the link. The Editor will take you to the page the link jumps to.
- You can wander through your site using a browser, such as Microsoft Internet Explorer, Netscape Navigator, or any other popular browser, and test each of the links. This way you'll be able to see first-hand that all the links work, including links to other sites on the Internet.
- You can have FrontPage verify all of your links in one step by using the Verify Links command on the Tools menu in the Explorer. This command is explained in Chapter 4. This command, however, only verifies that the targets of your links exist—it does not verify that what you linked to is what you *intended* to link to!

In addition, you can check that your links to all Microsoft Office documents are correct, and that they open up in the appropriate viewer. The best way to check this is, unfortunately, the slowest way—by opening each one.

Finally, you can check that your image files are positioned on your pages where you want them. You can do this in the Editor or in a browser. You should test-view them in the browser last, for the final check. Also use the browser to check for the speed that pages appear on your screen. Some might not appear as quickly as you think they will; it's best to test all the pages in your site in this manner.

You'll often get different results from testing a site locally than from testing the same site through a network or over the Internet because of variables that can affect speed and information transfer. If you can, test your site in as many ways as possible:

- Locally, on your own computer
- Over a network
- Through a firewall
- Remotely, over the Internet
- Through modems and other communication devices at different speeds
- On different operating systems
- With different browsers at different screen settings

Going Live with Your Site

As the World Wide Web grows, so does the hype surrounding it. Some sites today are on topics so trendy and involve budgets so big that you'd think they would have debuted at a Hollywood-type premiere. It's not uncommon for a web-site budget to top $1 million. Maybe you've got several thousand Benjamin Franklins to spare for the kind of party where you break bottles of champagne against your web server, but most organizations do not. Nonetheless, going live with a web site is still a milestone event, and when it comes time, you've got to know how to do it.

There are a few ways you can make your site accessible to your audience. One common way is to develop your site on the server it will be viewed on, and let people visit your site as it matures. The Under Construction icons are very useful for this purpose; they let viewers know that a page isn't in its final form just yet. These icons can instill in viewers a curiosity about what your site might look like in the future, which can lead them to come back for a visit. FrontPage can insert these icons if you use a wizard to create your site.

When you're not comfortable with people seeing your site under construction, and when there's simply not enough content to make a visit worthwhile, you can do one of two things: develop your site locally or limit end-user permissions.

Developing Your Site Locally The FrontPage Personal Web Server suits local development to a "T." It allows you to develop and test your intranet or World Wide Web site on your own computer or over a **LAN**. When your site is complete and you're ready to go live with it, you can copy it to its destination web server using the Copy Web command on the Tools menu in the Explorer. With this command, you can copy the site to any server that has the appropriate FrontPage Server Extensions installed. To copy a site to web servers that do not have the Server Extensions installed, you can use the FrontPage Publishing Wizard, which is explained in Chapter 9. The Copy Web command is explained in Chapter 3.

If you need to limit access even when developing locally, you can limit permissions; the next section explains how.

Limiting Permissions

Limiting permissions gives you, the web-site developer, the final say over who sees your site in its varying stages. No matter where your site is being developed, you can grant access only to those who you wish to work on the site. You limit access by using the Permissions command on the Tools menu in the Explorer. For details on using this command, see "Permissions" earlier in this chapter.

You can limit permissions to control who can view the site, no matter what kind of site you're developing—an intranet or a site on the World Wide Web. On the End Users tab of the Web Permissions dialog box, you can limit permission to users who are registered to use your site, or you can allow access to everyone. If you've limited permission to registered users only, someone on the Web who is not a registered user will not have access to your site, plain and simple. (You might want to limit access to a list of registered users while you are developing the site.) When your site is ready to go live, you can simply change the end-user permissions to allow access to everyone. For more information, see "Permissions" earlier in this chapter.

Updating Your Site

The World Wide Web is a perfect reflection of information technology in general today—it changes constantly. One day you can e-mail a friend about a great site you visited, and the next day your friend won't be able to see what you saw because it's already changed. Even corporate intranets reflect this changing nature, although not at such a rapid pace. One reason some sites change so often is because they're easy to change. Once they're up and running; it takes little effort to replace a graphic or change a link.

Another reason that sites change often is because audiences demand it. You must keep your site updated with the latest information, or else your viewers will not return. Visiting a site is like turning up a playing card that's face-down; if your audience doesn't see a different card now and then, they'll move on to a different game.

Updating large sites is time-consuming, however, and the process requires more time as site size and the frequency of updating increase. It's further complicated when development resources are geographically distant from the web server. You should have a plan for updating your site before you even begin to create your site. If you're planning a site now, or if you need to implement an update plan, read ahead for a few ideas on how to go about it.

Updating Content

You can use a similar process for updating content that you used for gathering the content originally, but watch for ways to streamline the process. For example, when getting approval for your content, you can try routing it to people in a different order if the process was slow the first time around. Or you can eliminate a step in the process if you determine that the step wasn't necessary; for example, the material might need only one editing stage, not two. Also, check employee schedules to make certain a folder doesn't sit on someone's desk while he or she is lying on a beach in Tahiti.

If your company requires you to route material through a legal department, perhaps *all* your material doesn't have to be routed there, or maybe some of the material you want to put on your site has already been approved for use elsewhere in the company. If you can save some of the material from being rerouted, you'll save time and energy that you can apply elsewhere.

Never forget to *plan ahead*. If you've put forth a major effort to implement a site that's to be updated monthly, and if you plan to create a test site for your new material before you go live with it every month, leave yourself plenty of time for that test. For example, if you first went live in May, and you have an update planned for June, allow enough time to develop and test the update before June 1 rolls around. That might mean that all content for the June release must be finalized by mid-May so you have enough time to test the site and fix any errors you find.

Consider the time it will take you and/or your team to write, edit, and approve content. You'll need resources from different departments around your company, and even if you or an assistant are the ultimate go-getter who loves to make personal office visits for every bit of information you need, make sure you allow plenty of time to gather that material.

Also keep in mind that in the corporate world, you'll often want to have a Plan B ready to go, because as Murphy's Law says, Plan A almost never works as it's supposed to.

Updating Content Remotely

Updating site content from a remote location is one of FrontPage's strongest attributes—few other web-site authoring tools offer this feature. It's easy to do; here's all you need:

- You need to be able to connect to the web server that contains the site you want to update

- The FrontPage Server Extensions must be installed for that server
- You must have FrontPage installed on the computer you're using remotely

If you utter a resounding "YES!" to all three of those requirements, it's time to lobby your boss to allow you to work on the site from your favorite beach in the Cayman Islands. Wheeewww!

Simultaneous Authoring

FrontPage makes changing the content of your site a simple task that can be performed by multiple authors at once. If you update content while you're on the go, piece by piece, you can be changing one page in your site while someone else works on another page. The danger, of course, arises when two or more authors attempt to make changes to the same page simultaneously.

To help avoid this problem, FrontPage issues a warning if someone is overwriting a page that someone else has edited since you started working on your copy. If you receive a warning like this, you'll need to decide which set of edits are retained. If you continue with your changes, the others might be lost. In the future, coordinate with the other person so that only one of you is working on a given page at one time.

Such complications can be avoided if your organization adheres strictly to the To Do List. In the To Do List, only one author is assigned a given task. If that author is not the one who should be performing that task, the task should be reassigned. Even if multiple authors are changing content on a site from separate locations, they still use the same To Do List for that site, and working on the same page simultaneously can easily be avoided if they are directed to work only on tasks assigned to them.

Updating for Traffic

Are you or your company prepared to receive heavy traffic on your site? If your site becomes a popular one on the Web, you'll need a high-volume web server to handle the hits. FrontPage makes it easy to move sites from one server to another, using the Copy Web command on the File menu in the Explorer. So if a server in one location is taking a beating and you have a higher-volume server that can handle increased traffic (and if the appropriate FrontPage Server Extensions are installed on that server), you can simply move your site to the new server using the Copy Web command on the Explorer's File menu. It's as easy as point-and-click. For more information on the Copy Web command, see Chapter 3. For more information on web servers and the FrontPage Server Extensions, see Chapter 9.

Coming Up

This wraps up Part 2, where you've learned the basics of using the FrontPage Explorer to view, manipulate, and manage your web site. In Part 3 you'll get familiar with the Editor and find out how to craft a site that no viewer will want to leave.

PART

3

Page Construction

Chapter 6
Crafting Your Pages

Allergic to HTML?

Back in the Old Days of the Web, when you created your own pages you had to format them using Hypertext Markup Language (HTML). You added the formatting to the page's content by inserting special codes around the text. Both the codes and the contents of your page were represented as simple text; only when you viewed the page with a Web browser could you see the results of the HTML coding.

Oftentimes to get a page to look just right, the HTML coding had to be very sophisticated. You might even say web pages had to be *programmed,* because HTML can go beyond just marking formats and be made to work like a programming language. It wasn't as simple as putting a few lines of instructions into an editor. (Many of us don't even think *that's* simple.)

Now, FrontPage has given the Web play a different cast, a different crew, and an entirely different set of directors. FrontPage doesn't require you to know any HTML to produce professional-looking pages for the Web or for an intranet. If you're editing a page and want to italicize a word or change the color of a heading, you just select the text, click a button, and *voila*—FrontPage creates the HTML coding behind the scenes.

If you want to, however, you can still work with HTML in FrontPage. For example, to take advantage of some of the advanced features of the newest generation of Web browsers (such as Microsoft Internet Explorer), you might need to write a line or two of simple HTML instructions to get exactly the results you want. But remember the word *simple,* because that's what FrontPage is all about—enabling you to create and manage a web site without having to have a computer science degree.

So far in this book you've seen how to create, view, and manage web sites in the FrontPage Explorer. Now it's time to get your hands dirty and find out how to use the FrontPage Editor to craft all the elements on your web site's pages to get just the look and feel you want. The Explorer enables you to create and manage web sites; the Editor enables you to create, edit, and link web pages.

The Editor in Brief: WYSIWYG

One reason the FrontPage Editor is so easy to use is that it presents pages in WYSIWYG ("what you see is what you get") format. This means that whatever you see in the Editor is what you or your audience will see when viewing the pages using a Web browser. In the days when every detail on a page had to be formatted with HTML codes, you would painstakingly make changes to the coding and then *hope* that the changes looked right when you actually viewed the results. You'd have to view your page, go back to working in HTML and make changes to your code, view the page again, and so on. Now all you need to do is make sure it looks right in the Editor *once*. What you see is what you get!

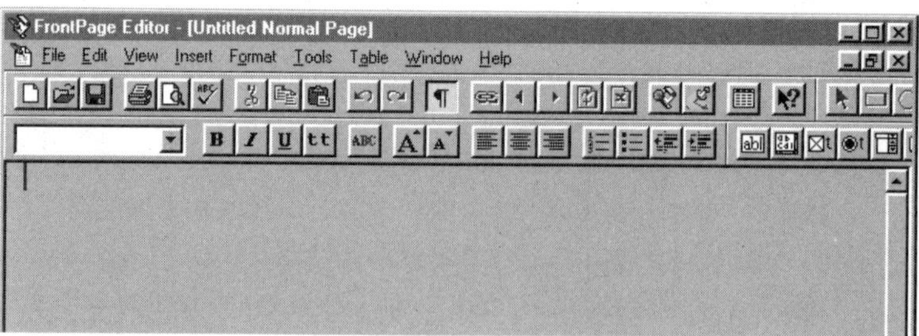

Using the Editor is much like using a word processor such as Microsoft Word. The Editor includes many of the standard buttons and commands found in Word, such as buttons for bold, italic, and underline; numbered and bulleted lists; undo and redo; and so on. You type text on the Editor's screen just as you do in Word. You can even insert tables and use **frames** very easily in the Editor—many other web-page authoring tools don't even support tables or frames, yet you can do this in the FrontPage Editor with a few clicks of the mouse.

And like Word, the Editor allows you to have more than one file open at a time. The Editor deals with pages, so it's correct to say you can have more than one *page* open at a time. This is useful for toggling back and forth between pages to ensure consistency, accuracy of information, and so on. The Editor also allows you to copy a page (and all of its formatting and HTML code) from the World Wide Web and edit it as you wish. This is useful if you own other sites and need to garner information from them quickly. Be careful, of course, about copying information from others' web sites—there are copyright laws to heed, and plagiarism should be left to those who don't mind shelling out the bucks for a defense attorney.

Launching the Editor

How do you get to the Editor? Let us count the ways:

- By double-clicking a page in Link view or Summary view in the Explorer. The Editor opens with that page in its main window.
- By selecting a task associated with a page in the To Do List window and then clicking the Do Task button. Again, the Editor opens with that page in its main window.
- By launching the Editor on its own (either from Microsoft Windows or by clicking the Show FrontPage Editor button in the Explorer). In this case, the Editor opens with a blank screen. You can then open a page using one of the Open commands on the File menu, and begin editing.

When the Editor launches, it appears in its own window, with toolbars and numerous menu commands at the top. It might look a tad formidable at first, but we'll describe what the toolbar buttons and commands do in this chapter. Before you begin to use the Editor, though, you should learn how to customize it so you can use it to your best advantage.

Adjusting Settings

Surely you have a preferred way to work on your computer. (Don't worry, we'll stop calling you Shirley.) For example, maybe you don't like working with toolbars—so what's the purpose of keeping them on the screen? Or maybe you like working in a smaller or larger window. Adjusting these elements in the Editor is easy; here are a few ways to tailor your environment.

Changing the window size It's often useful to maximize the Editor to a full screen so you can get the largest view of the page you're editing. To do this, click the Maximize button, which is the middle button of the three-button set in the upper right corner of the Editor's title bar when the window is not maximized. To restore the Editor to its previous location and size, click the Restore button that appears in the same position for maximized windows. That three-button set is the same one that you see in all Windows 95 and Microsoft Windows NT applications.

Click on the middle button in this three-button set to maximize the Editor to a full screen. If you don't see this button, the Editor is already maximized.

TIP

If you have multiple pages open in the Editor, you can also move from page to page by clicking the Forward and Back toolbar buttons.

You can also maximize and minimize individual pages in the Editor. To do so, click the Maximize button for the page. This button is the middle button of the smaller set of buttons in the upper right corner of the *page's* title bar. You can *minimize* a page by clicking on the button to the far left of the group of three. When you minimize a page, it's reduced to a button at the bottom of your window, which makes it easy to see that you can have multiple pages open in the Editor at once.

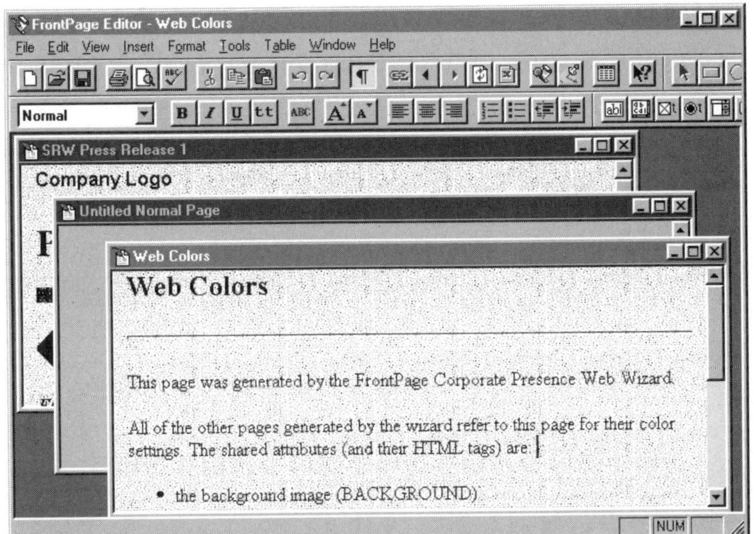

You can have several pages open at once in the Editor. Here, all the pages are normal windows, neither maximized nor minimized.

Working with toolbars The Editor includes the Standard, Format, Image, and Forms toolbars at the top of the screen. When they all appear together, they take up a fairly large chunk of space in the Editor window. If you don't need some of them, you can hide them. To hide a toolbar, choose that toolbar's name from the View menu to remove the check mark beside it. To show a hidden toolbar, choose its name from the View menu (to add a check mark beside it), and the toolbar will appear in the same position it held before it was hidden.

The Editor's toolbars can be placed anywhere on your screen. If you prefer to work with the toolbars off to one side or at the bottom of your screen, you're in luck. To move a toolbar, click on a region of the toolbar outside the buttons and drag it to its new position. To have a toolbar "float," drag it from the toolbar region to a position within the window. To "dock" the toolbar again, drag it back to the toolbar region at the top of the Editor window.

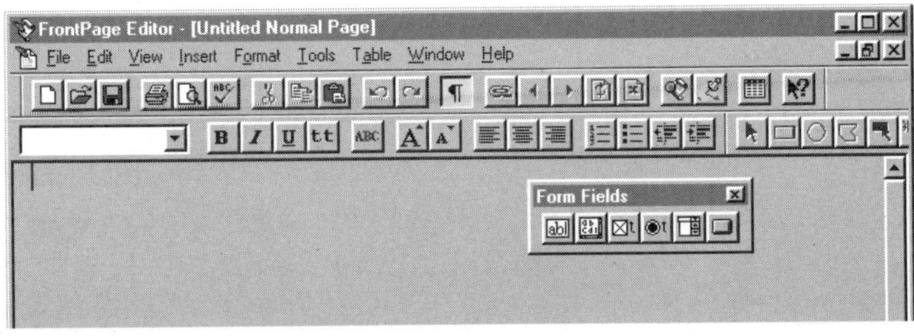

Showing and hiding the status bar and formatting marks

You can show or hide the status bar at the bottom of the Editor window by choosing the Status Bar command from the View menu. The Editor also uses formatting marks on the screen for some elements, such as headings, hard line returns, bookmarks, and form outlines. To show or hide these marks for the page you are currently working on, choose the Format Marks command from the View menu.

SHORTCUT

You can click the Format Marks toolbar button, which looks like a paragraph mark, to show or hide format marks.

Now that you've learned how to adjust some basic settings, it's time to get your feet wet.

Let the Construction Begin

This section describes most of the elements you can add to a page in the Editor. You can add all of the obvious page components, such as text, links, and headings, plus some that might surprise you—such as tables. You can also add images, which are another major component of a web page; the procedures are detailed in Chapter 7. You can also add forms and bots in the Editor; these procedures are fully explained in Chapter 8.

When adding elements to your pages in the Editor, follow this simple guideline: Think as you would when using a word processing application such as Word. The Editor mimics many of the procedures and techniques you use in Word to add and manipulate page elements. The menus and toolbars also closely resemble those in Word. If you've used a word processing application, you'll have no trouble using the Editor, and you'll learn it very quickly.

Navigating in the Editor

Once you have material on your page, you can use your keyboard to navigate in the standard ways. For example, you can use the PgUp and PgDn keys to move one screen up or down. Ctrl+Home takes you to the top of a page, and Ctrl+End sends you to the end of a page. You can also use the cursor keys to navigate on your pages, and you can use a scroll bar, if one is present, to move horizontally or vertically.

Text

Adding text to a page is as simple as typing it in. Let's go through the motions of adding some text:

1. Create a new page in the Editor by choosing New from the File menu. In the New Page dialog box, select Normal, and then click OK. A blank page appears on your screen, with the cursor blinking in the upper-left corner.
2. Type in the line, "Dan knows how to fish." Notice that the text begins on the far left side of the current line. If you don't want it to begin there, you can indent the text, center it, right-align it, and much more. For more information, see "Formatting Your Pages" later in this chapter.

Whatever you type on the screen is what you see in the browser. And just as in Word, to start a new paragraph you simply press the Enter key.

Cutting, copying, and pasting text You can cut, copy, and paste text (and any other elements, for that matter) in the Editor just as you do in Word. The Editor uses the Clipboard in the same way that Word does; you can cut or copy material to other pages in the Editor, or to other documents in other applications. Simply cut or copy the material, move to the destination document (opening it if necessary), and paste it in. Depending on the application you move the material to, you might lose some of the formatting when you move the material.

Deleting text Deleting text or other elements is also very simple, and you can do it in many ways. You can select the material you want to delete, and then press the Del key or choose Clear from the Edit menu.

SHORTCUT

The Editor uses common keyboard and toolbar shortcuts for cutting, copying, and pasting. Cut: Ctrl+X; Copy: Ctrl+C; Paste: Ctrl+V. You can also right-click to cut, copy, and paste.

TIP

If you want to reinsert material you've just deleted, choose Undo from the Edit menu or click the Undo toolbar button. For more details, see "Undo/Redo" later in this chapter.

You can also delete words and characters in front of and behind the cursor—to delete a word to the right of the cursor, press Ctrl+Del, and to delete a word to the left of the cursor, press Ctrl+Backspace. Try these shortcuts to get comfortable with them; they're some of the least-used keyboard combinations in the FrontPage Editor and in Word, but they can make your editing work go much faster.

Headings

One mark of an effective web-page design is the wise use of headings. Too many large headings can make a page difficult to read, and too few headings can make a page look dull and perhaps make it difficult to understand.

To show you a simple use of headings, let's try this exercise: Suppose you're creating a simple page titled "Company Sales" that serves as the opening page of the Sales section in your company's intranet site. You want the names of your company's salespeople to appear on the page, which will later serve as links to their own pages. Here's what you can do:

1. Create a new page in the Editor by choosing New from the File menu. In the New Page dialog box, select Normal, and then click OK. A blank page appears on your screen, with the cursor blinking in the upper left corner.
2. Choose Heading from the Insert menu. The Editor displays a submenu with choices for six levels of headings. The page heading should be fairly prominent, such as that of a Heading 1. Move your mouse to select Heading 1, and click. FrontPage adds space for the heading as a separate paragraph, placing it on its own line, ready for you to type the heading text.

> **TIP**
>
> You can also use the Style drop-down list on the Formatting toolbar to start a heading. For this procedure, you can select the heading level in the drop-down list while your cursor is on a blank line, and then enter the name.

3. Type in the main heading for the page, *Company Sales*.
4. Now you want to add the names of your salespeople to the page. Choose Heading from the Insert menu,

select Heading 3 on the submenu, and then click. A line formatted as Heading 3 appears below the title you just typed. Type *Judy*.

5. Repeat step 4 to enter the names of your other salespeople: Julie, Beth, John, and Bev. If you prefer, you can simply press Enter after you type each name; the next line is automatically formatted as Heading 3.

   Your page should look like the figure below.

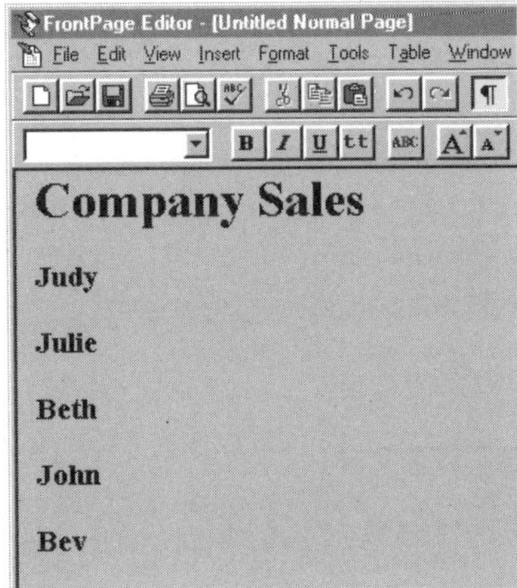

   Here are the sizes of headings you can choose from:

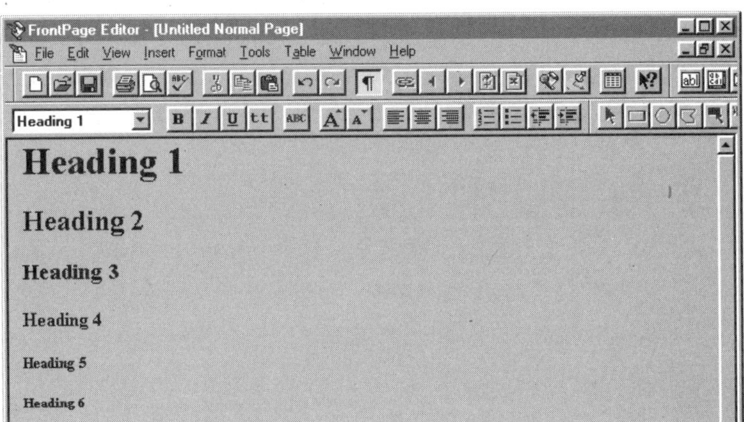

The user's Web browser will determine the exact formatting of the headings and might override FrontPage-specific formatting. No matter what, the formats are designed so that the more important headings (starting with Heading 1) stand out more than the less important ones (ending with Heading 6). Generally, the more important the heading, the larger the text, the more space above and below the heading, and so on. Some browsers even center some headings or italicize the less important ones.

Formatting existing text as a heading You don't always have to insert a heading before you type your heading text. Suppose you have a line of text that you want to make into a heading. It's this simple:

1. Position your cursor on a blank line. If you want to continue this exercise from the last procedure, press the Down arrow key after you type the name *Bev*.
2. Type the name *Jane*.
3. Select the name you just typed, and then select Heading 3 from the Style drop-down list on the Formatting toolbar. The name *Jane* is now formatted as Heading 3.

Lists

Everyone loves lists these days. What would our days be like without a Top Ten list of some sort? When you're designing your pages, consider using a list instead of cramming material into paragraph form; lists are much easier to read, so they tend to make your pages more user-friendly. If you use too many lists, though, your pages can become dry and tedious to read, and your audience will dash off to read the *Congressional Record* just to clear their minds.

The exact formatting of each kind of list is determined by the Web browser used to view the page. Here's a rundown of the kind of lists you can choose from:

- Numbered List—Presents items in numbered sequence, beginning with the number 1. This formatting is ideal for procedural lists.
- Bulleted List—Presents items with bullets. Bulleted lists are often used for related, nonsequential items. This is the basic bulleted list format.
- Directory List—Another bulleted list format. Some browsers recognize the coding for a directory list and

format the list items differently than for a simple bulleted list. Generally, this format is used for very short items. Many Web browsers do not support the directory list style.

- Menu List—Another bulleted list format supported by some (but not all) browsers.

Creating a list To create a list on your page (along with the list's formatting), do the following:

1. Position your cursor where you want the list to begin. You can position the cursor in the middle or at the end of a paragraph.

2. Choose List from the Insert menu, and choose one of the list types from the submenu that appears. Your choices are Bulleted, Numbered, Directory, or Menu. When you choose the type of list you want, FrontPage inserts a new line, formatting the first line of the new list with a number or a bullet; type the text for that first element.

SHORTCUT

You can convert existing text to a bulleted or numbered list by selecting it and then clicking the respective toolbar button.

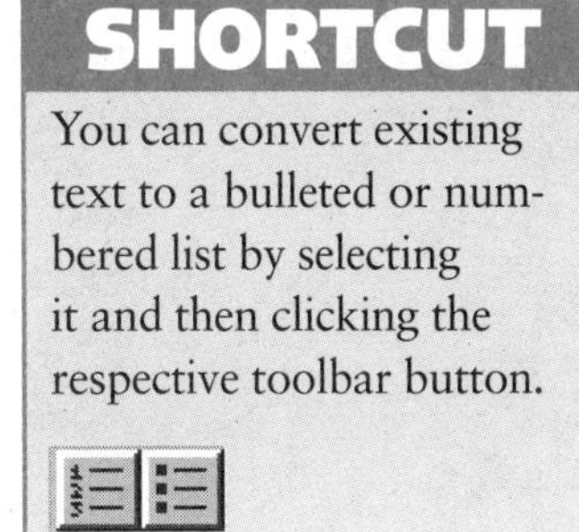

3. After you type the first element of the list, press Enter. The Editor inserts the next item in the list, and you can type that text in. Continue this process until you finish the list.

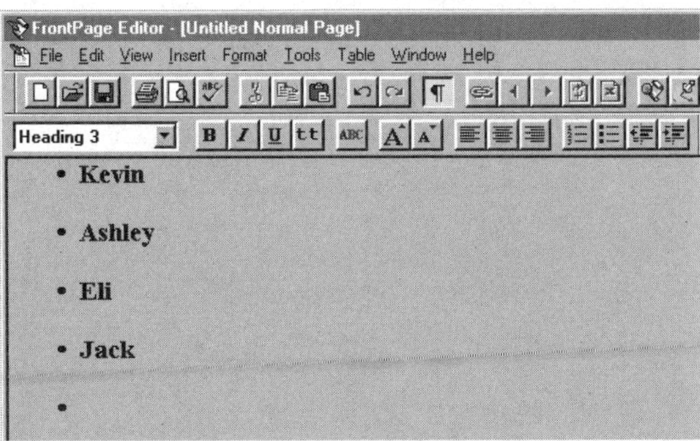

A bulleted list in progress. The author has just typed *Jack* and pressed Enter.

4. When you finish the list, press Ctrl+Enter. The Editor inserts a new line following the list and places the cursor at the start of that line.

Nested lists You might find occasion to use a list within a list, also called a *nested list*. It's easy to create: From within a list, position your cursor at the end of the line above where you want to begin the nested list, and then begin the new list with a command from the Insert menu. To end the nested list and return to the original ("parent") list, press Ctrl+Enter.

To avoid formatting confusion, it's best to insert a nested list *after* you've completed the list it's nested in. Here's a sure-and-safe way to create a nested list:

1. Create the parent list with all of its items. Don't worry about where you'll add the nested list.
2. Determine where you want to insert the nested list, and click at the end of the line immediately above that location.
3. Begin the nested list by choosing a list type from the List command on the Insert menu. This splits the existing list and adds the first entry for a second level of items (your nested list).
4. Complete the nested list, pressing Enter at the end of each line except the last one.

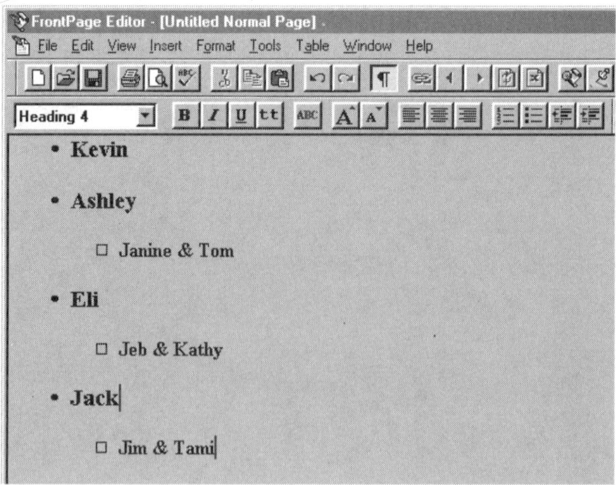

If you add extra lines to your list that you don't need, press the Backspace key as many times as you need to get the nested list and the parent list formatted properly.

Reformatting text into a list Suppose you have some text on your screen that you'd like to make into a formatted list. Just as in Word, you can do that easily in the Editor. Select the material you want to make into a list, and then click on the Numbered List or Bulleted List toolbar button, or choose a list type from the List command on the Insert menu. Each paragraph in the selection will become a separate list item.

Definitions

A **definition** is a page element you won't see in many other web authoring programs. This type of formatting is particularly useful for organizing a list of terms and their definitions (although you can use definitions in any way you like). In many ways, a series of definitions is a special type of list. Rather than numbers or bullets, a word or phrase is used to start each item. The remaining text for the item is formatted as the definition for that entry.

In many browsers, the word or phrase is positioned at the left margin and the definition text is indented next to it (similar to the way a bulleted list has the bullet at the left with the remaining text indented). In other browsers, the word or phrase appears on one line with the remaining text positioned below it.

Let's suppose a coffee shop has a list of its drinks on its World Wide Web site. The shop can use a definition term for the name of each drink, and then insert the definition following that. You can see what a short definition list might look like in the following figure, and then you'll get to build it in the procedure below.

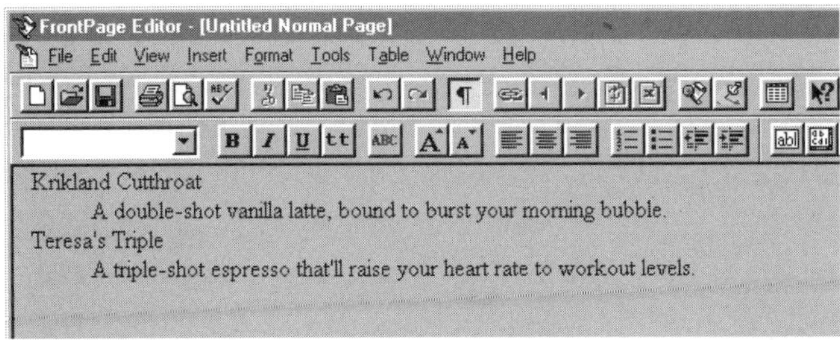

1. At the beginning of a blank line, choose Definition from the Insert menu. Then choose Term from the submenu.

2. Enter the words *Kirkland Cutthroat.*
3. Choose Definition from the Insert menu, and then choose Definition from the submenu.
4. Enter the following: *A double-shot vanilla latte, bound to burst your morning bubble.*
5. Choose Definition from the Insert menu, and then choose Term from the submenu. Enter the words *Teresa's Triple.*
6. Choose Definition from the Insert menu, and then choose Definition from the submenu. Enter the following: *A triple-shot espresso that'll raise your heart rate to workout levels.*
7. Press Ctrl+Enter to end the definition list.

Tables

Adding tables to a web page in the Editor is so fast and easy that you'll be playing the back nine while your competitors who use other web authoring tools are still glaring at their computers.

Tables in FrontPage have the same structure and are used in similar ways as tables in a Word document. In fact, constructing tables in the Editor is very similar to constructing them in Word. Tables consist of columns and rows of cells that can contain text, images, forms, or bots. Tables are used for arranging data systematically on a page, but you can also use them for other purposes, such as organizing the elements of your page (for example, images) in an orderly way.

If you create a table and find later on that you need to add or delete rows or columns, or change the size of cells, don't fret—it's easy to customize an existing table in the Editor. When you create a table, you don't have to consider cell width and height if you don't want to; as you add material to the cells, the height automatically expands to accommodate the material.

Creating a table First you'll learn how to create a simple table, and then you'll see how to customize the table so it does just what you want it to do.

1. Position your cursor where you want the table to begin, and then choose Insert Table from the Table menu. You'll see the Insert Table dialog box.

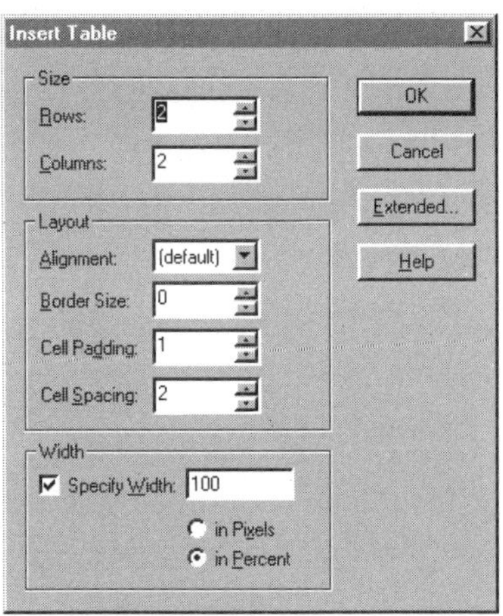

2. Enter the number of rows and columns you think you'll need in your table. You can add or delete rows and columns later.

3. Choose an alignment option for the table: at the right side of the page, centered, or at the left side of the page.

4. If you want a border around the table, enter the width in **pixels**. This setting is for the border that surrounds the entire table; each cell in the table also has a border representing the cell spacing (see step 6). If you do not want a border, enter 0. The exact format of all table borders is determined by the browser being used rather than by settings within FrontPage.

5. Enter a number, in pixels, for the cell padding. Cell padding is the space between a cell's contents and each of its borders. This number pertains to all cells in the table; cell padding cannot be set for individual cells. The default is 1.

TIP

If you don't want a border but you want to see the layout of your table as you work on it, you can choose the Format Marks command on the View menu or click the Show/Hide Paragraph toolbar button. You'll see cell outlines in the Editor that will not appear in a browser.

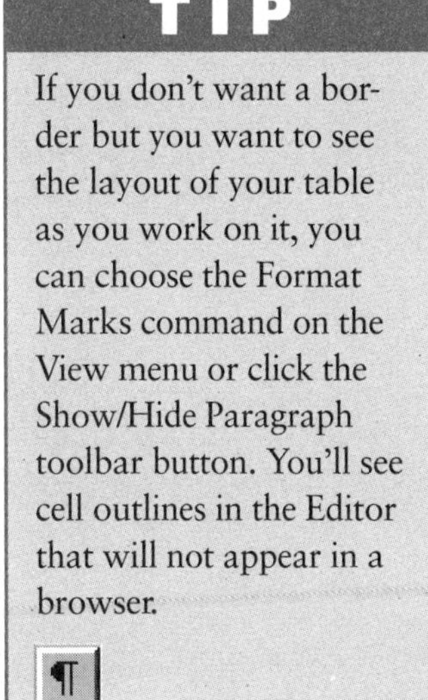

6. Enter a number, in pixels, for cell spacing. This controls the spacing between the cells in a table and is represented as a border around each cell (including those at the outer edge of the table). The default is 2.

7. Specify the width of the table. You can set the number in pixels or as a percentage of the page width. For example, if you set the table width to 50 percent, the table will span half the width of the page.

8. Click OK. The Editor creates the table and displays it on the page. FrontPage uses the number of columns and the width of the table to calculate the size of each of the individual columns.

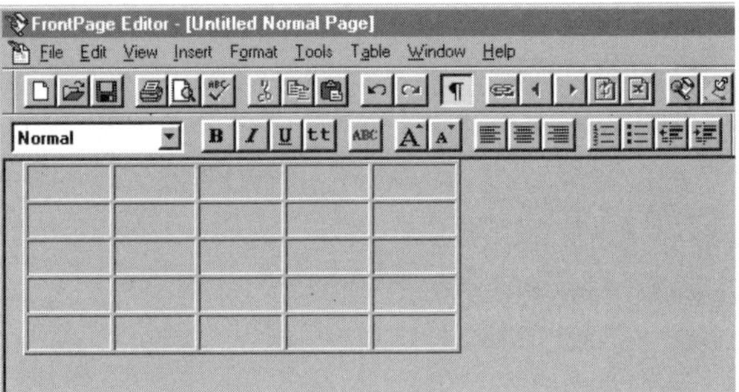

The table above is five rows by five columns. It is left-justified on the page and has 1-pixel border, 1-pixel cell padding, and 2-pixel cell spacing settings.

Adding text You can type in a table cell just as you would anywhere else on a page in the Editor. If you add more text than the cell is formatted to hold, the height of the cell expands to accommodate it.

Changing table properties At any time, you can change settings for table alignment, border size, cell padding, cell spacing, and overall table size by using the Table Properties command. Simply right-click on the table and choose Table Properties from the pop-up menu. The Table Properties dialog box opens.

To get a "test view" of what your table might look like with different settings, you can change some settings in the Table Properties dialog box and then click the Apply button. You can change the settings and click Apply as many times as necessary.

Changing cell properties You can also change some properties for cells, such as the alignment of text within them, their width, and the number of rows they span. Here's how to view and change these properties:

1. Select a cell or group of cells in the table. To select a cell, position your cursor in the cell and then choose Select Cell from the Table menu. To select multiple cells, select the first cell and then hold down the Shift key while clicking additional cells with the cursor.
2. Choose Properties from the Edit menu or right-click over the selected cell(s) and choose Properties from the pop-up menu. The Cell Properties dialog box appears. 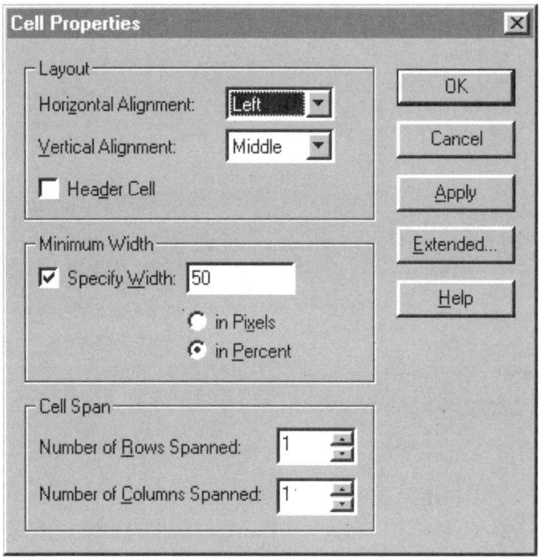
3. To change the alignment of text within a cell, alter the settings in the Layout section. For example, to align the text in the exact center of a cell, select Center for the Horizontal Alignment and for the Vertical Alignment.
4. Enter a new number in the Specify Width text box to change the width of the cell. If you want to decrease a cell's width, you must select the entire column the cell is in, and then change the width setting in the Cell Properties dialog box. You reach the dialog box in the same way that you do when you select a single cell. If you increase a cell's width, the row width changes accordingly.

5. In the Cell Span section, enter the number of rows or columns you want a cell to span. Changing this setting expands the cell to cross that number of rows or columns. This causes cells in the column to the right and/or the rows below to move to the right to make room for the enlarged cell. One reason you might want to expand a cell in this fashion is to fill the area with an image.

   For example, suppose you have a two-row, two-column table, and you want an image to fill the area below the top two cells. You can expand the bottom-left cell so it spans the two columns. As shown below, the bottom right cell is pushed toward the right to accommodate the expanded cell next to it.

> **TIP**
>
> If you want to insert an image into a cell but do not want to enlarge the cell so that it spans other rows or columns, don't worry. When an image is larger than the cell that contains it, you can click on the image to see it in its entirety. Of course, if the image doesn't fit on the screen, you'll need to use the scroll bars to view all of it.

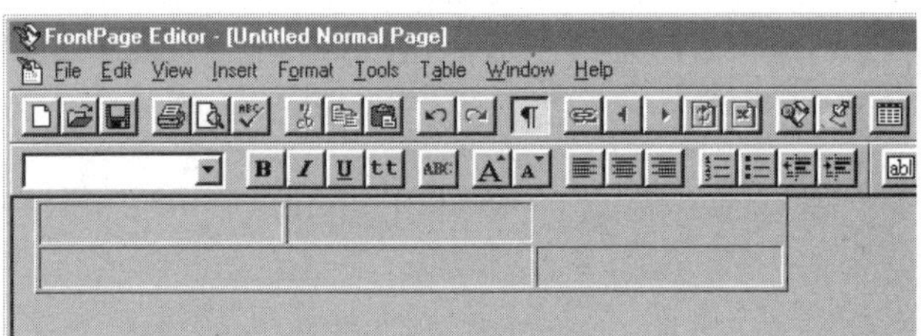

6. Change the settings you want, and then click Apply to view them before closing the dialog box. When you have the settings the way you want, click OK to exit the Cell Properties dialog box.

Creating header cells Often a header cell is used at the top of a column or at the left end of a row, and will contain a title for that row or column, but really a header cell is any cell that you want to make prominent in your table. Header cells are marked for special formatting; in FrontPage tables they contain bold text. You can turn any regular cell or cells into a header cell by doing the following:

1. Select the cell or cells you want to turn into header cells. To select multiple cells, select the first cell and then hold down the Shift key while clicking on additional cells.

2. Choose the Properties command from the Edit menu or right-click over the selected cell(s) and choose Cell Properties from the pop-up menu. In the Cell Properties dialog box, select the Header Cell check box, and then click OK.

Any existing text in a cell that becomes a header cell is shown in bold, and any additional text you type in the cell will also be bold. Browsers might treat header cell formatting in different ways.

Selecting rows and columns To select a row or a column, position the mouse pointer near the top of a column or near the left border of a row until it turns into a solid arrow, and then click. You can select multiple rows or columns by dragging the mouse.

Navigating within a table You use the arrow keys to move from character to character (or element to element) within a cell. You can also move between cells by using the arrow keys. Unlike in Word, you cannot use the Tab key to navigate within a FrontPage table.

Adding cells If you need to add a piece of information in your table but have nowhere to add it, you can always insert a blank cell. Inserting a cell into a table adds one more cell to the row it's inserted in, and can extend the row outside the original table boundary. In the following illustration, a cell was added to the right of the cell with *5.* in it:

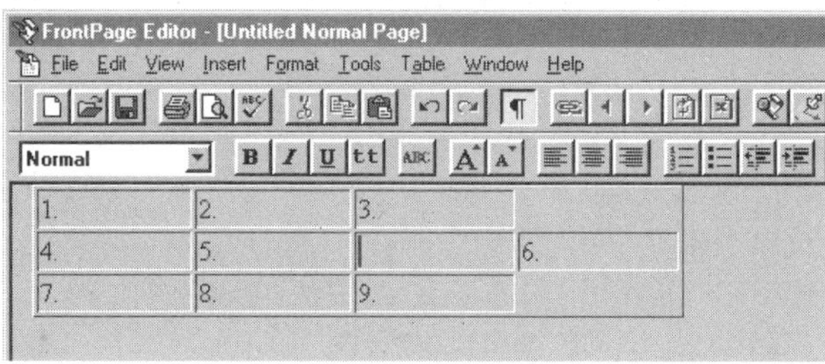

As you can see, inserting cells can make your tables asymmetrical, but that just might be your goal. To insert a cell, position your cursor in the cell directly to the left of where you want the new cell to appear, and choose Insert Cell from the Table menu.

Adding rows To add a row or rows to your table, do the following:

1. Select the row above or below where you want the new row to appear.
2. Choose Insert Rows Or Columns from the Table menu. You'll see the Insert Rows Or Columns dialog box.

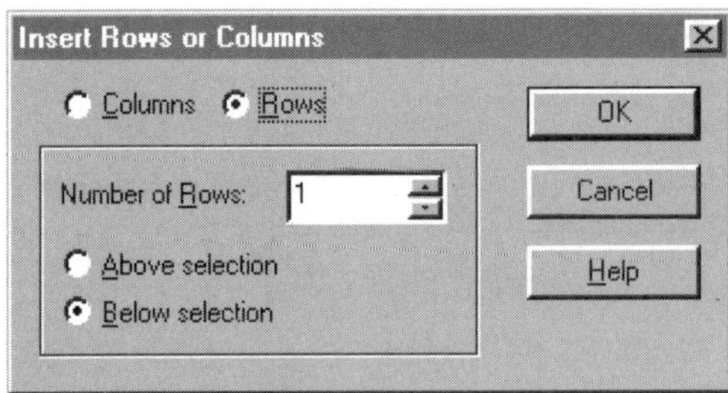

3. Select the Rows option, and enter the number of rows you want to insert. Then specify whether you want the rows to be inserted above or below the row you selected, and click OK.

Adding columns To add a column or columns to a table, select a column next to where you want the new column to appear, and then choose Insert Rows Or Columns from the Table menu. Follow the same procedure outlined above in "Adding Rows," but select the Columns option and enter the number of columns you want to insert.

Deleting rows or columns To delete a row or a column, select the row or column you want to delete, and then press the Del key.

Moving rows or columns Here's how to move a row or a column to another place in a table. In FrontPage, unlike in many other programs, when you paste a portion of a table, the pasted information replaces that in the new location. There is no way to insert a row or column from the Clipboard as a new row or column. For this example, we'll move a row, but the same procedure works for columns:

1. If there are no blank rows in the table, insert a row to serve as the destination row for the material you want to move. You will move your material from the original row into a blank row.

2. Select the row you want to move, and then choose Cut from the Edit menu.

3. Select the blank row you want to move the material to, and then choose Paste from the Edit menu. The material is pasted in the new row.

This procedure also works for material you want to copy from one row or column to another. You can also cut and copy multiple rows and columns at once in the same way.

> **WARNING**
>
> When you move rows or columns from one table to another, the number of cells in the rows or columns must be equal in both tables. FrontPage will not allow the copying or moving of material between rows and columns that do not contain the same number of cells.

Splitting cells To provide more detailed information in your table, or to clean up the formatting on a page, you might want to split a cell. When you split a cell, you divide a single cell into as many rows or columns as you need. Here's how:

1. Select the cell you want to split.
2. Choose Split Cells from the Table menu. The Split Cells dialog box appears:

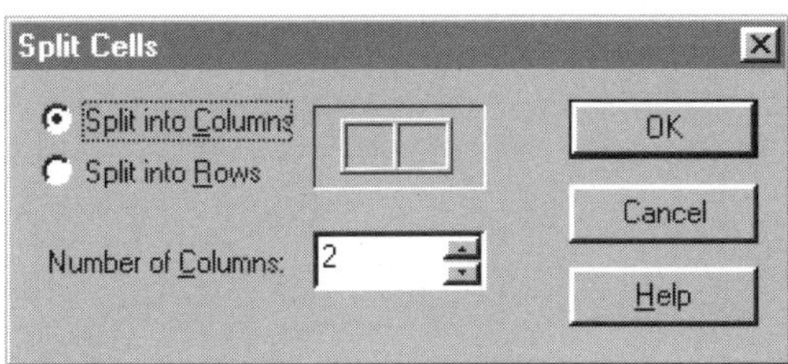

3. Specify whether you want to split the cell into columns or rows, and then enter the number of new columns or rows you want in that cell. Click OK.

Here's an example of a three-column table whose centermost column is split into three rows:

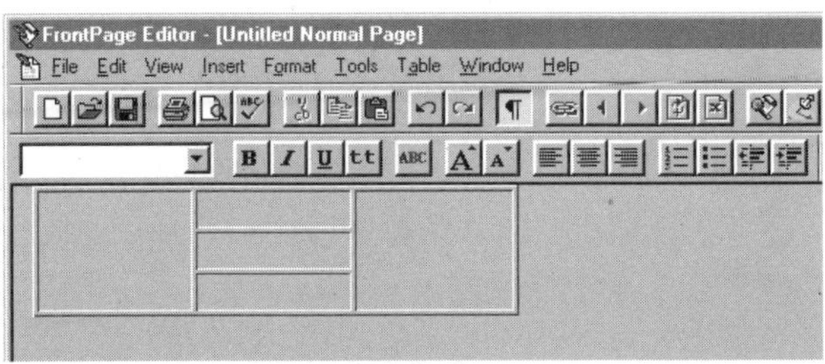

Merging cells There might be times when you want to combine material from several neighboring cells into one cell. This is called merging cells. Here's how to do it:

1. Select the cells you want to merge. To select multiple cells, select the first cell, and then click in the next cell while holding down the Shift key. When merging cells, you can select as many cells as you want, but they must all be in the same row or column.
2. Choose Merge Cells from the Table menu. The Editor merges the cells, displaying the information in the order of the cells that were merged. Any cell borders shared by the merged cells are removed, resulting in a larger cell. The content of each of the cells is formatted as a separate paragraph.

Adding images to cells To add an image to your table, choose Image from the Insert menu and use the resulting Insert Image dialog box. For detailed information on inserting images, see Chapter 7.

Inserting tables within tables The Editor allows you to insert a table within a table. You might want to use a table within a table to order your data in a special way. Or, you might want the look and feel of several bordered tables on a page. If you use tables for presenting thumbnail images for users to click on to obtain a larger version of the image, using a table within a table might help you to present the thumbnails in a more logical or graphically pleasing way than in an ordinary table.

Before you use the table-within-a-table strategy, consider if you can obtain the same results for your work by splitting cells. Keeping your table design as simple as possible will probably save you time when you troubleshoot any problems on your pages.

To insert a table within a table, position the cursor in the cell where you want the new table to appear, and create the new table via the Insert Table command on the Table menu. This process is described earlier.

At A Glance

The Editor

The Editor is where you let your creativity flow. In this WYSIWYG (What You See Is What You Get) environment, you can create web pages that dazzle your audience.

It's easy to create custom forms, manipulate text size and color, and make clickable image maps of all shapes and sizes.

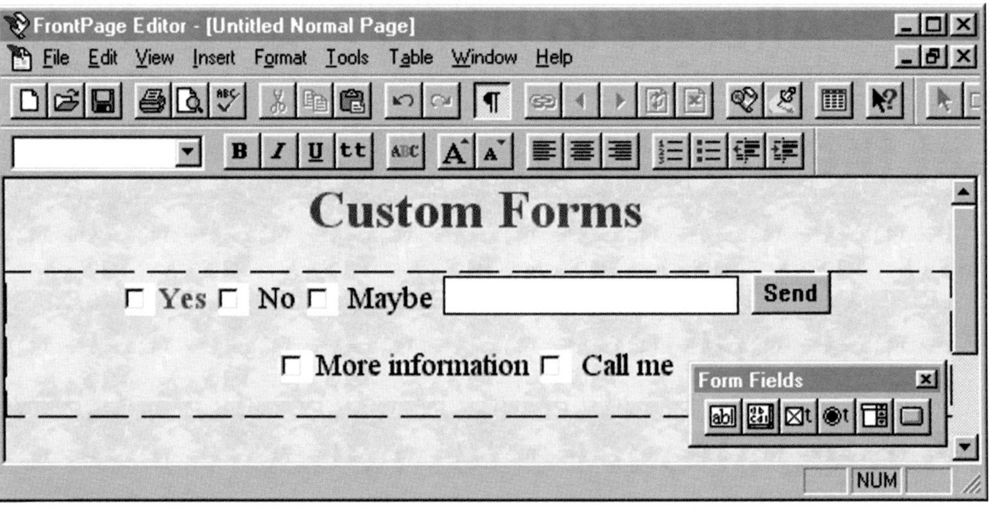

Create forms with the click of a button.

stomForms

Typeanyw

FrontPage gives you great type controls.

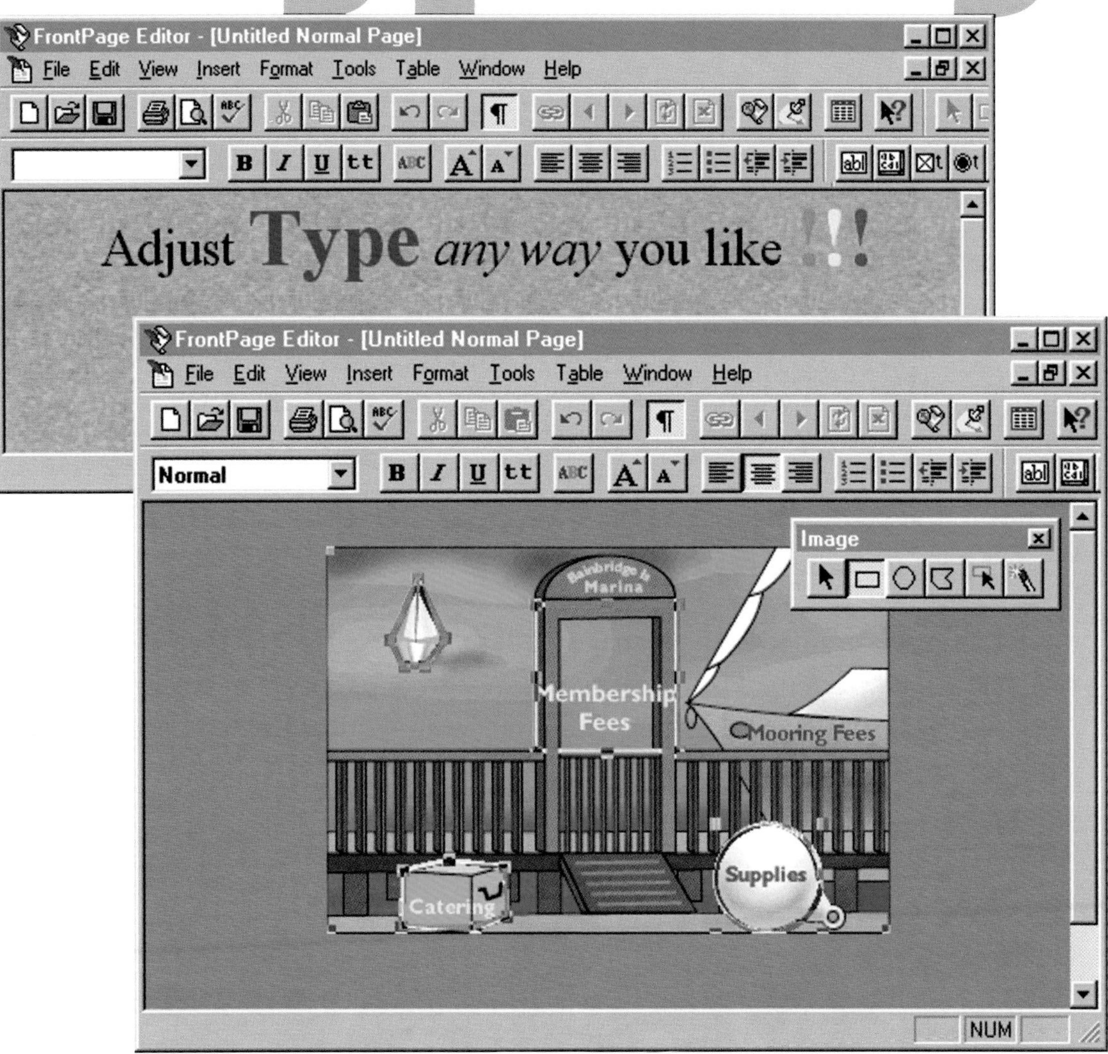

Clickable image maps. Any size, any shape.

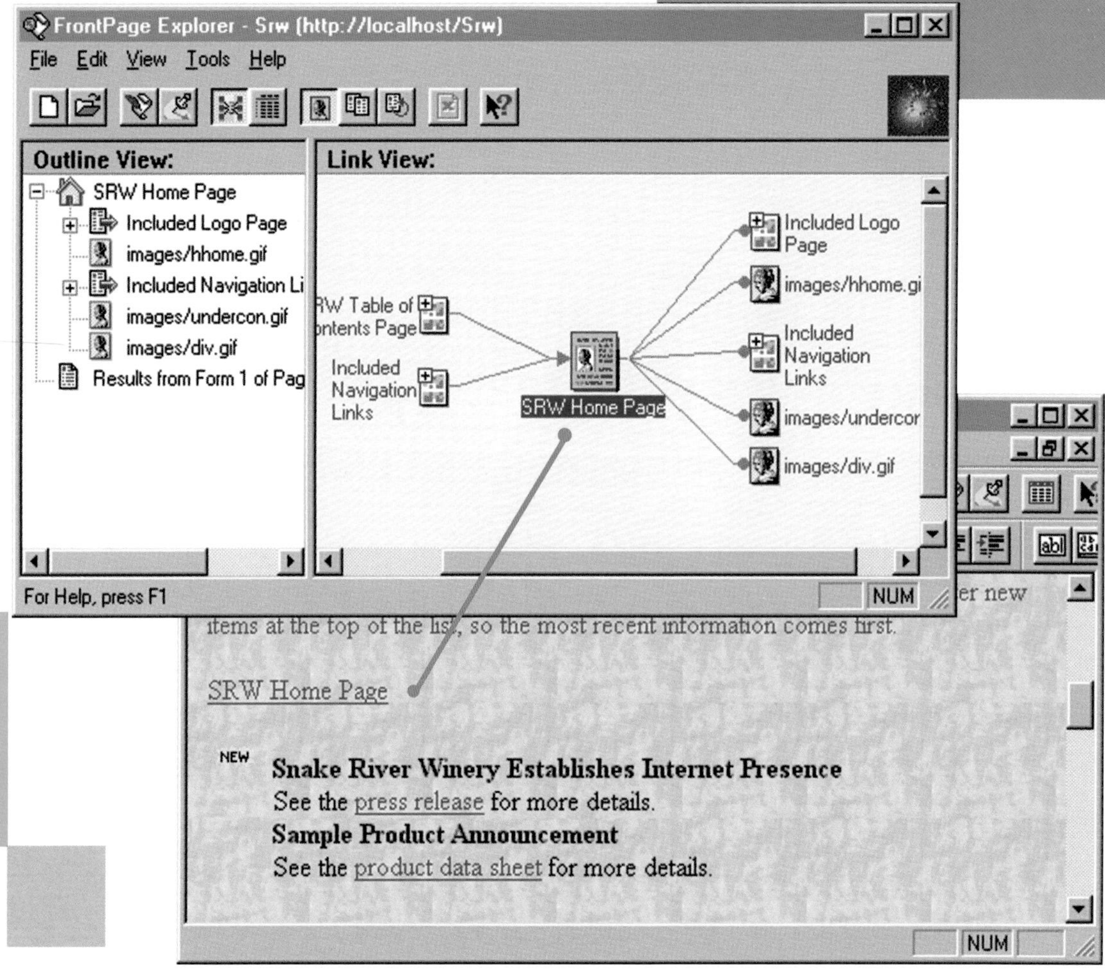

Drag and drop a link.

You can automatically create a text link by dragging and dropping a page or image from the FrontPage Explorer onto a page you're creating in the Editor. FrontPage takes care of all the details—including logging the URL of the link's destination.

The Explorer

View your site in different ways.

You create and manage your web sites in the FrontPage Explorer. Here you can see your web sites as you've never seen them before.

Summary view lists all the details of your pages and files, and Link view presents a graphical view of the links between your site's pages and images.

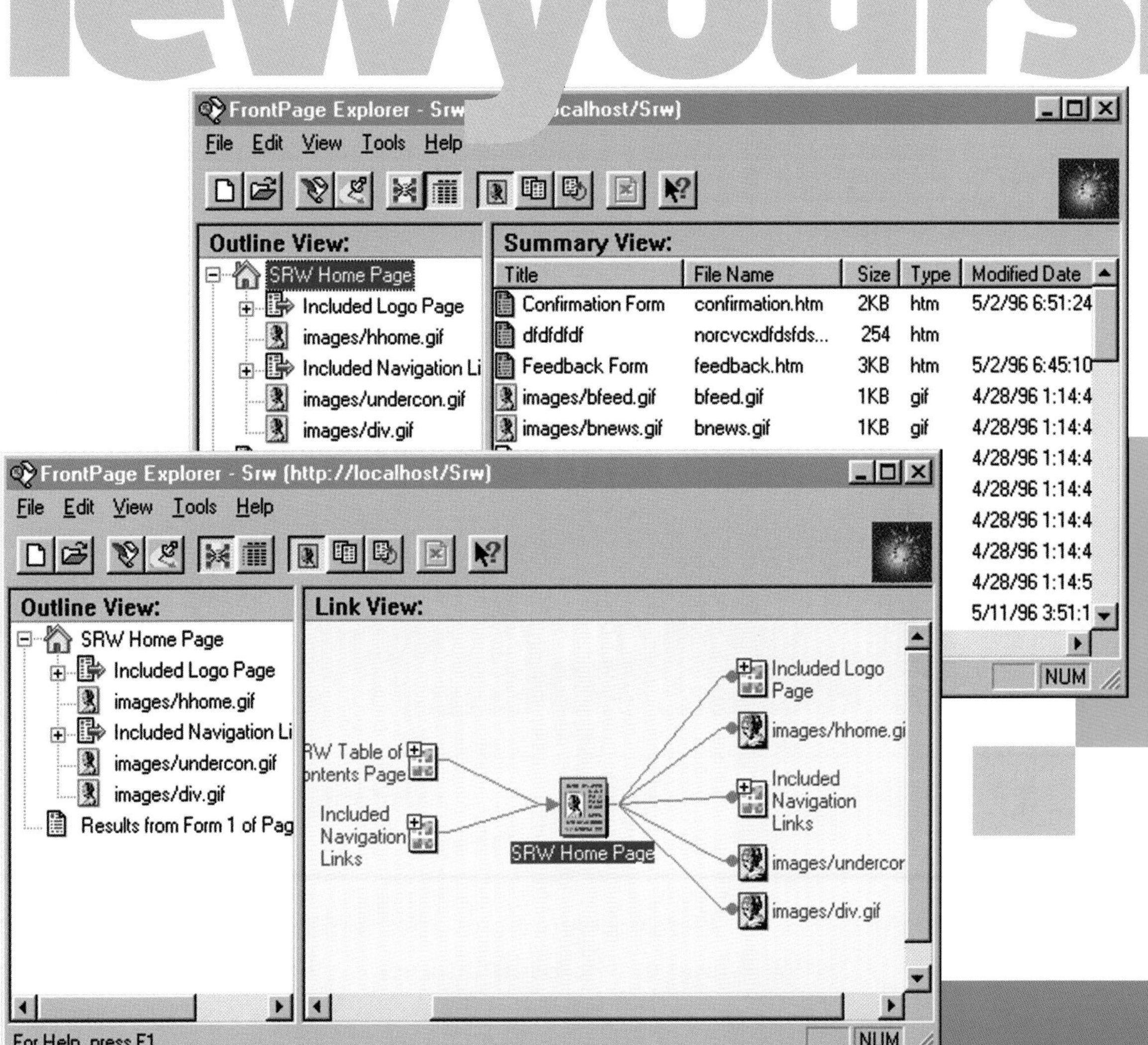

WYSIWYG

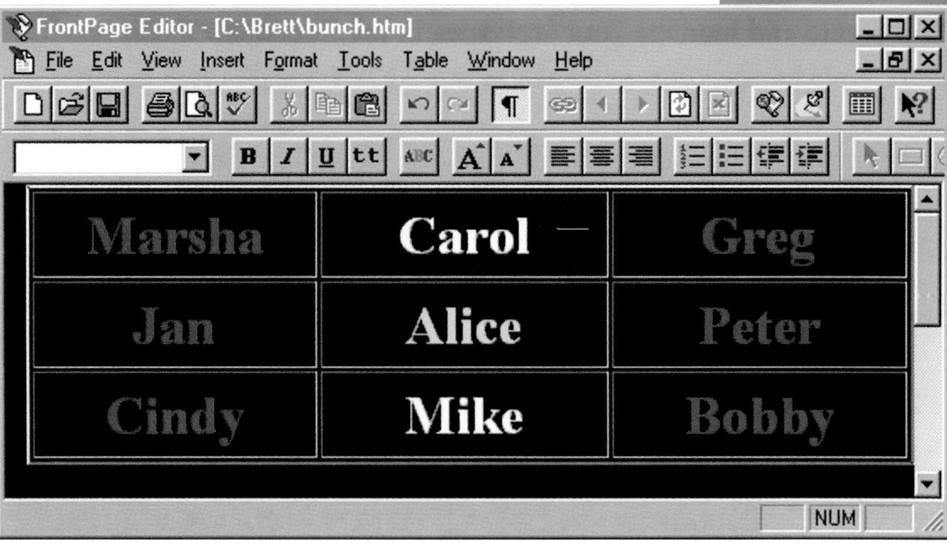

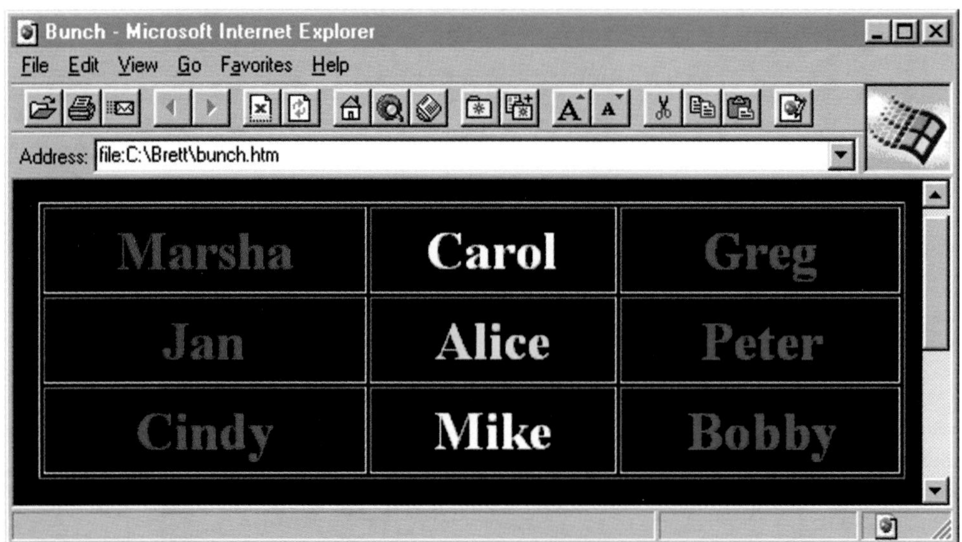

You can organize your information on a web page easily by using tables.

Here's a before-and-after look at a table in the Editor and in Microsoft Internet Explorer browser, showing that the Editor really is a WYSIWYG environment—What You See Is What You Get.

FrontPage and the Internet

Microsoft FrontPage is taking the lead in web-site publishing. Its two-tiered, client-server architecture gives you power and flexibility as you've never had it before. Leave the mind-boggling HTML behind if you want—FrontPage does the programming for you!

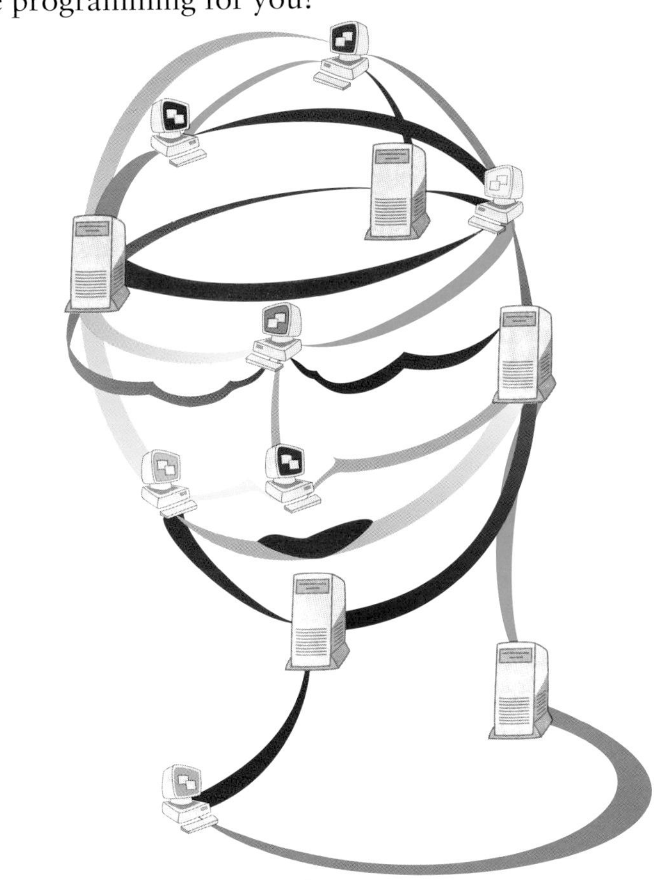

The To Do List (below) helps you keep track of all the tasks that need to be completed in a site. Even for small sites, the number of things to do can be overwhelming. Why bother with scribbled sticky notes when you can keep track of everything electronically?

FrontPage To Do List - Srw

Keep window open   Show history

Task	Assigned To	Priority	Linked To	Description
Customize Feedback Form	Dave	Medium	Feedback Form	adjust input areas in the form
Customize Home Page	Ollie	High	SRW Home Page	replace generic text with some
Customize News Page	Linda	High	SRW What's New Pa...	add your own public relations
Customize Products Page	Casey	High	SRW Products & Ser...	create data sheets for your ow
Customize Search Page	Reign Man	Medium	SRW Text Search Pa...	explain how to search for com
Customize TOC Page	Ina	Medium	SRW Table of Conte...	describe sections in more deta
Replace Logo Image	Randy	High	Included Logo Page	replace the image on this page

Do Task   Details...   Complete...   Add...   Close   Help

Keyboard Shortcuts

FrontPage Explorer

Create a new web site Ctrl+N
Open a page or image Ctrl+O
Delete a page or image Del
Edit properties Alt+Enter
Stop an operation in progress Esc
Close a dialog box Esc

FrontPage Editor

File Management

Create a new page Ctrl+N
Open a file Ctrl+O
Save a page Ctrl+S
Print a page Ctrl+P

Editing Pages

Undo an action Ctrl+Z or Alt+Backspace
Redo an undone action Ctrl+Y
Select all items on a page Ctrl+A
Find text Ctrl+F
Replace text Ctrl+H
Go to top of page Ctrl+Home
Go to bottom of page Ctrl+End
Scroll through a page Pg Up, Pg Down, and arrow keys
Edit an existing link or create a new link Ctrl+K
Delete a selected item Del
Edit properties Alt+Enter

Formatting Text

Make text bold Ctrl+B
Make text italic Ctrl+I
Underline text Ctrl+U
Increase font size Shift+Ctrl+>
Decrease font size Shift+Ctrl+<
Reset text formatting back to normal Ctrl+Spacebar

Inserting Lines and Spaces

Insert a line break Shift+Enter
Insert a non-breaking space Shift+Spacebar
Insert a hard space Shift+Ctrl+Spacebar

Other

End a list Ctrl+Enter
Check spelling F7
Follow a text or image link Ctrl+left mouse button
Move to an adjacent table cell Arrow keys
Stop an operation in progress Esc
Close a dialog box Esc

Frames

A **frame** is a region on a web page in which you can display other pages or images. In FrontPage, you create frames using the Frames Wizard; this process is described in Chapter 4.

Uses for frames Frames can be used in a wide variety of ways, and their use is limited only by your imagination. You should use a frame whenever you want particular contents on a page to remain static while other contents on the page change. A common use involves inserting a company logo in a frame at the top of a page, and using the rest of the page for other content.

Another use of frames on a World Wide Web page might involve presenting a list of your company's products in a frame on the left side of a page, and having each product appear on a page in a frame on the right side. The page in the left frame is static; you want the list of products to appear all the time. The page that appears in the right frame changes, according to what product the user clicks on in the left frame. You can associate each of the links on the page in the left frame with a target frame, which in this case is the right frame. Thus, when a user clicks on a link on a page in the left frame, the appropriate page appears in the target frame on the right side of the page.

You can create many similar pages for your company's intranet. One page might present a listing of each month of the year in the left frame, with each month linked to a sales report page for that particular month, which appears in the right frame.

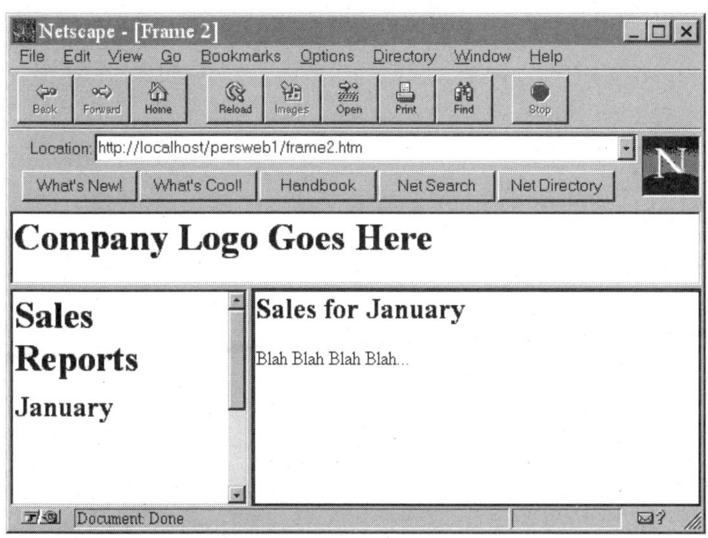

Frame sets All the frames you create on a page are collectively referred to as a **frame set.** A page that includes a frame set is saved by FrontPage as an HTML file, just like any other page. The pages and/or image files that *fill up* the frames are regular page and image files from the same site. You create these pages in the Editor and import the images into your site.

There's a major difference between editing frame-set pages and editing standard HTML pages in the Editor—you edit frame sets using the same wizard you used to create them. Keep this important fact in mind: You can never edit a frame or frame set directly in the Editor. You edit frames and frame sets using the Frames Wizard. The *content that appears in the frames*, however, is edited either in the Editor (for HTML pages) or in a third-party image editor (for images).

Editing a frame set You use the Frames Wizard when you want to change anything about a frame set, including adding, removing, resizing, and renaming frames; changing frame attributes such as margin width; and specifying different content to appear in a frame. You can reach the Frames Wizard in one of two ways. Suppose you want to open Frameset1.htm, which contains the frame set you want to edit. Here's what you can do:

- In the Editor, choose Open From Web from the File menu. In the Current Web dialog box, select Frameset1.htm, and click OK. To reach the Frames Wizard this way, you must have the web site that contains Frameset1.htm currently open in the Explorer.
- In the Explorer, double-click the page labeled Frameset1.htm in either Link view or Summary view. Or, in any view, you can right-click on Frameset1.htm and choose Open from the pop-up menu.

The Frames Wizard appears, ready for you to edit the frame set. Here's a rundown of the edits you can make to the frame set:

- Changing the layout of a frame set—To change the layout of a frame set, such as splitting or merging frames or changing the number of rows and columns your frames are divided into, use the Frames Wizard - Edit Frameset Grid screen, which is the first screen of the Frames Wizard.

- Renaming frames and changing other frame attributes —To rename a frame, change the margin width and height, or make a frame scrolling or nonscrolling, use the Frames Wizard - Edit Frame Attributes screen, which is the second screen of the wizard.

> **TIP**
>
> If you make changes to the frame set that you do not want to save, click Cancel anywhere in the wizard.

- Changing alternate content—To change the content that appears in place of a frames page in browsers that do not support frames, use the Frames Wizard - Choose Alternate Content screen, which is the third screen of the wizard.
- Renaming the entire frame set and changing its URL—To rename a frame set and/or change its **URL**, use the Frames Wizard - Save Page screen, which is the fourth and final screen of the wizard.

When you have entered all the information you want to change, click Finish in the final screen. FrontPage saves the frame set with your changes.

For more information on using the Frames Wizard, see Chapter 4.

Displaying a page in a frame To designate a page to appear in a frame, you create a link to the page and associate the link with the frame. This all happens in the Edit Link dialog box. For example, suppose you have a Table of Contents page with a word, *Sales*, that's linked to a page containing sales information. You want both pages to appear in different frames of a frame set (on the same page). Here's how to set this up:

1. Display the Table of Contents page in its frame by specifying its URL in the Source URL text box on the Frame Wizard - Save Page screen.
2. Select Edit to open the Table of Contents page in the Editor.
3. In the Table of Contents page in the Editor, right-click on the *Sales* link and choose Properties from the pop-up menu to bring up the Edit Link dialog box.

4. On the Current Web tab, enter the Page URL for the Sales page in the Page text box.

5. In the Target Frame text box, enter the name of the frame you want the Sales page to appear in.

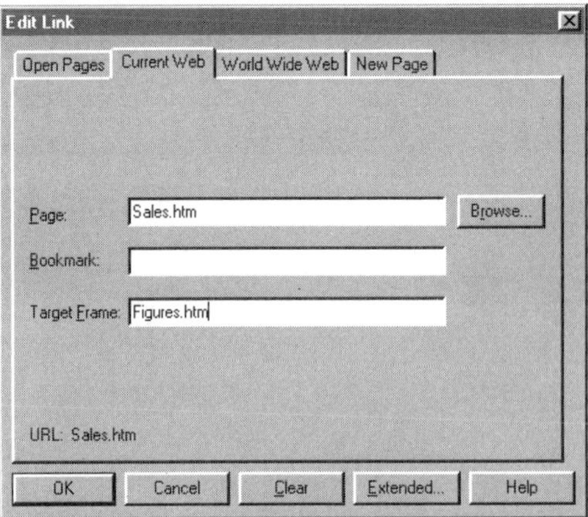

6. Click OK to close the Edit Link dialog box.

After this is set up, if the user clicks on the *Sales* link in the left frame, the Sales page will appear in the right frame.

Displaying form pages in a frame In the same way that you can direct a standard page to appear in a frame, you can direct the output of a form to appear in a frame, because the output of a form is a page itself. Here's how to set this up:

1. In the Editor, right-click on any form field and choose Form Properties from the pop-up menu.

2. In the Target Frame text box, enter the name of the frame you want the output of the form directed to.

3. Click OK to close the Form Properties dialog box.

Default target frames If you have a page with many links and you don't want to assign a target frame to every one of them, you can associate them with a default target frame. Default target frames specify a frame for any links on a page that are not associated with a specific target frame. The same applies for clickable images: For any links on an image that are not assigned a target frame, they can be assigned a default target frame. To find out how to assign a default target frame, see the facing page.

- For a page—With the page open in the Editor, right-click on the page and choose Page Properties from the pop-up menu. In the Page Properties dialog box, enter the frame name in the Default Target Frame text box, and then click OK.
- For a clickable image—In the Editor, right-click on the image and choose Properties from the pop-up menu. In the Image Properties dialog box, enter the frame name in the Default Target Frame text box, and then click OK.

Bookmarks

A bookmark is a set of one or more characters on a page that is the target of a link. Using links to bookmarks allows a viewer of your web site to jump to any point within a page (not just to the beginning of a page).

For example, suppose one of your pages consists of a five-section document, and you link to that page from somewhere else within your site. When a user follows that link, the top of the page (i.e., the top of the document) appears in the browser. But if the document includes bookmarks at the beginning of each section, you can create your links directly to those bookmarks. That way, a user can follow a link to a bookmark and jump to any of those sections instead of having to jump to the top of the document.

Bookmarks appear in the Editor as blue dashed underlines when Format Marks is selected on the View menu; otherwise, they do not appear. See "Links" on the next page for information on linking to bookmarks.

Creating a bookmark To create a bookmark, do the following:

1. Select one or more characters of text that will become the bookmark.
2. Choose Bookmark from the Edit menu. The Bookmark dialog box appears.

3. Enter the name of the bookmark in the Bookmark Name text box. Try to name your bookmarks intuitively, because later when you create a link to a bookmark you'll need to select the bookmark from a list. It'll help to be able to easily discern one bookmark from another. If your page already includes other bookmarks, they will appear in the dialog box.

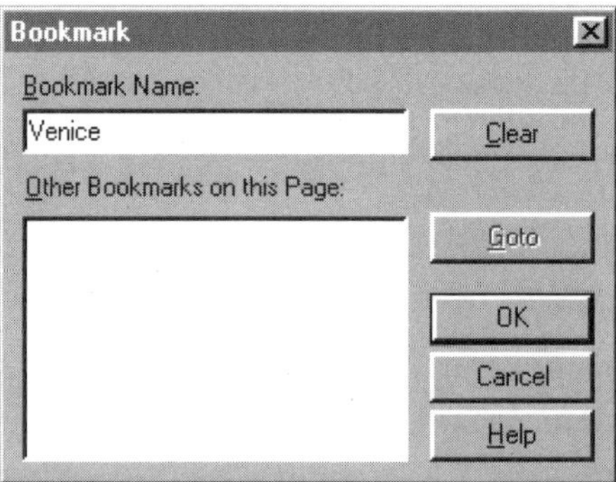

4. Click OK after you enter the bookmark name. The text for the bookmark will be indicated on screen if you choose Format Marks from the View menu.

Jumping to a bookmark Suppose you have a list of bookmarks on the current page in the Bookmark dialog box, and you want to jump to one of them. To jump to any bookmark in the list, select the bookmark and then click Goto. This is a quick and handy alternative for scrolling up and down a page to find your bookmarks.

Clearing a bookmark To remove a bookmark, select the bookmark and choose Bookmark from the Edit menu. In the Bookmark dialog box, click Clear. The dialog box closes, and the bookmark is removed.

Links

Links, sometimes called hotspots or hyperlinks, are connections from one point to another. Viewers of a site can click on a link and jump to wherever the link points to; this location is represented in HTML as a **URL**. You can link to and from text, images, other files (such as Microsoft Office files), or bookmarks. For information on creating links from images, see Chapter 7, and for information on changing the color of a link, see "Page Properties" later in this chapter.

Creating a link to pages or bookmarks To create a link, select the text you want to link from, and then choose Link from the Edit menu. The Create Link dialog box appears, with four tabs that allow you to link to different places.

> **SHORTCUT**
>
> You can quickly create or edit a link by selecting the text or link and then clicking on the Create Or Edit Link toolbar button.

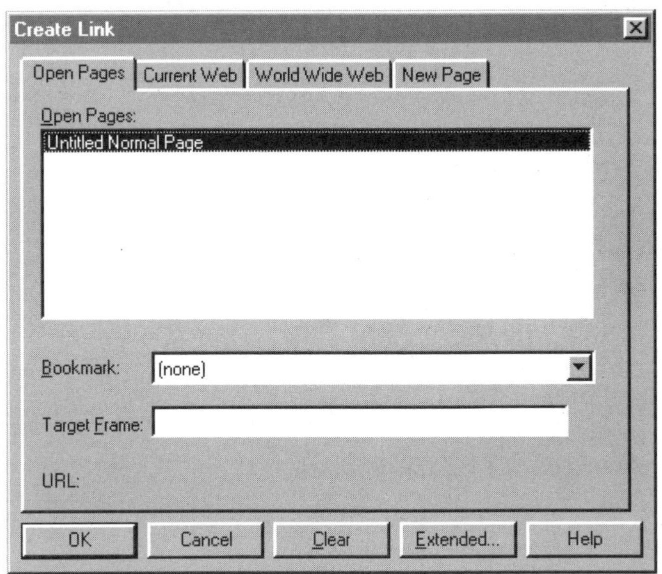

Here's how to use each of the tabs when creating links:

Open Pages tab—Allows you to link to any page currently open in the Editor, or to a bookmark on an open page. The Open Pages list box lists all currently open pages; select a page and click OK to link to that page. To link to a bookmark on a page, select the page (which causes FrontPage to list all of the bookmarks on that page in the Bookmark drop-down list box), select the bookmark from the drop-down list, and then click OK. As you work, FrontPage displays the relative URL of the current selection at the bottom of the dialog box.

Current Web tab—Allows you to link to any page or bookmark in the current web site (the one open in the Explorer). Click Browse to select a page as the target page of your link. If your target link is a bookmark, you can enter its name in the Bookmark text box for the page selected. Clicking the Clear button clears your selection. FrontPage displays the **relative URL** of the selection at the bottom of the dialog box. Click OK to create the link and close the Create Link dialog box.

TIP

If you want to create a link that allows users to send e-mail, select the mailto: protocol in the Protocol drop-down list on the World Wide Web tab. Then type the destination e-mail address following the protocol in the URL text box.

World Wide Web tab—Allows you to link to a Web URL. Select a supported protocol from the Protocol drop-down list. The Editor creates the protocol portion of the URL based on your selection. In the URL text box, enter the rest of the URL of the web page you want to link to. Clicking the Clear button clears your selection. Click OK to create the link and close the Create Link dialog box.

New Page tab—Allows you to link to a page in the current web site that has not yet been created. Enter a page title and a page URL in their respective text boxes. If you want, use the option buttons to select between opening the page immediately in the Editor or adding the page to the To Do List. The URL text box displays the relative URL of your selection; clicking the Clear button clears the selection. When you define such a link and click OK, FrontPage closes the dialog box and creates the page and the link to it.

Selecting a link All you need to do to select a link is to click anywhere within the hotspot. You can highlight text associated with a link to select it, but you do not need to. If the cursor is on a link, the toolbar buttons and menu items pertaining to links are enabled.

Removing a link To remove a link, select it and then choose Unlink from the Edit menu. The link is removed, but the former link's text remains.

SHORTCUT

Another fast way to reach the Edit Links dialog box is to right-click on a link and then choose Properties from the pop-up menu.

Editing a link To change a link's destination, select it and then choose Link from the Edit menu. Change the destination in the Edit Link dialog box that appears. For more information, see "Creating a Link to Pages or Bookmarks" on the previous page.

Dragging a link from the Explorer Here's one of the neatest features in FrontPage version 1.1. If you have the Explorer and the Editor open simultaneously, you can create a text link to a page by dragging the page from the Explorer to a location on a page displayed in the Editor. Here's how to do it:

1. Size the Editor and Explorer windows on your screen so that (1) the target for the link appears in the Explorer window, and (2) the page on which you want the link to appear is shown in the Editor. You can drag a link from any Explorer view, and the link itself can be to a page, an image, or a file (such as an Office document). One of the easiest ways to arrange your windows is to minimize all windows except the Explorer and the Editor, right-click over the taskbar background, and choose Tile Vertically from the pop-up menu.

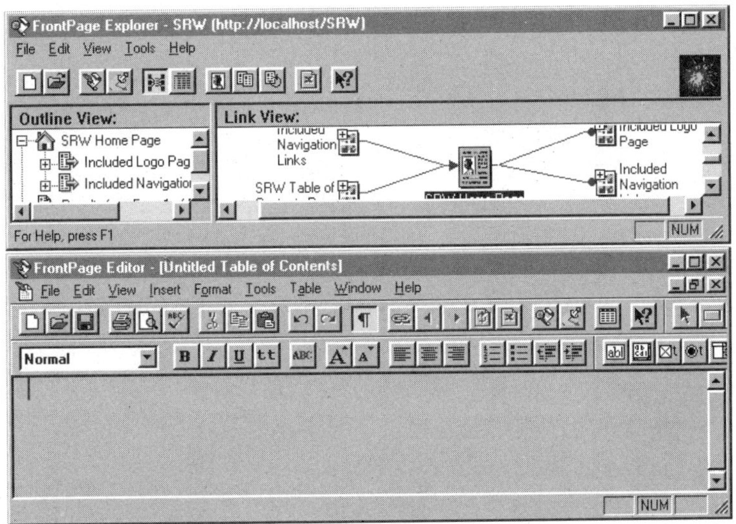

The Editor and Explorer are open and ready for the drag operation.

2. Click the icon or file in the Explorer that will be the link's target, and drag it onto the page in the Editor. The cursor changes to a link cursor, which is an underlined capital *L*. Position the cursor at the exact spot where you want the link to appear on the page in the Editor, and release the mouse button. The name of the target is inserted and a link is created from that text to the target itself. There's no more work to do—FrontPage takes care of designating the link's destination for you.

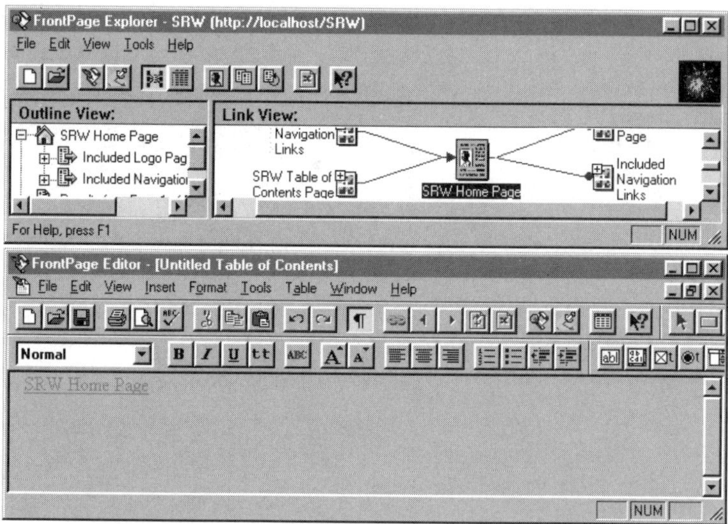

The SRW Home Page was just dragged from the Explorer onto the page in the Editor. The mouse button has just been released, creating the link.

Formatting Your Pages

Once you've got the material you want on your pages, you probably want to fine-tune it. Your paragraphs don't have to stay left-aligned, your text doesn't all have to remain the same color and size, and the links and background of your pages don't have to remain the same, either. You can change all of this, and more, very quickly in the Editor.

You've probably noticed many web pages that use plain, black text of the same size and plain, boring paragraphs. With FrontPage, you can format your pages so they really stand out. It's like adding those hidden ingredients to a recipe—next to most others, your pages will be like your grandmother's apple pie next to a frozen pie.

FrontPage uses levels, and not actual values such as point size, for settings of elements such as headings and font size. For example, a Level 1 heading is the largest heading you can use in FrontPage, a Level 2 heading is slightly smaller, and so on. Headings decrease in point size as their level number decreases, but you don't have to be concerned with setting specific point sizes in relation to one another in FrontPage if you're using several different levels of headings. It's much easier to work with a smaller set of heading and font-size levels than it is to work with many possibilities of point size.

Character Formatting

The Editor gives you many options for formatting characters in different sizes, colors, and styles. You can change some of this formatting with toolbar buttons, but all of the options are included in the Character Styles dialog box. Here's how to reach that dialog box, and what you can do with the options:

1. Select the text you want to change, and then choose Characters from the Format menu. You can also right-click on the text and choose Format Characters from the pop-up menu. If you don't highlight any text before choosing these commands, after closing the dialog box any text you type at that location will be formatted according to the settings you've made in the dialog box.

2. Set any of the following options, and then click OK to exit the dialog box.

Regular styles Choose from Bold, Italic, Underlined, Strike-Through, and Typewriter Font. Use these styles when creating new text. Typewriter text characters are all the same width. You can use typewriter-text font to represent computer code or user input.

Special styles Because the pages you open might contain special styles, FrontPage includes many such styles in this section of the dialog box. Use regular styles, not special styles, when you create new text. The special styles might not display in a browser as they do in the Editor, because many browsers do not support many of the styles. If you want to apply a special style, you can choose from the following:

> Citation—An italic style that can be used for the name of a manual, section, or book.
>
> Sample—A typewriter-font style.
>
> Definition—An italic style used for defining terms.

SHORTCUT

You can also make your text bold, italic, underlined, or typewriter text by using their respective toolbar buttons. Using the toolbar buttons applies the same bold and italic styles that you can specify in the Regular Styles section of the Character Styles dialog box.

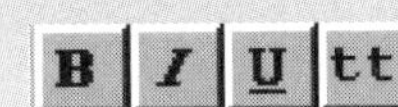

Blink—A style that makes text blink in a browser. Many Web browsers do not support blinking text, however.

Code—A typewriter-font style that can be used to represent code.

Variable—An italic style that can be used to mark variable names.

Bold—A simple bold style.

Italic— A simple italic style.

Keyboard—A typewriter-font style that can be used for user-entry text.

SHORTCUT

You can also adjust font size by clicking on the Increase Text Size and Decrease Text Size toolbar buttons.

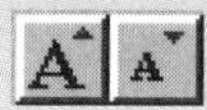

Font size Seven sizes are available in the Font Size drop-down list. Approximate point sizes are given for each of the font sizes; actual sizes can vary depending on a browser's settings.

Color You can make your text any of 48 standard colors supplied by FrontPage. In the Character Styles dialog box, select the Set Color check box, and then click the Choose button. Click on a color in the Color dialog box to select it, and then click OK to return to the Character Styles dialog box. If you want to use a custom color, click the Define Custom Color button in the Color dialog box.

SHORTCUT

You can reach the Color dialog box quickly by clicking the Text Color toolbar button.

Superscript and subscript FrontPage supports authoring of superscript and subscript styles. These styles are supported by some browsers, but not by all.

To set a superscript or subscript style, select Superscript or Subscript from the Vertical Position drop-down list, and then set its numeric level. The numbers correspond to varying heights that the superscript or subscript can appear at, and not to the size of the superscript or subscript. Selecting a superscript level of 1, for example, sets the superscript slightly above the sentence. A number 2 superscript sets up shop a little higher than a number 1, and so on. You can set 100 different superscript and subscript levels.

Paragraphs

Creating a new paragraph To create a new paragraph, press the Enter key. A blank line will appear, and you can type in text in the same style as the preceding paragraph. For example, if you're typing in the Normal style, when you press Enter the new paragraph will also be in the Normal style.

To insert a new paragraph with a different style, do the following:

1. Place your cursor at the place where you want the next paragraph to begin. This can be at the end of a previous line or in the middle of a paragraph.
2. Choose Paragraph from the Insert menu, and choose one of the following styles from the submenu: Normal, Formatted, or Address. Normal is the default style, Formatted is a style that uses the Typewriter font, and Address is an italic style. The Editor inserts a blank line, and you can begin typing in the new style.

If you insert a new paragraph in the middle of a paragraph, the Editor splits the original paragraph into two parts and adds the new paragraph between the two, keeping the original style for both parts. For example, inserting a Formatted paragraph in a Normal paragraph results in a paragraph containing the first portion of the Normal paragraph, followed by the new Formatted paragraph, and then the remaining portion of the original Normal paragraph.

Changing paragraph styles Suppose you want to change the style of a paragraph from Normal to Address. There are several ways you can do this. First highlight the paragraph whose style you want to change (or simply place your cursor somewhere within the paragraph), and then do one of the following:

- From the Style drop-down list (at the far left of the Formatting toolbar), select the new style for your paragraph.
- Choose Paragraph from the Format menu. Select the new style for your paragraph in the Paragraph Format dialog box, and then click OK.

- Right-click on any text and choose Format Paragraph from the pop-up menu. Change the style in the Paragraph Format dialog box, and then click OK.

The Paragraph Format dialog box gives you numerous format options, including Normal, Formatted, and Address, as well as all six heading styles. The Style drop-down list contains these plus five list styles.

Indenting a paragraph When you indent a paragraph in the Editor, the entire paragraph receives the indent. To indent a paragraph, position your cursor anywhere in the paragraph and click the Increase Indent toolbar button. To remove an indent, click the Decrease Indent toolbar button.

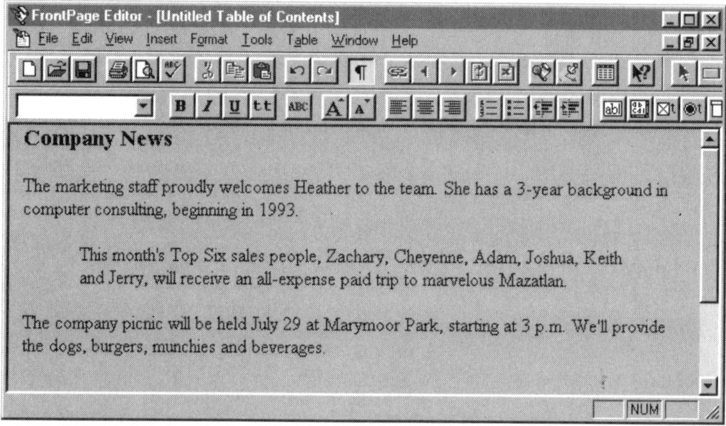

The middle paragraph above is indented.

> **TIP**
>
> If you're changing the style of a paragraph in the Paragraph Format dialog box, you can also change the paragraph's alignment there at the same time.

Aligning a paragraph You can make a paragraph left-aligned, centered, or right-aligned with the click of a toolbar button. Just position your cursor anywhere in the paragraph, and then click the Align Left, Center, or Align Right toolbar button. You can use these buttons to align paragraphs on a page or to align text in a table cell. Left-aligning a paragraph leaves a ragged right margin, right-aligning a paragraph leaves a ragged left margin, and centering a paragraph leaves both sides ragged and centers the paragraph within its margins.

Line Breaks

A line break forms a new line on a page without creating a new paragraph. In other words, when you insert a line break, the next line starts below the previous line with the formatting used for the other lines within the paragraph. When you start a new paragraph, it too begins on the next line, but it is formatted as the first line of the paragraph (perhaps with indenting or some additional spacing to separate the new paragraph from the previous one).

Inserting a line break To insert a line break, position your cursor where you want the line break to appear, and choose Line Break from the Insert menu. From the Break Properties dialog box that appears, select among the following:

Normal Line Break—Adds a line break and does not clear any images from the left or right margins. In other words, even if there is an image in either the right or left margin, the new line starts immediately below the line break.

Clear Left Margin—Adds a line break, and if an image is in the left margin, moves the line following the line break down until the margin is clear.

Clear Right Margin—Adds a line break, and if an image is in the right margin, moves the line following the line break down until the right margin is clear.

Clear Both Margins—Adds a line break, and if an image is in one or both margins, moves the line following the line break down until both margins are clear.

Formatting a line break To change the way a line break works with images, right-click on it and choose Properties from the pop-up menu. This displays the Break Properties dialog box, where you can change the type of line break.

Deleting a line break You can treat a line break as any other character. You can delete it with the Backspace or Del key.

Horizontal Lines

Using horizontal lines on a page is a neat way to separate sections, topics, or other elements. You can insert shaded or solid horizontal lines and format them in a few ways.

Inserting a horizontal line To insert a horizontal line, position your cursor where you want the line to appear, and then choose Horizontal Line from the Insert menu. A line appears, formatted the same as the last horizontal line that was inserted in the Editor. If you're inserting a line for the first time, it will span the width of the page, have a shadow, and be two pixels high.

Formatting a horizontal line To change the appearance of a horizontal line, right-click on it and choose Properties from the pop-up menu. The Horizontal Line Properties dialog box appears:

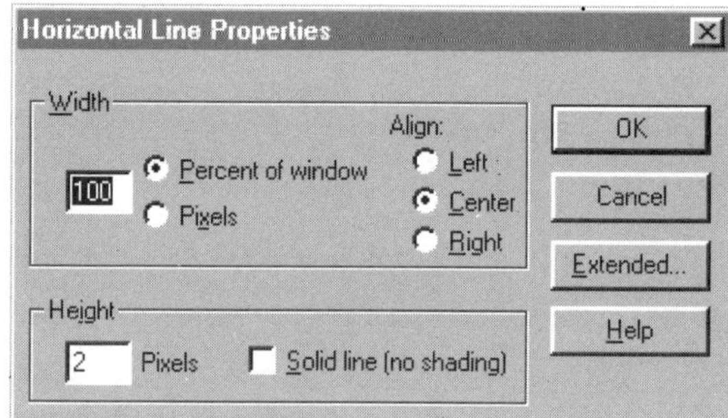

In the Width section, specify the length of your line as a percentage of the screen width, or as a length in pixels, and specify Right, Left, or Center alignment. Then enter the line's thickness in pixels in the Height section, and specify whether you want the line to appear as a solid line. Solid lines appear in black, and shaded lines (the default) appear shaded with the page's background color. Click OK to accept your settings and close the dialog box.

Deleting a horizontal line To delete a horizontal line, select it and then press the Del key or backspace over it.

Page Properties

Setting Page Properties You can set the properties for a page in the Editor by choosing the Page Properties command from the File menu or from the pop-up menu that appears when you right-click on the page. In the Page Properties dialog box, you can set a page's background image or color, a default color for text, and default colors for links. You must have a page open in the Editor in order to set these properties. (To open a page or create a new page, see the next section.) Here's a primer on the properties:

1. Enter a page title and a URL if none are present. You'll only need to change these if you've created a new page and haven't named it or given it a URL, or if you want to change either of these properties.

2. Customize the colors and background of the page. You have several ways of doing this:

   Get Background and Colors from Page If you go this route, you can start with the same background colors, images, and custom colors for links that exist on another page. Select the check box, and then click the Browse button to specify the page you want to use for this purpose. If you've already set up those properties elsewhere, this saves you time by not having to set them up again for the current page.

   Background Image Here you can specify an image to use as your page background; most browsers will tile this image automatically. You've probably seen this on the Web; a tiled background can be effective if it adds to the "viewability" of a page and does not impair text or other images on the page. Once a background image has been selected, you can set some of its properties by clicking the Properties button.

   Use Custom Background Color You can specify a background color for your page if you don't want to use a tiled image. You might also consider using another color with more flair. Just make sure your text and images are easy to read against whatever color you select. Click the Choose button to select your color from a color palette.

   Use Custom Text Color Here you can specify the default color of the text that appears on your page. Click the Choose button to select a default color from

> **TIP**
>
> To adjust the properties of an existing background image, open the Page Properties dialog box and click the Properties button in the Background Image section. This brings up the Image Properties dialog box. See Chapter 7 for information on this dialog box.

a color palette. Black is a safe standard, but don't hesitate to experiment with other colors that might look good against the background you selected. Sometimes a dark blue is a nice alternative against a gray or white background. Any text that is formatted in a different color will override the default color specified here.

Use Custom Active Link Color The active link color is the color of a link as it is being clicked. Click the Choose button to select your color.

Use Custom Link Color You can specify a color to use for all links on a page that have not been visited. Click the Choose button to select your color.

Use Custom Visited Link Color Links change to this color after they have been followed. If a link appears on more than one page, following one triggers the visited link color for all instances of that link in your site.

3. For those of you who need to set extended HTML or meta-tags to the page, you can do so by clicking the Extended or Meta buttons. Extended attributes consist of HTML coding that FrontPage does not directly support, and meta-tags supply information about the document but do not affect the page appearance. If you don't know what these are, don't fret—chances are you'll never have to worry about them.

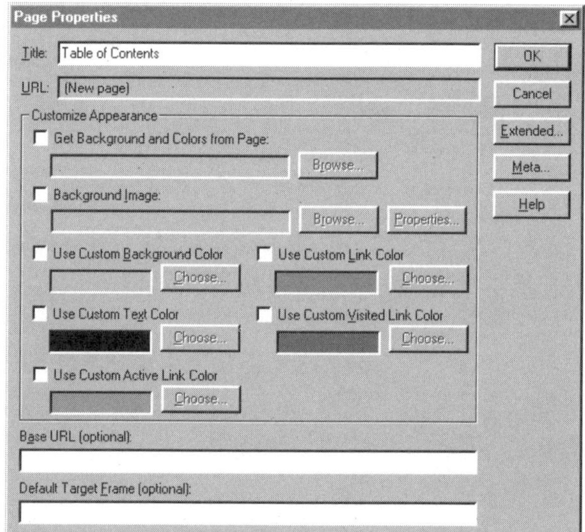

4. Click OK.

Working with Page Files

Standard file management commands in the Editor are similar to their counterparts in the Explorer, except they work at the page level, not at the web-site level. For example, you save or close a page in the Editor, while you save or close a site in the Explorer. In addition, you can perform a few different tasks with files in the Editor, such as printing.

A web site's pages and files are stored on a web server. On the web server(s) that you're using with FrontPage, they're stored in the Content directory. FrontPage creates a subdirectory for each web site you create, which includes further subdirectories to store files of different types, such as image files and page files. All page files have the HTM extension, which indicates they are HTML pages. In this section you'll learn how to use the Editor's file management commands.

Creating New Pages

Creating new pages in the Editor is easy, and FrontPage allows you to create numerous kinds of pages with its templates and wizards. Most often, you'll create new pages to add them to a web site that is currently open, but you're not limited to that scenario. You can also create a new page, save it separately, and add it to any other web site later on. (See "Saving Pages" later in this chapter for more information.)

1. To create a new page, choose New from the File menu. You'll see the New Page dialog box:

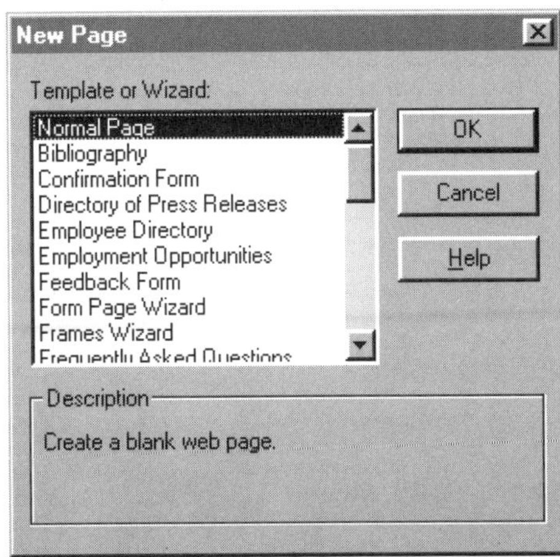

SHORTCUT

You can quickly create a new page by pressing Ctrl+N on your keyboard, or by clicking the New button on the toolbar.

2. Select a page template or wizard from the list, and click OK. If you want to edit a blank page, select the Normal page template. You can find full descriptions of the templates and wizards in Chapter 4.

Opening Pages

The various Open commands in the Editor allow you to open existing pages stored as files in your system, pages from your current web site (if it is open in the Explorer), and even pages from sites on the Web itself. This gives you countless options for adding new material to your site; you can add any page that you have access to, including those with the following extensions: TXT (text files), RTF (rich text format files), or HTM (HTML). You have the following possibilities:

Opening a page from your file system Say you're editing your web site, and you need to add a page that is saved as a file but not saved as part of a web site. For example, suppose someone in your organization is creating custom pages for several different web sites and saving them separately for others to add to their respective sites as they need them. If you want to add a page like this to your site, here's how to do it:

1. Choose the Open File command from the File menu. The Open dialog box appears:

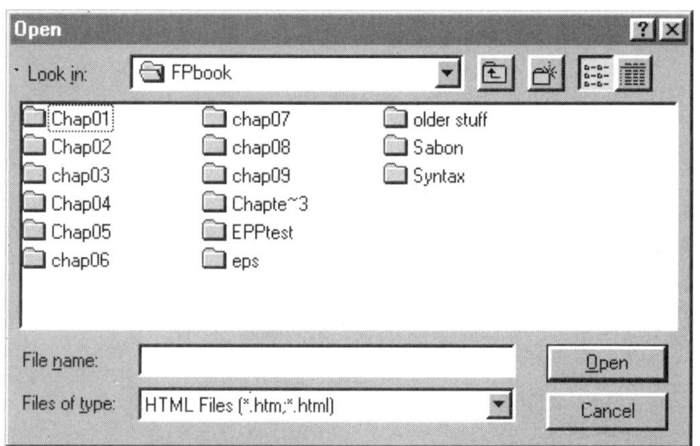

2. In the Files Of Type list box, select the type of file you're looking to open—RTF (rich text format), TXT (text), HTML, or All Files for files with different extensions. Then browse your file system for the file, select it, and click OK.

> **SHORTCUT**
>
> You can quickly access the Open dialog box from the Editor by pressing Ctrl+O or by clicking the Open button on the toolbar.
>
> 

If you open a file with an extension that the Editor does not recognize, you'll see the Open File As dialog box. Here you'll have the option to open the file as an HTML, RTF, or TXT file. If this dialog box leaves your brain feeling a little fuzzy, keep this in mind: The Editor can only read open page files in one of these three formats. The only use for this dialog box is for identifying files that have a different extension and are therefore not recognized by FrontPage.

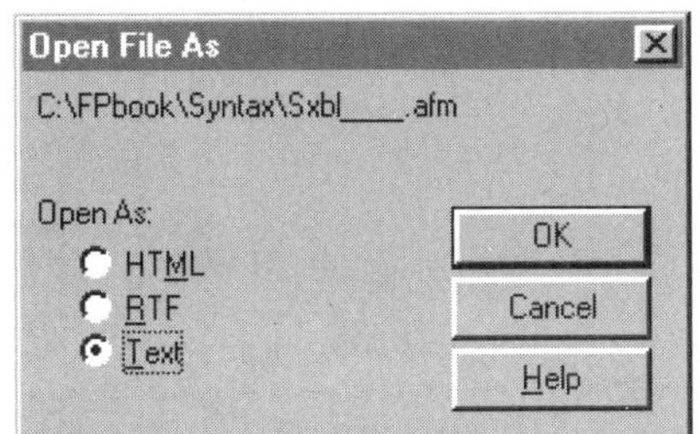

The Editor will try to open actual HTML files as they are, without conversions, and display all of their elements. However, if the file contains HTML code that FrontPage does not recognize, the Editor will preserve it in an HTML Markup bot. (For more information on HTML Markup bots, see Chapter 8.)

If you are opening a page stored as a text file, you'll see the Convert Text Dialog Box, which gives you several nifty options:

- One Formatted Paragraph—Gathers all the text in the file and presents it in one paragraph of formatted (Typewriter font) text.
- Formatted Paragraphs—Converts each paragraph to formatted text.
- Normal Paragraphs—Converts paragraphs to the Normal style, which is the default paragraph style in the Editor.

- Normal Paragraphs with Line Breaks—Converts paragraphs to Normal text and preserves line breaks, which force a new line on the page without creating a new paragraph.

When opening RTF files, the Editor makes the following conversions:

- Bulleted and numbered lists are retained, but numbering style might be lost.
- Tables are converted to formatted text; they lose any justification and centering.
- In-line graphics are converted to GIF files and are linked to the document.
- All footnotes are placed at the end of the page; footnote references are linked to their topics.
- Bold and italic fonts are retained.

Opening a page from the current site If you need to edit a page that's part of the current web site in the Explorer, there are two easy ways to do it: You can go to the Explorer, find the page, and open it from there (perhaps by double-clicking on it). Or (an even easier way), you can open it in the Editor by choosing the Open From Web command from the File menu.

When you choose the Open From Web command, you'll see the Current Web dialog box, which lists the titles and URLs of the pages in the site. Select a page and click OK, and the page opens in a new window in the Editor for you to edit to your heart's desire. There's also a third way to open a file from a current web site, described next, but it's a little more difficult.

Opening a page from any site You can open any page from any web site you have access to—including those on intranets and the Web. All you have to know is the page's address. Here are the details:

To begin, choose Open Location from the File menu. In the Open Location dialog box, type the address of the page you're after, and then click OK. The address can be of two types:

- Page URL—In simplest terms, a page URL is the name of a page, including its extension; for example, *index.htm*.

If you supply a page URL in the Open Location dialog box, you'll only be able to open pages from your current web site.

> **TIP**
>
> It's easier to use the Open From Web command to open pages from the current web site, as explained in the previous section, because using the Open Location command requires you to know and type in the exact name of the page.

- Absolute URL—An absolute URL is the full address of a page, including the protocol, host name, directory name, and filename. With absolute URLs, you can open pages from any system that can create a connection to that site. For example, say your organization is running a web site called BusinessSite1 with the Personal Web Server, which includes a press release page (with the page URL PR3.htm) that you'd like to edit. If you have access and editing privileges to the web site, to open that page in the Editor simply choose the Open Location command and type in the absolute URL—for example, *http://localhost/BusinessSite1/PR3.htm.* It's that easy, even for bringing up Web pages in the Editor.

FrontPage might display a warning that the address you supplied is not a valid **IP address.** If you see this warning, check the address and try it again. Make sure you typed the correct characters; you'll need at least *http://* at the beginning of the address. Be sure to use forward slashes instead of backslashes in the address.

If you're attempting to open a page from the Web and you get this error message, you might not be connected to the Web. Make sure your connection is live from your terminal, and then try again.

Closing Pages

To close a page in the Editor, choose the Close command from the File menu. FrontPage will save and close the page in one of the following scenarios:

- If you opened the page from a web site that is currently open, the Editor prompts you to save any changes to the page and then closes it.

- If you opened the page from a site that you've since closed in the Explorer, FrontPage will tell you so and ask you whether you want to save the page to the site that's currently open in the Explorer, if one is open. To save the page to the site you opened it from, you must reopen the site in the Explorer.
- If you don't have any web sites open in the Explorer, you'll be prompted to open a site and close the page again, so FrontPage can save the page as part of that site.
- If you opened the page from a file that's not part of a site, the Editor will close that file after prompting you to save any changes.

Saving Pages

Save your work in the same way that people in Seattle drink their coffee: early and often. Murphy's Law *will* strike you when it hurts the most; there will be times when the power goes down, or when your officemate, Kristina Klumsy, rips the power cords from the wall sockets with her size 10 blue suede shoes. The Editor gives you three kinds of saving options:

- Save—Saves the active page in HTML format, to a web site or to a file.
- Save As—Copies and saves the active page to a new page in the current web site or to a file.
- Save All—Saves all pages that are open in the Editor.

Saving for the first time No matter which command you use, if you haven't saved the page before, you'll see the Save As dialog box, which gives you several options for how to save your file. You can also use the Save As command to save a page to a different location or with a different name.

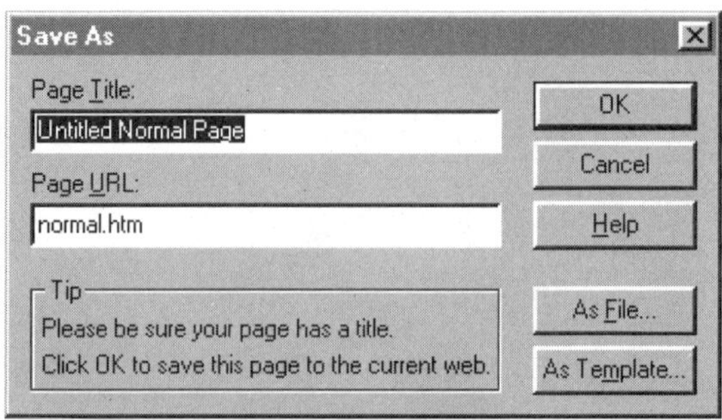

Here's how to use the Save As dialog box:

- Enter a page title and a page URL if you want to save the file as part of the site that's currently open in the Explorer. Give your page a unique and intelligent name so you can recognize it easily among other page names. After you enter that information, click OK.
- If you want to save the page as a file, either to any FrontPage web site in the Content directory on your web server or to anywhere else (such as to a floppy disk), you don't need to fill in the title or URL. Click the As File button. This takes you to the Save As File dialog box, where you can type the filename and specify the location where you want the file saved. You can specify an extension as part of the filename, but if FrontPage does not recognize the extension, it will save the file with an HTM extension.
- You can also save the page as a template from the Save As dialog box. For details on this, see Chapter 4.

SHORTCUT

You can quickly save a page by pressing Ctrl+S or by clicking the Save button on the toolbar.

Using the Save and Save All commands When you use the Save and Save All commands, FrontPage saves each page either to a web site or to a file, depending on where it was opened.

Saving Images

When FrontPage saves a page, it saves the HTML coding as an HTM file, and any images on the pages in their image format (either **GIF** or **JPEG**). For each image you insert from a file or from another site, FrontPage will ask you how to save it when you're closing the page. You can either save images as part of the current site open in the Explorer, or elsewhere as separate files.

Saving images to a web site When you're saving a page to a web site, and the page you're saving includes images you've inserted, you'll see the Save Image To Web dialog box appear for each image.

In the Save As URL text box, the name of the file you inserted will show up as a default name; you can type a different name if you wish. The buttons available at the bottom of the dialog box depend on whether the current web site already includes an image with the filename you've specified. Here are your options:

- The site does not have an image with the filename—If this is the case and you want to save the image, you can click the Yes button to save it. If you'd like to save the page *without* saving the image, click the No button.
- The site does have an image with the same filename—In this case, you have two options: You can click the Replace button to overwrite the image in the web site with the current image, or you can click the Use Existing button to keep the existing image in the site and *not* save the current image in place of it. If you're unsure whether you want to overwrite an image in your site, you can always give the image a different name to be safe.

> **WARNING**
>
> When you replace an image in your web site with another image, you overwrite *all instances* of that original image in your site.

Clicking the Yes To All button saves all images on the page to the current web site, with their current filenames. If one of the remaining files has a filename that's currently in your site, you'll be asked to confirm to replace the image with the new image.

Saving images to a file If you're saving a page as a file, you'll be prompted to save any new images that you've inserted on the page since you last saved it. These images are saved as separate files in the directory of your choice. For each image, you'll see the Save Image To File dialog box.

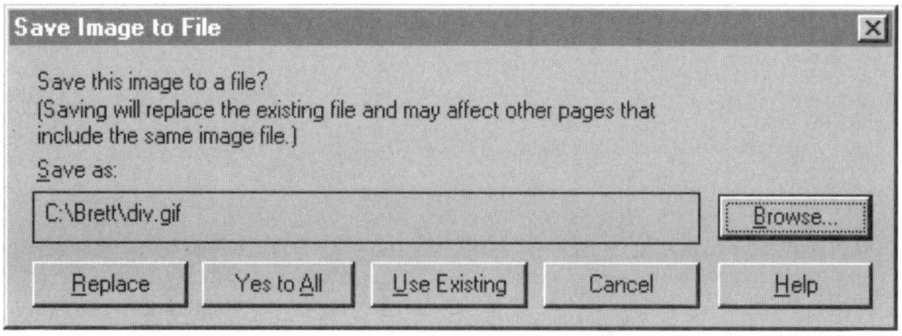

The options for saving the image are similar to those in the Save Image To Web dialog box. The buttons available at the bottom of the dialog box depend on whether the page has already been saved. Click the Replace button to overwrite the file with the current image. Click the Replace All button to perform this task for all new images inserted in the file since the last save. Or, click the Use Existing button to *not* overwrite the file with the current image. If you'd like to save the image as another file or save it in a different directory, click the Browse button. From there, select the file you want to overwrite, or specify a different directory and/or filename for the current image, and then click OK.

Printing Pages

Sometimes it's good to see a hard copy of a page you're working on, even if it's just to get a different "feel" for the page. Often you'll see things differently on hard copy versus on-screen. Many of us are used to working in the traditional "paper" office as opposed to the "paperless" office. It's hard to break old habits, isn't it?

> **WARNING**
>
> If your page is wider than the paper you're printing on, portions of the page might not be printed. In these cases, you can try printing the page in Landscape orientation.

If you're armed with a color printer, you've got an incredibly useful tool for seeing your web site on paper, especially when it comes to determining effective color combinations on a page.

The Editor prints your pages as they appear on-screen, provided that your paper size is large enough to accommodate the page. The next two pages explain how you can use the Page Setup, Print Preview, and Print commands to produce a paper version of the page you are working with.

Page Setup Choose Page Setup from the File menu to set up the headers, footers, and margins of your printed page. These settings can be used to make your printed page easier to read and keep track of. You'll enter settings in the Print Page Setup dialog box, which looks like this:

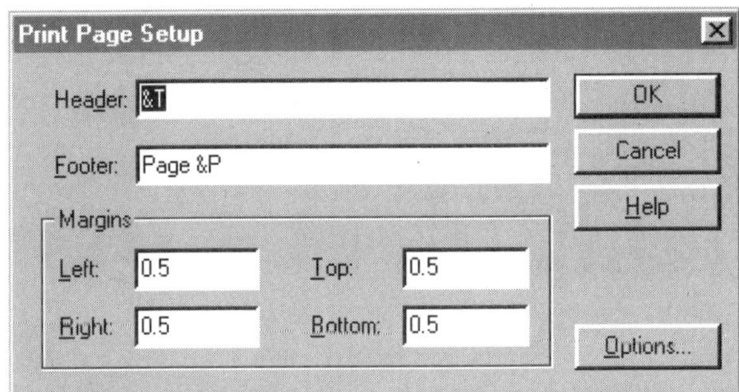

If you accept the default settings of the header and footer (shown as *&T* and *Page &P*), the Editor will print the page title as a centered header at the top of each printed page, and the current page number (with the word *Page*) as the footer. This emphasizes the difference between a web page and the printed page. A single web page might extend across several printed pages. Of course, your pages do not need to be numbered, but FrontPage numbers its printed pages in case you need to keep track of them.

TIP

If you do not want headers or footers to appear on your printed pages, leave their text boxes blank in the Print Page Setup dialog box.

Clicking the Options button in the Print Page Setup dialog box takes you to the Print Setup dialog box for your printer. The Print Setup dialog box is different from the Print Page Setup dialog box—it is controlled by Windows and allows you to change settings for your printer such as page orientation, paper size, and so on. When you're satisfied with your printer settings, click OK to return to the Print Page Setup dialog box.

Print Preview You can choose the Print Preview command from the File menu at any time to see what your page will look like when printed. This is not necessarily what the page will look like in a Web browser, however, so be careful not to rely on Print Preview for that purpose. After previewing the page, you might want to return to the Print Page Setup dialog box to adjust the margins or the headers and footers.

When the Editor shows your page in Print Preview, it presents a series of view-adjustment buttons at the top of the screen. You can zoom in or zoom out, and you can view the next page, previous page, or a two-page, side-by-side view. You can also print directly from Print Preview by clicking the Print button. To exit Print Preview without printing, press the Esc key or click the Close button.

SHORTCUT

You can click the Print Preview button on the toolbar to preview your page at any time.

Print Choose Print from the File menu to print your page. The standard Print dialog box will appear on your screen; if you need to change printer settings, click the Properties button. You can change printer settings in the Properties dialog box that appears.

When you're satisfied with your printer settings, click OK in the Print dialog box to print your page. If your web page runs longer than the length of paper you're using, the Editor will print it on multiple pages.

SHORTCUT

Press Ctrl+P or click the Print toolbar button to reach the Print dialog box quickly.

Utilities and Useful Commands

You'll find numerous utilities and other commands in the Editor to make your work a little easier, and maybe even save your rear end if you make a mistake somewhere along the line. These commands can be accessed either on the menus or via toolbar buttons.

Undo/Redo

Do you ever wish you could take back some of the mistakes you've made in your life? The Undo command can't help you with most of those things, but it can save you on the job. Use Undo to reverse the last action you made on a page, up to the last 30 actions. To undo an action, choose Undo from the Edit menu or click the Undo toolbar button.

To reverse the effect of an Undo command, you can choose Redo from the Edit menu or click the Redo toolbar button. You can redo up to the last 30 Undo commands.

Following a Link

> **SHORTCUT**
>
> For a fast and easy way to follow any link on a page, you can press Ctrl and click on the link. The cursor will change to a dot with a right-pointing arrow.

You can use the Editor as a mini-browser by using the Follow Link command. To see the actual page, file, or bookmark that a link goes to, select a link and choose the Follow Link command from the Tools menu.

If the link leads to another page, the Editor opens that page if it is not already open. If the link is to a file, such as a Microsoft Excel document, the Editor opens the application configured for the file type and presents the file in its native environment.

Show Explorer and Show To Do List

If the Explorer is open, you can bring it to the front of the desktop by choosing the Show FrontPage Explorer command from the Tools menu. If the Explorer is not open, you can start it with this command. The Show FrontPage Explorer toolbar button carries out the same commands.

If the To Do List is open, you can bring it to the front of the desktop by choosing the Show To Do List command from the Tools menu or by clicking the Show To Do List toolbar button. You must have an open web site in the Explorer to use the To Do List. If the To Do List isn't open, this command opens it. For more information on the To Do List, see Chapter 5.

Add To Do Task

If you want to add a task to the To Do List, you can choose the Add To Do Task command from the Edit menu. You'll see the Add To Do Task dialog box.

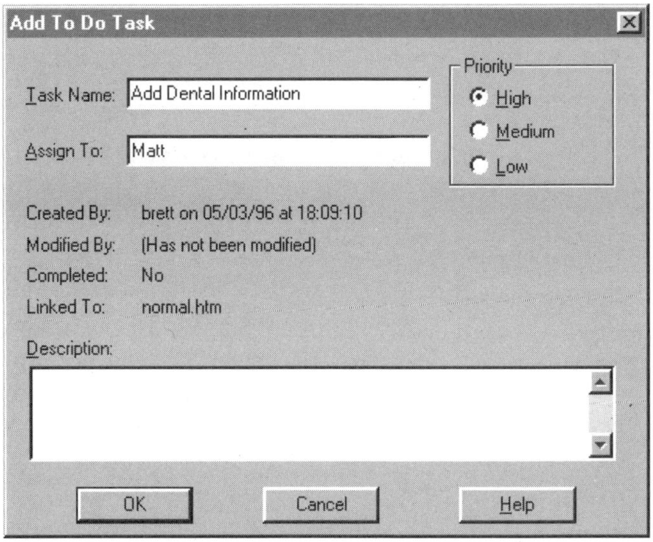

You can add details to the task that appears on the To Do List, such as the task name, who it's assigned to, its priority, and a description. The task will be linked to the active page in the Editor. Chapter 5 discusses using the To Do List.

Spell-Checking

FrontPage is equipped with the Microsoft Word spell-checker, which provides added consistency between Word documents and FrontPage web sites. You can check the spelling of selected text or of the entire active page. Here's how:

1. To spell-check a selection of text, highlight it. To spell-check the entire page, no highlighting is necessary.
2. Choose Spelling from the Tools menu, or press F7. The spell-checker begins at the top of the page if no text is selected. If it finds no unrecognized words, it presents a dialog box informing you that the spell-check is complete.
3. If there are words that the spell-checker doesn't recognize, you'll see the Spelling dialog box. Use the buttons as follows:

   Ignore Ignores the current word and searches for the next unrecognized word.

   Ignore All Ignores all instances of the current word and continues.

Change Replaces the selection in the Not In Dictionary text box (the unrecognized word) with the selection in the Change To text box.

Change All Changes all instances of the current word on the page with the contents of the Change To text box.

Add Adds the selection in the Not In Dictionary text box to the custom dictionary and makes no changes to the word.

Suggest When enabled, suggests alternative words, based on the spelling of the unrecognized word, that are contained in the dictionary.

Cancel Closes the dialog box and quits the spell-check. Changes that have been made to the page and to the custom dictionary remain.

Help Launches the Spelling Command online help topic.

The spell-checker does not check the spelling in a file included on the page by an Include bot. You must open these files separately to check their spelling. For more information on Include bots, see Chapter 8.

Find/Replace

Unlike in Word, when you use the Find command in FrontPage you do not have the option to open the Replace dialog box when you find matching text. If you know you need to replace a selection of text with another, you must use the Replace command.

Use the Find command to find instances of text on an active page. To use the command, choose Find from the Edit menu, or press Ctrl+F. The Find dialog box appears:

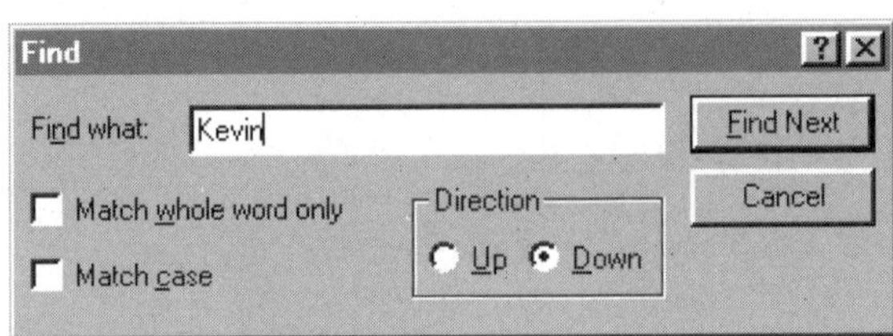

Type in the text you want to find. If you only want to find whole words, select the Match Whole Word Only check box. For example, if every word on your page is *the*, and you search for *t*, you won't find any instance of *t* if the Match Whole Word Only check box is selected. If the box is not selected, every instance of the letter *t* will be found.

Select the Match Case check box if you only want to find text that exactly matches the case of the selection you're searching for. You can specify the direction of the search, Up or Down, from the insertion point. When an instance of the selection is found, click the Find Next button to continue searching. Click Cancel to close the dialog box and stop the search.

To replace text with other specified text, use the Replace command on the Edit menu, or press Ctrl+H. The Replace dialog box appears:

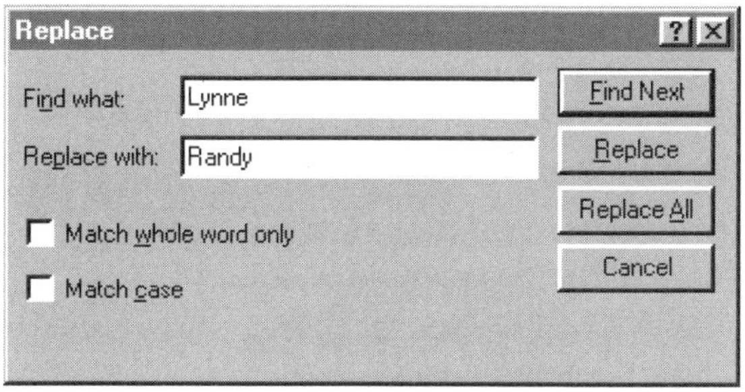

Type what you want to replace in the Find What text box, and enter your replacement text in the Replace With text box. To find text only if it matches a whole word or only if it matches the case of the text you're searching for, select the appropriate check box. To replace all instances of the text on the page, click the Replace All button. To locate the first matching instance, click the Find Next button to begin the search. When the Editor finds an instance of the text you're looking for, the text is selected on the page. To replace the text, click the Replace button. To move on without replacing the text, click the Find Next button.

Viewing HTML Code

You can view the HTML code for an active page by choosing the HTML command from the View menu. The View HTML window that appears is read-only; you cannot change the code here. However, if you want to edit the code for other purposes, you can copy the contents of the window to the Clipboard and open it in another application, such as Notepad or WordPad.

You have two choices for the kind of HTML you view: Original and Generated. Original HTML is the code for the page when it was opened or last saved; generated HTML is the additional code for the changes you've made to the page that have not yet been saved.

Moving Among Currently Open Pages

Use the Forward and Back commands from the Tools menu to move among pages that are currently open in the Editor. The pages are listed at the bottom of the Window menu in the order that they were visited. You can also use the Forward and Back toolbar buttons.

Reloading a Page

To refresh an active page in the Editor with the last saved version of that page, choose the Reload command from the Tools menu or click the Reload toolbar button. This command is handy when you've made changes to a page that you do not want to save, and you want to start over from the last version that was saved. It's also handy for viewing changes made to a page by another person. In either case, you'll be prompted to save changes you've made to the page before the page reloads.

Stopping an Action

To stop an action in the Editor, choose the Stop command on the Tools menu or click the Stop toolbar button. This command is handy for ending actions that are taking a long time to finish or that might be "hung up," such as communications between the Editor and a web server.

Coming Up

With that, the grand discussion of formatting comes to an end, and so does this chapter on creating pages. In the next chapter, you'll learn how FrontPage works with images.

Chapter 7
Working with Images

Getting into Graphics

All the great writing you can muster is just one component of a compelling web site. To make your site really stand out in the ever-growing Web crowd, you'll need to add some graphics. In other words, you'll want to add logos, illustrations, photos, and so on, to really pull your viewers in.

Working with these graphics (also called images) in FrontPage is a piece of cake, and FrontPage helps you go beyond just adding pictures to a page. With FrontPage you can create interactive images, such as images with clickable **hotspots**. And, with some simple HTML trickery, you can add animation or video to your web site. But first things first—let's talk about image formats.

What You'll Be Working with, or WYBWW

As you might already know, graphic formats are all referred to by an acronym or by the file extension associated with the format, and the names can get a little confusing. You've got BMP, GIF, EPS, TIF, JPEG, WMF, and a few others. While working on your web site in FrontPage, however, you'll be dealing primarily with two types of images, **JPEG** and **GIF**. Both are compressed graphic formats and are the most commonly used in web-site development.

The JPEG (Joint Photographic Experts Group) format is a scaleable compressed format that can deliver high compression with very little image degradation. It's not uncommon for an image to lose some of its crispness in electronic form, especially when it's converted from one format to another. Because JPEG images handle compression and image degradation well, they're ideal for a web environment in which they are often resized, converted, or otherwise altered. The JPEG format is most suitable for photographs or images with 256 colors or more. (FrontPage looks at the number of bits used to represent each color in the image, also known as the file's **bit depth**. Images with 8 bits of color information per **pixel** are capable of supporting 256 different colors. More bits equal more colors supported.)

The GIF (Graphics Interchange Format) format uses a different compression scheme than JPEG and is used mainly for images that contain 256 colors or less. When you import RTF documents into a FrontPage web site, FrontPage converts all graphics in the document to GIF images.

FrontPage allows you to perform a little chicanery with GIF images in a web site, using transparency. All images, including GIF images, are rectangular. But when using transparency, any one color in a GIF image can be set not to appear, allowing the background to show through where the color was. For example, suppose your web page has a white background, and on the page is a GIF image of a black rectangle with a red circle in it. If you set black to be transparent, the white background will show where the black was, and you'll see a red circle on the page. With transparency, you are not limited to using rectangular images on your pages, and you have more freedom to give your pages the look you want. We'll get into the "how" of transparent graphics a little later in this chapter.

Bringing in Those Graphics

Okay, now that you know a little bit about image formats used in web-site development, it's time to find out how FrontPage works with them. First, if you want to spruce up your pages with images, you've got to know how to get them on your pages in the Editor. To do this, you use the Image command on the Insert menu, which is as easy as the following three steps.

1. In the Editor, place the cursor where you want the image to appear.
2. Choose Image from the Insert menu. You'll see the Insert Image dialog box.

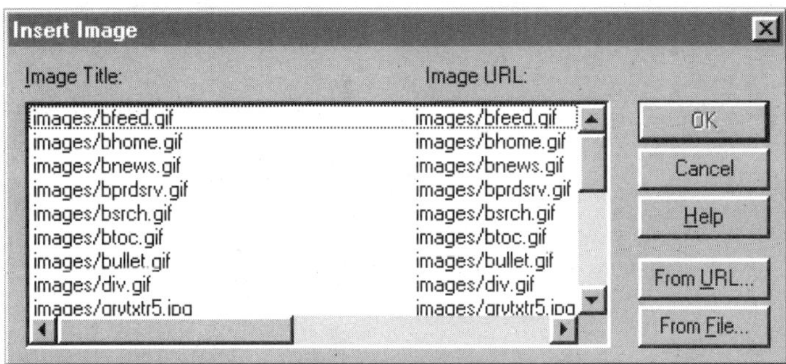

3. You can select an image from one of three sources, listed below. When you select the image, FrontPage inserts it on your page with the cursor blinking after it.

   From the current site The list box in the Insert Image dialog box shows all of the images that have already been inserted into the current site (the one open in the Explorer). Each image is listed by its name and **URL.** To insert an image from the current site, select it from the list and then click OK. If there are no images in the site, the list box will be empty.

   From a different site Click the From URL button and you can insert an image from a different site on your web server or from a site on the World Wide Web. When you click the button, you'll see the Open Location dialog box. Type in the **absolute URL** for the image, and then click OK. For more information on the Open Location command, see Chapter 6.

   From a file If the graphic you want to insert resides on a floppy disk, a hard drive, or a network, you can insert the image by clicking the From File button. When you click this button, the Insert dialog box appears. Locate the image, select it, and click the Open button to insert the image on your page. FrontPage gives you the option to save the image with your web site when you save the page.

FrontPage will import most of the popular graphic formats. If an image is not already in JPEG or GIF format, FrontPage automatically converts it to one of those formats, depending on the image's bit depth.

The Graphics Are In—Now What?

Once you insert an image, FrontPage gives you many ways to manipulate it from within the Image Properties dialog box. Here you'll find useful information about your image, such as its type, dimensions, file size, and much more.

Changing Image Properties

To alter the image and the way it appears on the page, you can manipulate that information to your heart's content. If you want to change any of the image properties, here's what to do:

1. Select an image in the Editor by clicking on it.
2. Choose Properties from the Edit menu. You'll see the Image Properties dialog box.

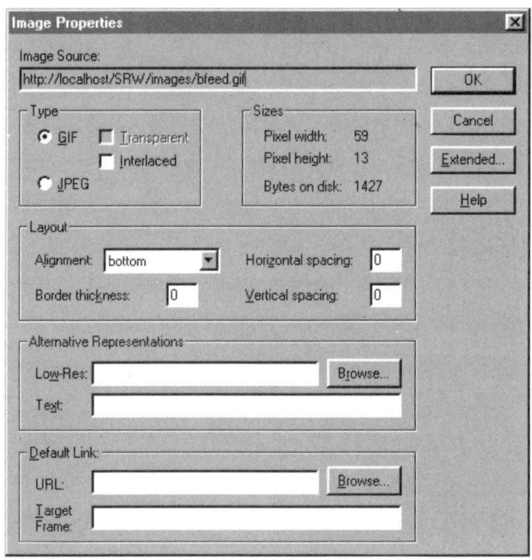

The Image Properties dialog box offers many ways to configure your image.

3. Adjust the settings as necessary. When you finish adjusting the settings, click OK. Remember that the settings are not permanent; you can always return to the Image Properties dialog box to change them. The following is a detailed look at the settings in the dialog box. (Use the Extended button to attach any HTML **extended attributes** to the image.)

> **SHORTCUT**
>
> You can double-click on an image or right-click on the image and choose Properties from the pop-up menu to reach the Image Properties dialog box. With an image selected, you can reach the Image Properties dialog box quickly by pressing Alt+Enter.

Image Source This text box displays the image's **page URL** if the image is in the current web site, its **absolute URL** if the image is from the World Wide Web, or its full filename if the image is in a file. This is for informational purposes only, and cannot be changed.

Type This section displays the type of image selected, either GIF or JPEG. The selected option is the image's current format. By selecting the other option, you can convert the image to that format.

When the GIF option is selected, you have two options for presenting the image: Transparent and Interlaced. You can use one or use both at the same time.

Transparent—Available only for GIF images, this check box is selected if a color in the image is currently specified as transparent. Deselect the check box to return the transparent portions of the image back to their normal color and make the image nontransparent. Later in this chapter, you'll find out how to make a color transparent (which automatically selects this option).

Interlaced—If the Interlaced check box is selected, the image will progressively render in the browser. A progressively rendered image slowly comes into focus as it downloads into a browser.

When the JPEG option is selected, the Quality text box appears.

Quality—You can adjust the image quality by entering a number between 1 and 99. A higher number means less compression, resulting in a better quality image, but it also means a larger image and slower performance. (The larger file takes longer for the browser to download.) A lower number means more compression, resulting in an image with lower quality but faster performance. By default, the Quality setting is 75.

Sizes This section displays the height and width of the image in **pixels**, as well as the image's file size in bytes. These numbers cannot be changed from the dialog box.

Layout In the Layout section, you control the position of the image on the page.

Alignment—Specifies a type of alignment between the image and the text around it. You can align the image in several ways.

Bottom: Aligns the text with the bottom of the image, so that the text begins at the bottom of the image.

Middle: Aligns the text with the middle of the image.

Top: Aligns the text with the top of the image.

Absbottom: Aligns the image with the bottom of the current line.

Absmiddle: Aligns the image with the middle of the current line.

Texttop: Aligns the top of the image with the top of the tallest text in the line.

Baseline: Aligns the image with the baseline of the current line.

Left: Places the image in the left margin and wraps the text preceding the image down the right side of the image.

Right: Places the image in the right margin and wraps the text preceding the image down the left side of the image.

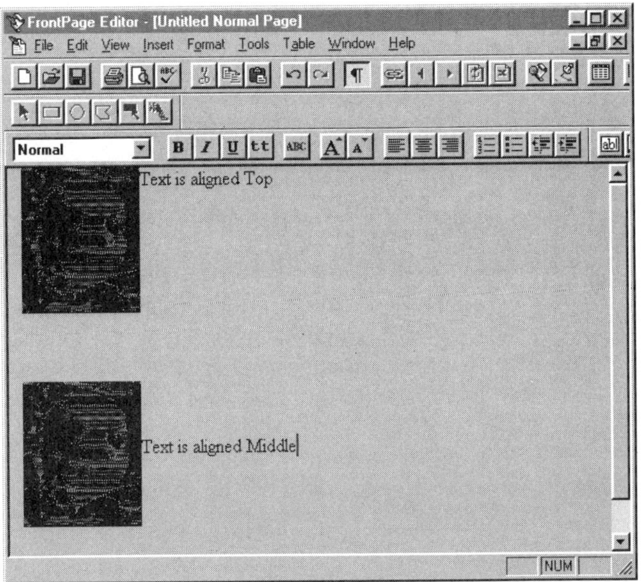

These settings apply only to images that appear on the same line as text. If an image is the only element on a line, the setting will default to Bottom.

Border Thickness—Specifies a black border around the image; the width of the border is expressed in pixels. To change the width, select the number in the text box and type in the new number.

> **TIP**
>
> You can also position the image on the left side, center, or right side of a page by using one of the alignment toolbar buttons in the Editor. The image alignment is **WYSIWYG** in the Editor, so you can see how the image will look from within a browser.

Horizontal Spacing—Sets a specified horizontal spacing in pixels from the image to the nearest image or text on the current line, on both sides of the image.

Vertical Spacing—Sets a specified vertical spacing in pixels from the image to the nearest image or text on the line above and/or below it.

Alternative Representations Not all browsers support images, and most browsers can be set to disable images. Some browsers can display a low-resolution image in place of the larger image while the larger image downloads from the server. For all these cases, you can supply an alternative representation for the image.

Low-Res—Specifies a lower-resolution image to display in place of a higher-resolution image while the latter is downloading. Click the Browse button, and in the Insert Image dialog box that appears, select the image and then click OK. For you HTML buffs, this alternate image is the same as the LOWSRC attribute.

Text—Specifies text that will appear instead of the image if the user's browser cannot display images or is set to disable the displaying of images. This is useful if you anticipate that some users will view your site without its graphics. (Actually, it's wise to anticipate this.) In some browsers, this text will appear while the image is loading.

Default Link You can turn part or all of your image into a **hotspot** that links to other locations. (See the next section to learn how.) If an image has multiple hotspots, you can set a default link for the parts of the image that are not covered by a hotspot.

To set a default link: Click the Browse button, and you'll see the Create Link dialog box. For your link, you can select from a list of currently open pages in the Editor; pages or files in the current web site; pages or images from the World Wide Web; Gopher, Newsgroup or FTP sites; or a new page. Set your link, and then click OK to return to the Image Properties dialog box.

To change a default link: If the image already has a default link, when you click the Browse button you'll see the Edit Link dialog box. You can change the link in the same way that you set it—by selecting from among currently open pages in the Editor; pages or files in the current web site; pages or images from the World Wide Web; Gopher, Newsgroup or FTP sites; or a new page. Set the link, and then click OK to return to the Image Properties dialog box. You can also set a target frame as a default link. For more information, see Chapter 6.

Cool Stuff You Can Do to an Image

Once an image is on your page, you can do many things with it beyond setting or changing its properties. For example, with FrontPage you can create a clickable **image map** from a **GIF** or **JPEG** image, allowing you to specify one or more portions of the image as a **hotspot** that links to other locations. Or, maybe you want to drop out the background of your image so that the cool background on the page shows through; this process is known as making an image **transparent**.

To create and adjust the image map and transparent effects of your images, you use the Image toolbar.

The Image toolbar contains six buttons. From left to right, they are the Select, Rectangle, Circle, Polygon, Highlight Hotspots, and Make Transparent buttons.

If you don't see the image toolbar in the Editor, choose Image from the View menu. Likewise, to hide the toolbar, choose the same command. The toolbar floats, which means you can move it anywhere you want on your screen, even outside the Editor. To move the toolbar, click inside the toolbar in an area not occupied by a button and drag the toolbar to its destination. You can dock the toolbar by dragging it and dropping it anywhere in the toolbar region of the Editor.

Creating Hotspots: Clickable Image Maps

You can turn part or all of an image into a hotspot that links to other locations. For example, if you own a toy store and advertise your products on the Web, why not use an image of a teddy bear as a link to the section highlighting your stuffed animals? Or, in an intranet, you can use an image of a dollar bill as a link to the Sales section.

You can create image maps in FrontPage in a matter of seconds. Here's how:

1. Select the image that you'll be creating the hotspot on. Notice that the Image toolbar becomes active and the Select button is depressed.
2. Decide which areas of the image you want "hot." For example, on an image of a house you might want the user to be able to click on the door and jump to an image of the foyer. If possible, make sure that the entire portion of the image you want to work with is visible on the screen.
3. Click the Rectangle, Circle, or Polygon toolbar button, depending on the kind of hotspot you want to create. The Rectangle and Circle buttons create rectangular and circular hotspots, respectively, and the Polygon button allows you to create a hotspot of any shape. When one of these buttons is depressed, the cursor changes to a pencil when it's over an image, indicating that you're ready to draw the hotspot.
4. Carefully draw the hotspot around the portion of the image that you want to be clickable. Here's a rundown of how:

   Rectangular and circular hotspots Position the cursor near where you want the hotspot to appear. Click and drag the cursor to draw and size the hotspot.

   Polygonal hotspots Position the cursor where you want to begin drawing the hotspot. Click and drag to draw one side of the polygon. Release the mouse button, and then click and drag again to draw another side, which begins at the point where you just released the button. Continue drawing sides until your hotspot is complete; it's complete when you draw and connect the final side to the original point where you first clicked and dragged.

   Once the hotspot is drawn, you can always move and resize it if it's not quite what you wanted. See "Moving and Resizing Hotspots" on the facing page.

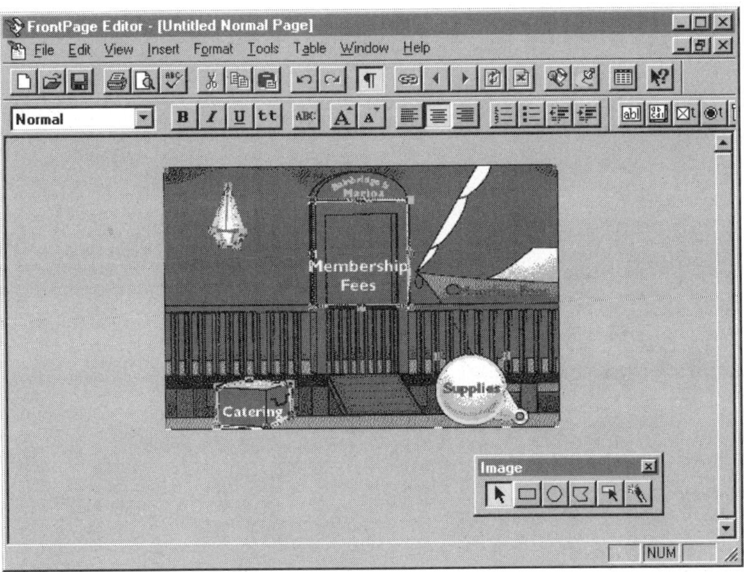

You can create hotspots in all shapes and sizes.

5. As soon as you draw the hotspot, the Create Link dialog box appears. This is where you set the target link for your hotspot. You can link to currently open pages in the Editor; pages or files in the current web site; pages or images from the World Wide Web; Gopher, Newsgroup or FTP sites; or a new page. If you add a link to a page that doesn't exist yet, FrontPage can add the task of creating the page to the To Do List. Set the link, and then click OK.

Moving and Resizing Hotspots

Once you draw a hotspot on an image, you have complete control over its size and location. You can click and drag it to anywhere on the image, or use the arrow keys to move it and adjust its location. To resize a hotspot, select it and then click and drag a size handle (one of the small squares at the corners of the hotspot).

> **TIP**
>
> To return a hotspot to its original position, press the Esc key; this is similar to an Undo command. You must use the Esc key *before* you release the mouse button.

Editing a Hotspot Link

TIP

You can press the Tab key to jump between hotspots on an image; you can press Shift+Tab to select the previous hotspot.

To change the target link of a hotspot, double-click the hotspot to bring up the Edit Link dialog box. You can also right-click on a selected hotspot and choose Properties from the pop-up menu to reach the Edit Link dialog box. Change the target link, and then click OK.

Highlighting Hotspots

Sometimes it's difficult to see all the hotspots you've created, especially on a complex image. Click the Highlight Hotspot toolbar button to see all the hotspots on a selected image. The image is removed and replaced with a white background, and only the borders of the hotspots are shown, as illustrated below. The toolbar button toggles between the two views.

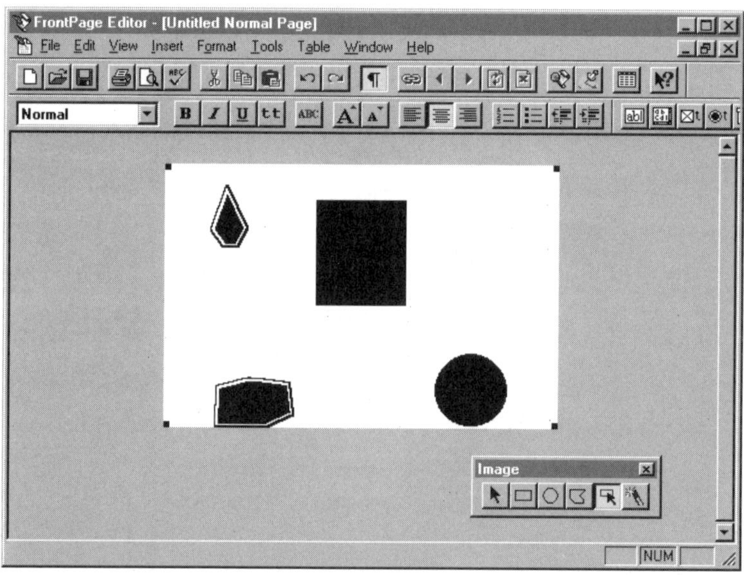

An image containing hotspots, with the Highlight Hotspot toolbar button selected.

Client-Side Image Maps

FrontPage makes use of client-side **image maps.** Normally, for an image map link to work, the **client** (e.g., a **browser**) needs to communicate with the server to figure out where the link goes to. With client-side image maps, the link destination information is stored in the image map at the client end, so the image map is no longer server dependent. This results in less communication between the client and the server, taking pressure off the server and reducing the time it takes to download the target of the hotspot to your browser. In the past, you were required to have the FrontPage Server Extensions (explained in Chapter 9) installed on the server in order for image maps to work.

If your site will be viewed in a browser that doesn't support client-side image maps, FrontPage can be configured to generate the correct HTML code and place the burden back on the server, in the slower, old-fashioned way. You set image maps in your web site as client-side image maps via the Web Settings command in the Explorer. This process is explained in Chapter 3.

Transparent Colors

Okay, so you've been on the edge of your seat, waiting patiently, to find out how **transparency** works. The truth is, it doesn't take a Houdini to make a color disappear in an image. The last button on the Image toolbar is the Make Transparent button, which enables you to make one color in a selected GIF image transparent, allowing the background to show through. JPEG images cannot be made transparent.

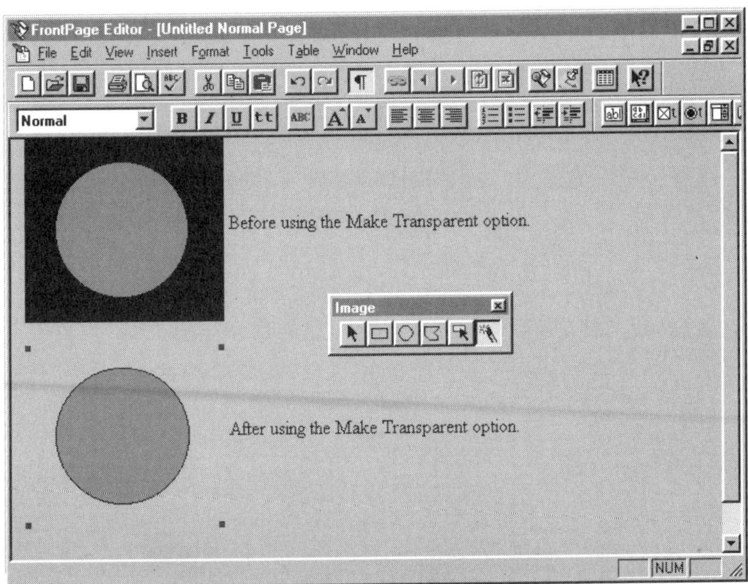

An image before using the Make Transparent option and after using the option.

Here's how you do it:

1. Select an image to activate the Image toolbar.
2. Click the Make Transparent button. Once you click this button and move the mouse pointer over the image, the pointer changes to the Make Transparent pointer.
3. On the image, click on the color you want to make transparent.
4. Voila—every part of the GIF that contained that color is now transparent, and the background of the page shows through the image.

> **WARNING**
>
> If the image you're making transparent is in JPEG format, FrontPage displays a warning dialog box telling you that the image must be converted and asking if you really want to convert it. If you click Yes, the image is automatically converted to a GIF.

Only one color at a time can be transparent in a GIF image. If you choose a new transparent color on an image that already has one transparent color set, the first transparent color reverts to its original color.

GIFs are used for transparency because they contain fewer colors and more solid areas to make transparent. Because JPEG images can contain a wide tonal range, using transparency on a JPEG image would be similar to poking holes sporadically through a photograph with a pin. The image would be transparent only where the holes appear.

Worried about Performance?

The infrastructure is not yet in place for the Internet to handle a high bandwidth of traffic while shuttling information speedily enough to satisfy most users. Until that day, you'll have to adjust the design and content of your site so it appears quickly enough on most users' screens. Here are a couple of ways you can make images and backgrounds download faster in a browser.

Speeding Up Your Images

If you want users to see those impressive graphics you just brought in, you need to make sure they're built for speed. The last thing you want is for users to become frustrated as they watch their screens draw and redraw a bunch of slow graphics. Keep in mind the following tips for making your files smaller and increasing the speed at which they appear in a browser. You'll need to use a third-party image editor to manipulate your images.

- Try using a GIF format with a lower **bit depth**. The smaller the bit depth, the faster the speed.

Bit Depth	Number of Colors
8 bit	256 Colors
7 bit	128 Colors
6 bit	64 Colors
5 bit	32 Colors
4 bit	16 Colors
3 bit	8 Colors

Various bit depths and their corresponding number of colors.

- If you're using Photoshop, convert from RGB to indexed color and use the adaptive palette with no dither.

The key is to experiment. You might notice some flattening of colors, but you'll also notice a decrease in file size. It's a judgment call, but it's one you'll have to make if you want faster graphics.

Creating Speedier Backgrounds

If you want that cool background to appear quickly, and eventually you will, these tips can help you speed things up:

- Browsers will tile background images, so make those images small.
- Don't put too much detail in a background. Remember that in most cases text will have to be read on top of it.
- If you use a GIF image for a background, make sure it's noninterlaced.

As crazy as this might sound, some people don't like to wait for graphics *at all,* so remember to take advantage of the alternative text feature (explained earlier in this chapter), and think about designing your pages so those "graphics haters" out there can still navigate through your web site.

As Promised, Some HTML Fun

Although FrontPage is designed for nonprogrammers, those who know HTML can have a little fun behind the scenes. Here are some examples of items you can add to your pages with a little HTML code.

Adding Animation and Video to Your Site

Using a simple line of HTML and the HTML **bot**, you can easily embed animation and video clips on a page. To implement this in your web site, you need to have an AVI (Audio Video) file and a GIF file. Before you panic, keep in mind that FrontPage makes this as painless and simple as possible.

Here's the process: First you need to designate a place on your page for the video to run. That's where you insert the HTML bot onto your page. In the bot you add the HTML code, which consists of one line. In the code, you use the HTML attribute DYNSRC (Dynamic Source) added to the IMG tag to identify the video clip, and you assign the SRC attribute to a GIF. This technique designates the GIF file that the browser will display until the animation is loaded and ready to run. (This can be a "still shot" of the first frame of the animation or video.)

Although you don't have to designate a GIF to be displayed, there are several advantages to doing so. For example, if the user's browser doesn't support video, the GIF file will just sit there, looking pretty, as a placeholder. If you don't designate a GIF file in this way, the area where the animation will run will be blank until the animation begins.

Here's what to do:

1. Insert an HTML bot at the place on the page where you want the animation or video clip to appear. To insert the bot, choose Bot from the Insert menu in the Editor, select HTML Markup in the Insert Bot dialog box that appears, and click OK. For more information on bots, see Chapter 8.

2. In the HTML Markup dialog box, type in the following code exactly as shown below. You'll be substituting exact variables for *XX* in the next step.

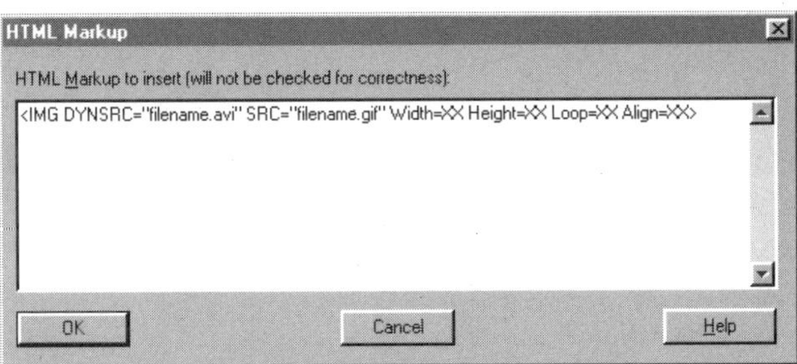

3. Substitute the following in your code:

- In place of *filename.avi*, type the name (and location, if it's not within the directory containing your web site) of the file you want to insert. To make things easier, include the AVI file in your web site.
- In place of *filename.gif*, type the name (and location, if it's not within the directory containing your web site) of the GIF you want to insert.
- In the expressions *Width=XX* and *Height=XX*, set *XX* to the width and height of the animation or video (in pixels) that will be displayed in the browser.
- In the expression *Loop=XX*, set *XX* to the number of times you want the video clip to play. If you set *XX* to 1 or INFINITE, the video will loop indefinitely. If you only want to play the clip once, omit the LOOP variable.
- In the expression *Align=XX*, set *XX* to either TOP, MIDDLE, or BOTTOM. The surrounding text will align with the corresponding area of the video.

4. Click OK to exit the HTML Markup dialog box.

In the Editor, the HTML bot you just entered will be displayed on screen as <?>. When you build your pages, it's important to keep in mind that <?> will be replaced in the browser at run time with the video displayed in the size you specified in the code. To test the HTML code you just entered, save the page and open it in a browser that supports the IMG DYNSRC tag.

When you open the page in the browser, the GIF image should be displayed first in the area reserved by the placeholder. Then, by default, as soon as the video clip is completely downloaded, it will start to play. To make the video interactive, you can add the MOUSEOVER attribute, as in the example below. When you do so, the video clip will begin to play when the mouse pointer is first positioned over the image.

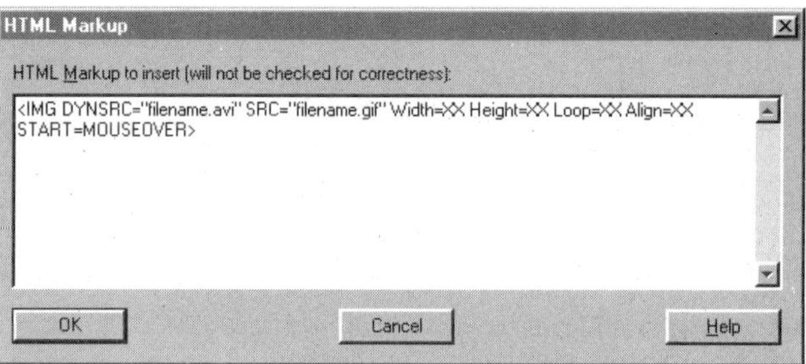

With the addition of the MOUSEOVER attribute, the video clip will play when the user positions the mouse pointer over the image.

Adding Background Sound

To add a MIDI or WAV file to a page in your site, insert an HTML bot anywhere on the page and insert this line of code:

<BGSOUND=“filename.mid”>

Substitute the name and extension of your MIDI or WAV file in place of *filename.mid*. The sound file will play once, after it's downloaded to the browser. To play the sound file more than once, add the LOOP attribute as described above. You cannot use the MOUSEOVER attribute with a background sound.

This is some basic HTML code for a simple implementation of video and sound in your site. With a little research you can use HTML, and the HTML Markup bot, to manipulate images and add sounds to your entire web site in many different ways.

Coming Up

You just got a glimpse of how bots work. The next chapter details this powerful FrontPage feature, along with FrontPage forms. With bots and forms, you can add numerous functionality features to your web sites.

Chapter 8
WebBot Components and Forms

Take It Easy

Traditional hunters and gatherers knew how to make the most of their time—they conserved their energy by optimizing their food gathering, tool making, and other tasks. In fact, they knew how important it was to rest—the work output in many historic hunting and gathering cultures averaged about four 10-hour days per week, or less. They allocated much more time for leisure activities and rest than we do today.

FrontPage lets you live a life like that again—you'll save so much time by using FrontPage's bots and forms to create your web sites that you'll be able to live in a cave and gather roots for dinner if you want to. It might be a little rough, though—there won't be an outlet to plug your television and food processor into, so you won't be able to watch *Friends* and *Seinfeld* while you're chopping up those roots. Think you can handle it?

What Are Bots?

FrontPage's WebBot components, also know as **bots,** are drop-in programs that add functionality to a web site. For instance, you can add a Search bot to a page with a few clicks of the mouse, and instantly your page has a full search engine for your users. Using the traditional way, a web-site developer would have to do the following:

1. Create an **HTML** form that initiates the search.
2. Install a third-party full-text search engine on the web server.
3. Write a **CGI** program on the web server that connects the HTML form to the full-text search engine.

With bots, you can forget all of this—there's no more need for complicated HTML and/or CGI programming to create sophisticated, interactive web sites.

You add bots to a web page by using the Bot command on the Insert menu in the Editor. When you insert a bot, you'll see one or more dialog boxes that let you configure it, and then the bot is inserted on the page where your cursor was positioned. Some bots are associated with **forms**, which are described later in this chapter.

The following sections provide a brief look at what you can do with bots.

Implementing Search Functionality

To give your users the ability to look for matching words or phrases in the text of a site's pages or in the text of all the messages in a discussion group, you can insert a Search bot on your page. The Search bot can be configured to check every word used within the site for a match. (This feature is called *full-text searching.*)

Adding a Search bot The Search bot creates a form that allows users to enter one or more words to locate in the site:

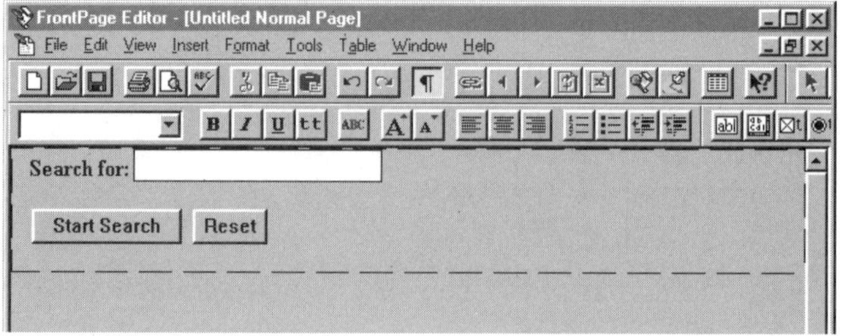

FrontPage doesn't actually have to examine each page of the site; instead, it searches a list of words that's maintained by the FrontPage Server Extensions. FrontPage returns a list of pages that contain the word or words the user is searching for. To add the ability to search for matching words or phrases in your site, do the following:

> **TIP**
>
> If you want to exclude certain pages from a search, you can store them in the _private directory under the directory for your site on the web server. FrontPage does not search any directory with a name that starts with an underscore.

1. In the Editor, position your cursor at the place on your page where you want the upper left corner of the search form (the label, the text boxes, and buttons created by the Search bot) to appear.
2. From the Insert menu, choose Bot. Then select Search in the Insert Bot dialog box, and click OK. You'll see the Search Bot Properties dialog box: 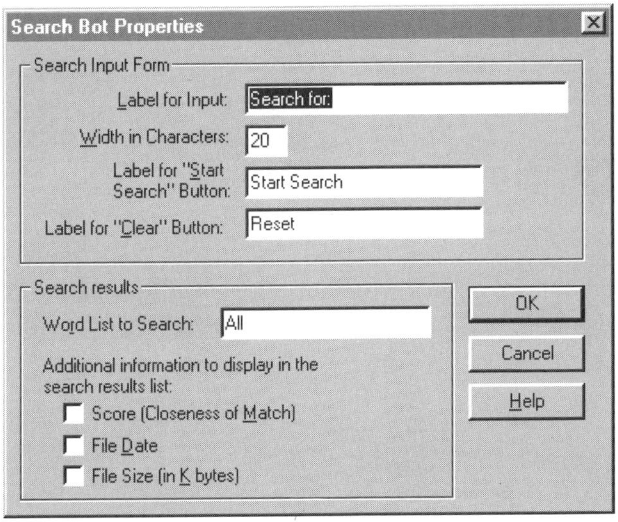
3. In the Label For Input text box, enter the text you want to use for the label of the text box. The default is *Search for:*.
4. In the Width In Characters text box, enter the width in characters of the input field—this is the maximum number of characters the user can enter to search for.
5. In the Label For "Start Search" Button text box, type the text that will appear on the button that starts the search.
6. In the Label For "Clear" Button text box, type the text that will appear on the button that clears the search.

7. In the Word List To Search text box, enter *All* if the search is intended for an entire web site, or enter the name of a discussion group directory if the search is intended for a discussion group.

8. You can also select check boxes to display the following information in the search results list:

   Score This indicates the quality of the match, or how closely the results match what you searched for.

   File Date This indicates the date and time the document containing the match was most recently modified.

   File Size This indicates the size of the document containing the match, in kilobytes.

9. When you finish entering the information in the Search Bot Properties dialog box, click OK. FrontPage inserts the search form on your page in the Editor.

Creating a Timestamp

To insert a timestamp, which denotes the date and time the page was last edited or automatically updated, you use the Timestamp bot. This bot inserts on your page the date and/or time of the last change.

Adding a Timestamp bot To insert a timestamp on your page, do the following:

1. In the Editor, position your cursor at the place on your page where you want the timestamp to appear. Often, the bot is placed following a phrase such as *This page was last modified*.

2. From the Insert menu, choose Bot. Then select Timestamp in the Insert Bot dialog box, and click OK. You'll see the Timestamp Bot Properties dialog box:

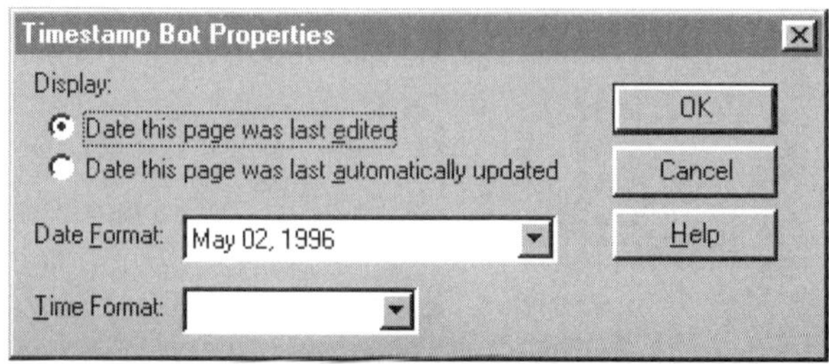

3. In the Display section, select the option for the date you want to display: the date the page was last edited or the date the page was last automatically updated. There's a slight difference in meaning between "edited" and "updated": A page is considered to be edited when it is changed and saved to the web server, and it is considered to be updated when its HTML is regenerated—but not necessarily saved to the web server. This occurs when pages are included within pages, and when the included page changes and results in the regeneration of HTML of the first page.
4. From the drop-down list boxes, select a format for the date and time that you want displayed by the timestamp. If you don't want to include the time, select None from the Time Format drop-down list.
5. When you finish entering your information in the Timestamp Bot Properties dialog box, click OK. The timestamp is inserted on your page. You can then format the text used for the timestamp information using the standard tools within the Editor.

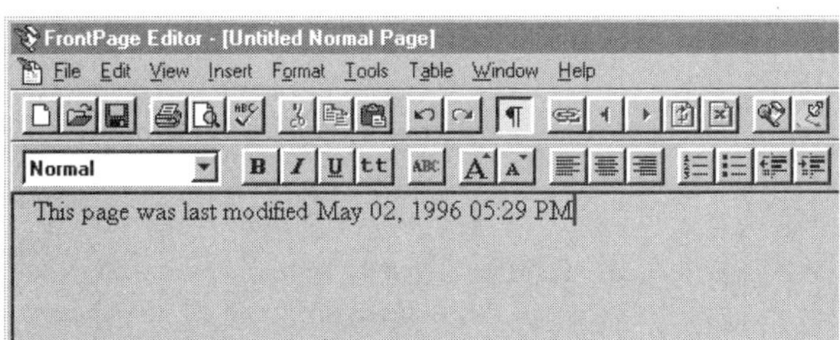

Including a Table of Contents

You can use the Table of Contents bot to create an outline for your web site, with links to each page. You can direct the bot to update the outline each time the site's structure changes.

Adding a Table of Contents To insert a table of contents (TOC) on your page, you can do the following:

1. In the Editor, position your cursor at the place on your page where you want the TOC to appear.
2. From the Insert menu, choose Bot. Then select Table Of Contents in the Insert Bot dialog box, and click OK.

You'll see the Table Of Contents Bot Properties dialog box:

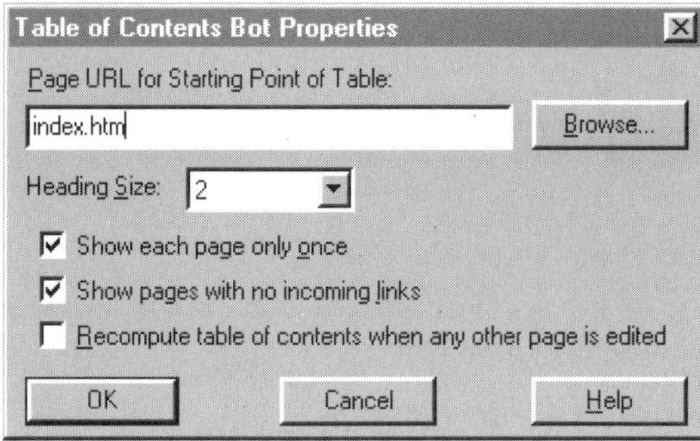

3. Enter the **page URL** of the page you want the TOC to begin with. The TOC will include all pages that have links that originate from the page you select. Specify the **home page** of your web site if you want a full TOC. If you have a site open in the Explorer, you can click the Browse button to see a list of pages in the site. If you do so, select a page in the Current Web dialog box, and then click OK.

4. In the Heading Size text box, enter a heading style for the first entry in your TOC, or select a style from the drop-down list. You can select a number from 1 (the largest size) to 6 (the smallest size), or select None if you want no heading style applied.

5. You can select check boxes to have FrontPage do the following:

   Show each page only once Select this check box to allow each page to appear in the TOC only once. If a page in your site has multiple links that can be traced back to your starting page, it can appear more than once unless you check this option.

   Show pages with no incoming links Select this check box to include orphan pages in your TOC (pages that are not linked to any page that appears in the TOC).

   Recompute table of contents when any other page is edited Select this check box to automatically recreate the TOC whenever any page in your site is edited. If your site is large and if pages are edited often, this can be time-consuming. You can manually recreate a TOC by opening and saving the page containing the Table of Contents bot.

6. When you finish entering your information in the dialog box, click OK. Your TOC appears on the page in the Editor. You cannot format the individual entries in the TOC, and the changes you can make to the formatting of the group of entries are limited.

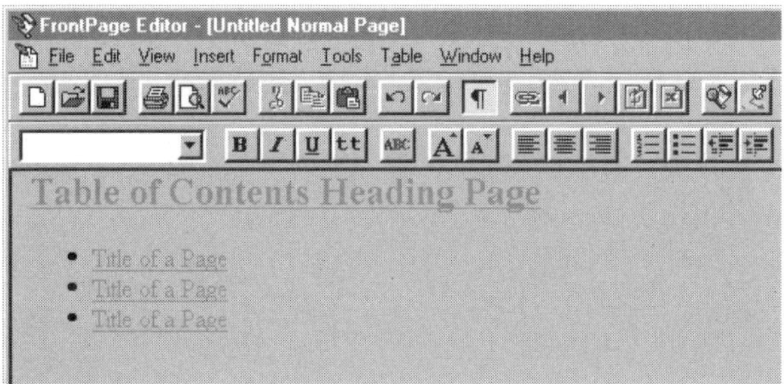

Adding Your Own Code to a Site

With the HTML Markup bot you can add nonstandard HTML commands and other emerging technologies to any page. You type the text in the bot, and then the text is saved to the web server as HTML code when the page is saved. An example of using this bot to add animation, video, and audio functionality to a site is discussed in Chapter 7.

You're on your own when you use the HTML Markup bot; the text you type is not verified by FrontPage as valid code.

You can also use the HTML Markup bot to add Visual Basic script, Java applets, and ActiveX applications to your web site.

Presenting One Page on Another Page

With the Include bot, you can present the entire contents of a page wherever you want on another page. The page you insert must be a page from the current web site. The Include bot differs from the Scheduled Include bot (discussed on page 200) in that it presents a page on another page *at all times,* and not just at specified times.

Suppose you have a "Site in Summary" section in your company's web site, which presents the most important pages in the site in one place. This kind of section might be good to include for viewers who are "on the go" and who only need to see certain pages of your site. Plenty of business people don't even have the time to look at specific pages of your site one by one—if they're scanning numerous sites for information in addition to their other daily tasks, you can understand how their time is limited. Your "Site in Summary" section can be a one-page section, in which you use several Include bots, one for each page you want to pull in from the rest of your site. The content of those pages will be presented in full, one after another, and all of the content will be scrollable as a single page.

Adding an Include bot To insert the contents of a page using an Include bot, do the following:

1. In the Editor, position your cursor at the place on the current page where you want the inserted page to appear.
2. From the Insert menu, choose Bot. Then select Include from the Insert Bot dialog box, and click OK. You'll see the Include Bot Properties dialog box:

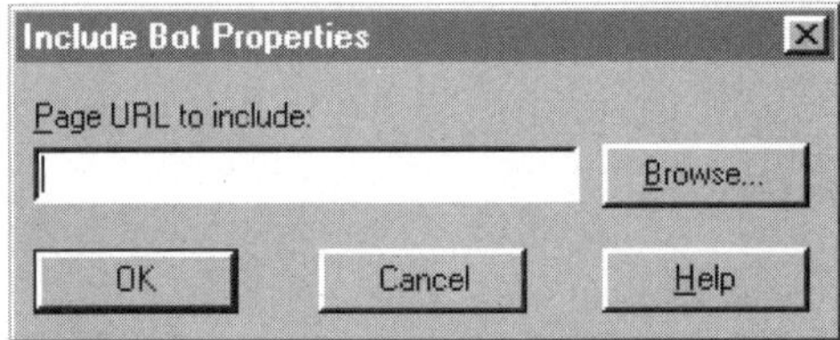

3. In the Page URL To Include text box, enter the page URL of the page you want to have appear. You can click the Browse button to see a list of pages in your site; if you do so, select one and click OK.
4. After you enter the page URL, click OK. The contents of that page are inserted on your page in the Editor.

Making Images Appear at a Certain Time

You can use the Scheduled Image bot to make an image available to users during a specified time period. The image is displayed on a page when the time period begins, and it's removed when the time has expired.

For example, suppose you're presenting a documentary on your web site over the course of a week, and you want your viewers to see a different photo on each of the seven days, in chronological order. To avoid having to update the image manually every day, you can insert several Scheduled Image bots to make those photos appear automatically when you want them to.

> **TIP**
>
> A Scheduled Image bot works only if a change is made to the site on each day the image is scheduled to appear or disappear. For example, you can change the value of a **configuration variable** (also called a *parameter*). You can name a configuration variable to represent the day of the week and change the value of the variable every day, thus changing the site. See Chapter 3 for information on changing parameter values.

Adding a Scheduled Image bot

To make an image appear during a specified time period, do the following:

1. In the Editor, position your cursor at the place on your page where you want the image to appear.
2. From the Insert menu, choose Bot. Then select Scheduled Image in the Insert Bot dialog box, and click OK. You'll see the Scheduled Image Bot Properties dialog box:

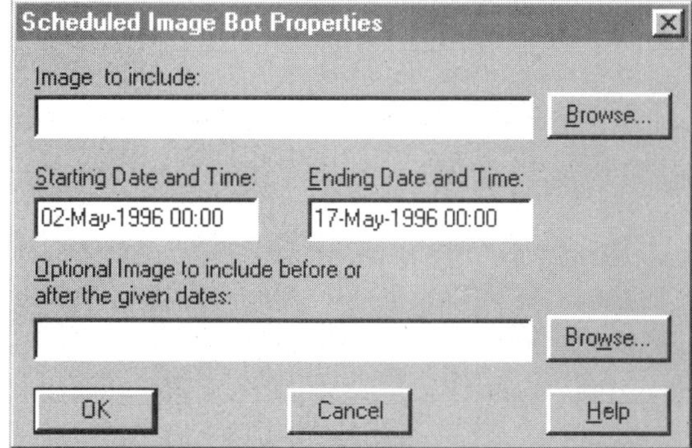

3. In the Image To Include text box, enter the name of the image you want to have appear. You can click the Browse button to see a list of images available in the currently open site in the Explorer; if you do so, select an image and then click OK.
4. Enter the starting date and time and the ending date and time for the period that you want the image specified in the Image To Include text box to appear.
5. You can also present an optional image to appear in the same location before and after the scheduled image appears. If you want to do so, type the name of the

image in the text box near the bottom of the dialog box, or click Browse to see a list of images available in the current site. This image can be a placeholder image, which fills up the space when the scheduled image does not appear.

6. When you finish entering your information in the Scheduled Image Bot Properties dialog box, click OK.

If you're within the time period you specified for the image to appear, the image will appear on the page. If you specified the image to appear at a future time (a more likely scenario), the words *Expired Scheduled Image* will appear in the bot on the screen in the Editor (but not in a browser). If you see these words, don't worry—the image will appear at its scheduled time.

Making Content Appear at a Certain Time

You can use the Scheduled Include bot to make specific content available to users in the same way that the Scheduled Image bot works with images. In fact, using the same documentary scenario discussed in the previous section, you can make an entire file available—that way, you can present an entire day's worth of the documentary at a time if you want. The Scheduled Include bot inserts an entire page at a time.

Like Scheduled Image bots, Scheduled Include bots work only if a change is made to the site on the day the content is scheduled to appear. For more information, see the Tip on the previous page.

Adding a Scheduled Include bot To insert the contents of a page using a Scheduled Include bot, do the following:

1. In the Editor, position your cursor at the place on your page where you want the content to appear.
2. From the Insert menu, choose Bot. Then select Scheduled Include in the Insert Bot dialog box, and click OK. You'll see the Scheduled Include Bot Properties dialog box, as shown on the facing page.

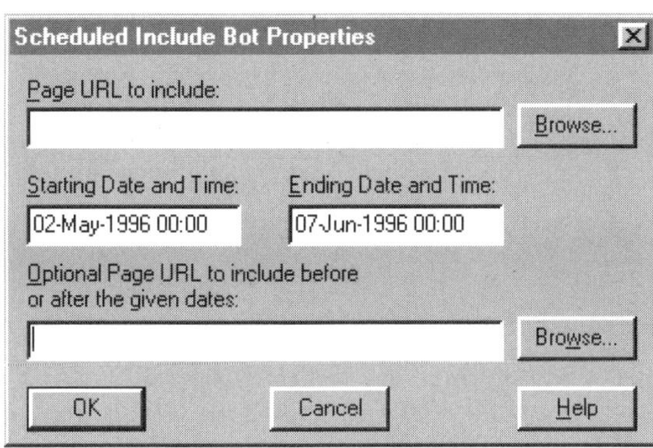

3. In the Page URL To Include text box, enter the page URL of the page you want to have appear. You can click the Browse button to see a list of pages in your site; if you do so, select one and click OK.

4. Enter the starting date and time and the ending date and time for the period that you want the page to appear.

5. To present the contents of another page in the same location before and after the scheduled page appears, type the name of the page in the text box at the bottom of the dialog box, or click Browse to see a list of pages currently available in your site. You can specify that a simple placeholder page appear at these times, which fills up the space when the scheduled page does not appear.

   As a simple example, you can produce a page that contains only the text *Thursday's Page*. (No links are necessary when you are including another page.) On Thursdays, the scheduled page will appear, but on every other day of the week the Thursday's Page page will not appear.

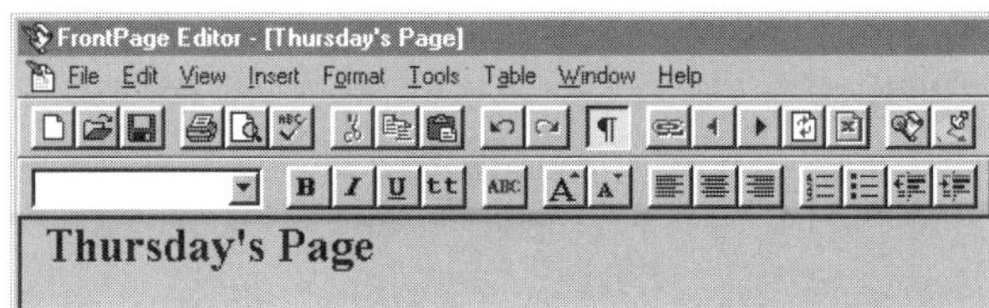

6. When you finish entering your information in the Scheduled Include Bot Properties dialog box, click OK.

Making Notes to Yourself in Your Site

To make notes to yourself as you build or update your site in the Editor, you can use Annotation bots. Text presented in Annotation bots appears in the Editor but not in a browser.

For example, if you know you want some images to appear in a certain order on a page, but you don't want to make notes on a piece of paper that you can lose, you can quickly insert an Annotation bot containing that information at the place on the page where you need to see it.

Annotation bot text is displayed in purple in the Editor, with the same size and other attributes of the current paragraph style.

Adding an Annotation To insert an annotation on your page that will show only in the Editor, do the following:

1. In the Editor, position your cursor at the place on your page where you want the annotation to appear.
2. From the Insert menu, choose Bot. Then select Annotation in the Insert Bot dialog box, and click OK. You'll see the Annotation Bot Properties dialog box:

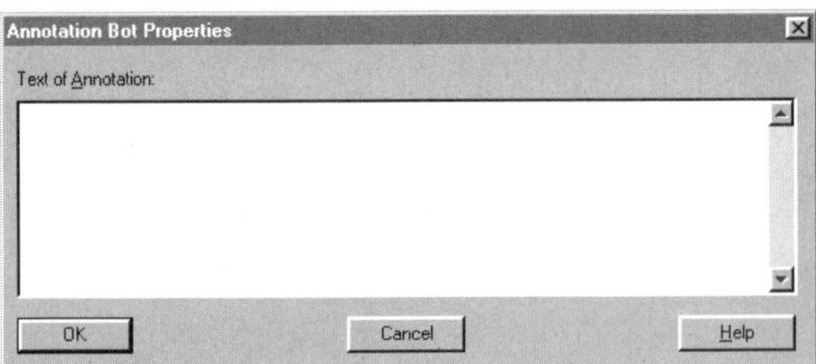

3. Type your annotation in the Text Of Annotation text box, and then click OK. The text will wrap when it reaches the end of a line; if you press Enter, you'll exit the Annotation Bot Properties dialog box, just as if you click OK.

Confirming User-Entered Information

When you are using your site to collect information from users, you want to do everything you can to make sure that the information they provide is correct. There's no way to have FrontPage check the accuracy of what they type, but you can give them an opportunity to edit the text that they've entered. Not only does this give them an opportunity to correct any typing errors, but it emphasizes that the information they provide is important. Maybe they'll read it a second time to make sure it really says what they mean.

If you've seen web pages or other forums where information that you've input is presented to you later for your confirmation, you've seen an example of this process. If you find that some of the information is incorrect, you can usually go back to the original page and change it, and if all the information is correct, you can click a button to say so. The Confirmation Field bot manages this process of presenting the information back to the viewer. (For more information on confirmation pages, see "Creating a Confirmation Page" later in this chapter.)

The Confirmation Field bot presents the contents of one form field—a single item such as name, age, or occupation—on a form **confirmation page**. (We'll discuss **forms** and **form fields** later in this chapter.) Each form field requires a separate Confirmation Field bot, but several bots can be combined on a single page. So if a user has entered lots of information in different form fields, you can use a page of Confirmation Field bots to replicate that information in one place for the user to confirm.

Adding a Confirmation Field bot To insert a Confirmation Field bot on a confirmation page, do the following:

1. In the Editor, position your cursor at the place on the confirmation page where you want the bot to appear.
2. From the Insert menu, choose Bot. Then select Confirmation Field in the Insert Bot dialog box, and click OK. You'll see the Confirmation Field Bot Properties dialog box:

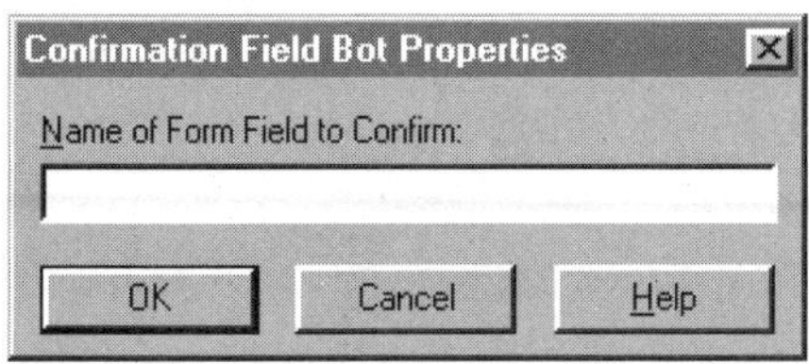

3. Enter the name of the form field whose contents you want to confirm, and then click OK.

In the Editor, the bot appears as a set of brackets surrounding the name of the field you just typed in. In a browser, the field's contents are shown to the user in place of the bot. You need to provide the text on the page to make sure the users know what information is being shown back to them.

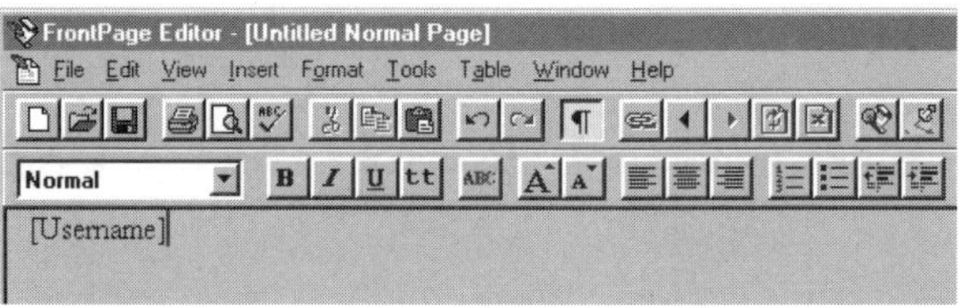

Inserting a Configuration Variable

You can insert the contents of a **configuration variable** (also called a *parameter*) on a page by using the Substitution bot. This is useful for many purposes, including the noting of who created or modified a page, or of the URL of the page.

Adding a Substitution bot Here's how to insert the value of a configuration variable using the Substitution bot:

1. In the Editor, place your cursor on the page where you want to insert the Substitution bot.
2. From the Insert menu, choose Bot. Then select Substitution in the Select Bot dialog box, and click OK. You'll see the Substitution Bot Properties dialog box:

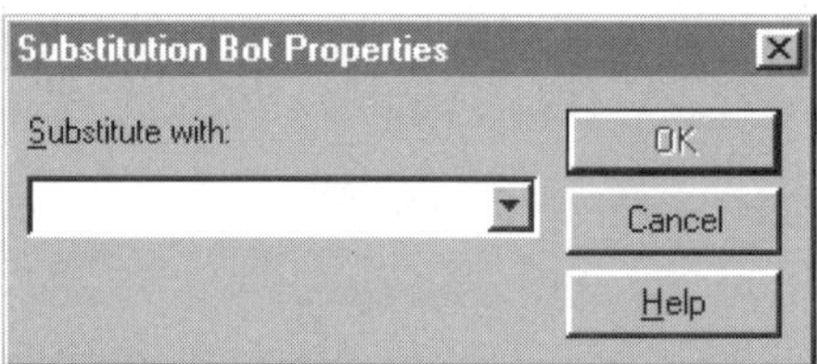

3. From the drop-down list, select a configuration variable, and then click OK. If you've added parameters to your site, they will appear in this drop-down list. The bot appears on the page in the Editor, filled in with the value of the configuration variable.

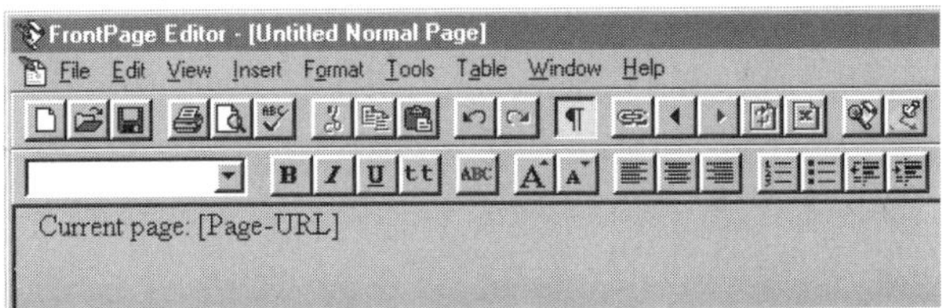

This use of the Substitution bot automatically substitutes the current page's URL where the bot is inserted. The Page URL will appear in the browser. The author typed *Current page:* on the page.

For more information on adding configuration variables and setting their values, see Chapter 3.

Editing a Bot's Properties

If you want to update a bot or change the way it works, you don't have to replace the entire bot—you can change its properties instead. To edit a bot's properties, simply right-click on the bot (you'll know you can do this by the appearance of the Bot cursor), and choose Properties from the pop-up menu. The Properties dialog box for the bot appears; you can make your changes here. When you finish, click OK to exit the dialog box and return to your page in the Editor.

Creating and Using Forms

A **form** is a collection of text and **form fields** that allows users to provide information to you. FrontPage form fields include one-line text boxes, scrolling text boxes, check boxes, option buttons (called *radio buttons* in FrontPage), and drop-down menus. You can also add push buttons (also known as *command buttons*) to your form to perform actions.

You use a combination of these form fields to collect the information you want. For instance, perhaps you want to find out what users think of your web site or the products showcased in your site. In an intranet setting, forms can be used to gather and store employee identification information. Users provide answers to your questions in the form fields.

You create a form whenever you add a form field to a page. Some templates (such as the User Registration, Feedback Form, or Survey Form templates) and some wizards (such as the Discussion Group Wizard) create pages that already contain forms.

Forms use applications called *handlers* on web servers that take the data from the form fields and store it in files that you specify. The handler can also respond to the user when it receives the input, by presenting a confirmation form so the user can confirm the information he or she submitted. So, in a sense, the handler is a go-between for the form and the web server. A handler can be a custom **CGI** script, Save Results bot, Registration bot, or Discussion bot. (These bots are discussed in "Assigning a Form Handler" later in this chapter.)

Creating a Data-Collection Form

Once you know how to create a form, the process will seem fairly simple, but learning it can be a little tricky. We'll step through the process by modifying two pages created using FrontPage's Feedback Form and Confirmation Page templates. The templates already contain working examples of forms and confirmation pages; we'll create more examples on these pages so you can learn how to build them yourself.

When you add each form field to your page in the exercises below, a dialog box immediately appears for you to configure the field. Each dialog box contains Extended and Form buttons. Don't be concerned with these buttons during the exercises. The Extended button is used when you want to add extended HTML attributes to the field that are not supported by FrontPage, and the Form button takes you to the Form Properties dialog box for the form you're working in.

Let's get going with some preliminaries:

Creating a Feedback Form page We'll begin by creating a Feedback Form page in the Editor.

1. In the Editor, create a new page using the Feedback Form template. Choose New from the File menu, select Feedback Form from the list of wizards and templates in the New Page dialog box that appears, and click OK.

2. When the page appears in the editor, save it; title it *Feedback Form,* and give it the page URL *feedback.htm.* We'll refer to this page from now on as the Feedback Form.

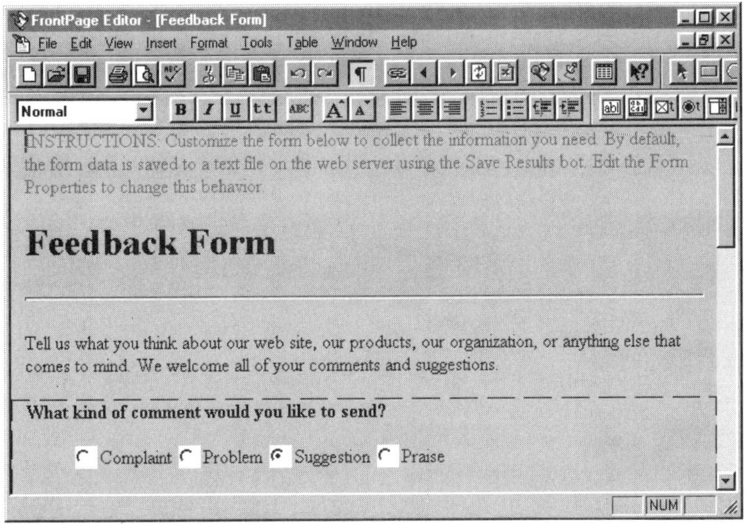

The Feedback Form includes several fields. In fact, it includes each of the five field types, plus two push buttons:

Option button Further down on the page, the buttons under the line "What kind of comment would you like to send?" are option buttons (radio buttons). These buttons act as a group; you'll find out more about their group functions shortly. Each of the buttons was added to the form separately, and the text for each was typed next to that button. You use option buttons when you want the user to be able to select a single option from a group of options. (You can also use a drop-down menu for this purpose.)

Drop-down menu The menu below the line "What about us do you want to comment on?" is a drop-down menu. You can customize the menu choices when you modify the item properties. A drop-down menu allows the user to select one or more items from a list (which is why these form fields are often called drop-down list boxes).

One-line text box The text box next to the drop-down menu is a one-line text box. Users can type text in this box, but cannot exceed the boundaries of the box. You set the width of this box as part of its properties.

Scrolling text box The large box under the line "Enter your comments in the space provided below:" is a scrolling text box. This type of text box is used to allow users to type lengthy comments.

Check box The box near the bottom of the page next to the line "Please contact me as soon as possible regarding this matter" is a check box. When a user clicks a check box, a check mark appears in it. Use check boxes when you are offering the user a Yes/No choice.

Push button The two buttons at the bottom of the Feedback Form labeled *Submit Comments* and *Clear Form* are push buttons. A user clicks these buttons to perform either of these tasks.

Now we'll replicate some of these fields and the buttons directly below them on the Feedback Form, to show you how to create them.

Creating an option button group Let's create a group of two option buttons that resembles the group of four on the Feedback Form.

1. Position your cursor following the option button labeled "Praise" below the line "What kind of comment would you like to send?" Press Enter twice, creating two new lines.

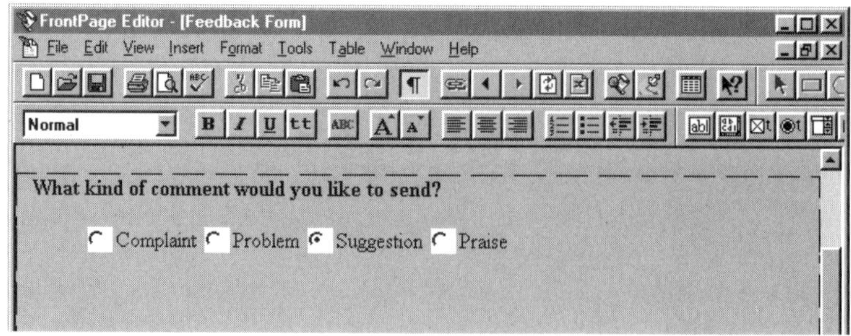

2. With the cursor on the second blank line you just created, click the Radio Button button on the Forms toolbar. (Remember, FrontPage uses the term *radio button* rather than option button.) If the Forms toolbar is not visible, choose the Forms Toolbar command from the View menu.

The Radio Button Properties dialog box appears:

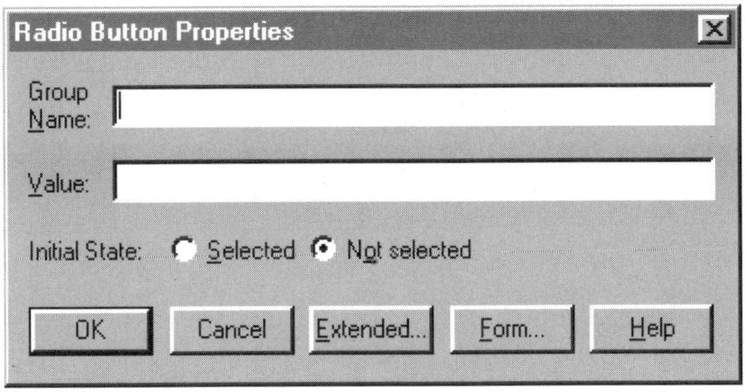

Radio Button Properties

Group Name:

Value:

Initial State: Selected Not selected

OK Cancel Extended... Form... Help

3. Fill in the following information, and then click OK:

   Group Name Enter the word *CommentType.* This is the name given to the group of option buttons you'll be creating. You'll use this name later on the confirmation page. If you give the same group name to a series of buttons, only one of them can be selected by a user. Assigning the same group name is what actually creates a group of option buttons.

   Value Enter the word *Compliment.* The word will appear on the confirmation page if the user selects this option when he or she is using the Feedback Form. You'll see how this works shortly.

   Initial State Select the Selected option. When the user sees the Feedback Form, this option will be selected as the default. Only one option button in a group can be initialized as Selected (because only one option in a group can ever be selected). FrontPage doesn't require you to initialize any option button as Selected; this is your choice.

TIP

Once a field appears on the screen in the Editor, you can right-click it and choose Properties from the pop-up menu to see its Properties dialog box. From there, you can change any of its settings.

4. Click on the page next to the option button, and type the word *Compliment.* You've just created an option button that, when selected, indicates that the user is sending a compliment back to you.

5. In the same fashion, create another option button directly to the right of the Compliment button. (You might want to press the Spacebar to create a little space between the buttons.) Give it the same group name *(CommentType),* but give it the value of *Criticism.* Select the Not Selected option for its initial state. Click OK to exit the Radio Button Properties dialog box.

6. Type the word *Criticism* following the option button. The option button is now complete.

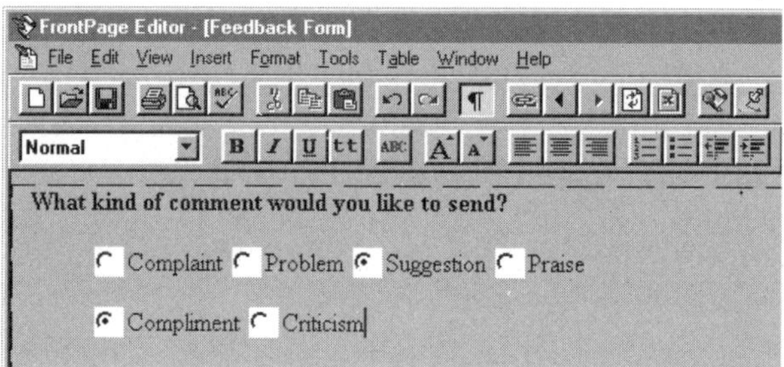

Make sure you save your changes as you go along.

You've just created a two-button group called CommentType. If you look at the properties for the buttons directly above (the Complaint, Problem, Suggestion, and Praise buttons), you'll see that their group name is MessageType. You've just created a similar group. You can create any option button group in the same way.

Creating a drop-down menu Next we'll create a four-element drop-down menu directly below the existing one.

1. Position the cursor following the one-line text box below the sentence "What about us do you want to comment on?" and press Enter twice, creating two blank lines.

2. With the cursor on the second blank line you just created, click the Drop-Down Menu toolbar button.

You'll see the Drop-Down Menu Properties dialog box:

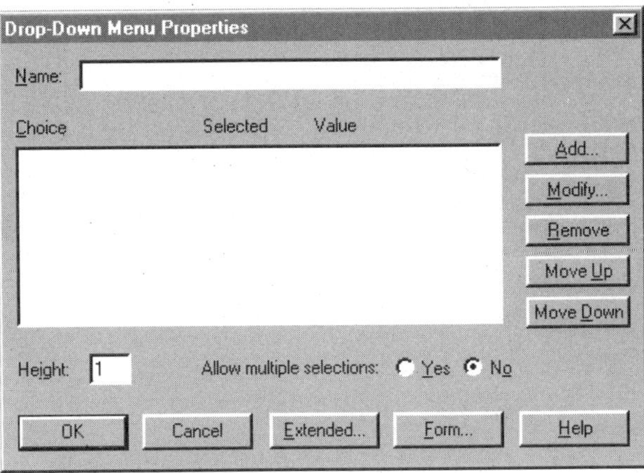

3. Enter the name *Topic* in the Name text box. You'll use this name later on when you configure the confirmation page.

4. Click the Add button to add an element to the box. You'll see the Add Choice dialog box:

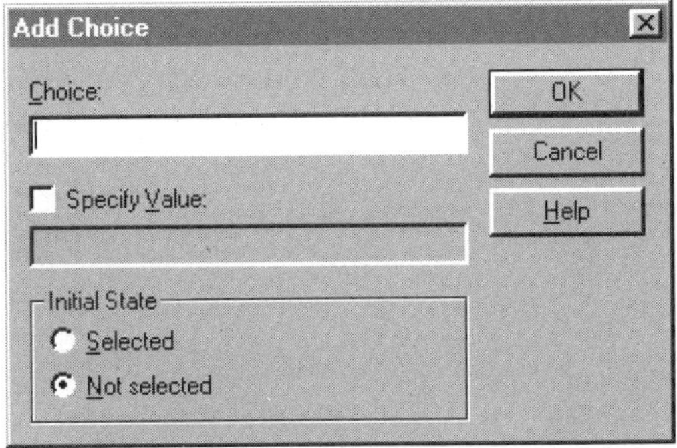

5. In the Choice text box, enter the word *Site*. By default, the value of this element is the same as its name; if you want the value to be different from the name, select the Specify Value check box, and then enter the value. In the Initial State section, select the Selected option. This sets the Site element as the item displayed in the drop-down menu when the user first sees it in a browser.

   Click OK when you finish entering information in the Add Choice Dialog box.

6. Add three more elements in the same fashion, named Technical Support, Prices, and Other. For each one, select the Not Selected option in the Drop-Down Menu Properties dialog box. The width of the drop-down menu will automatically expand to accommodate the widest element you add.

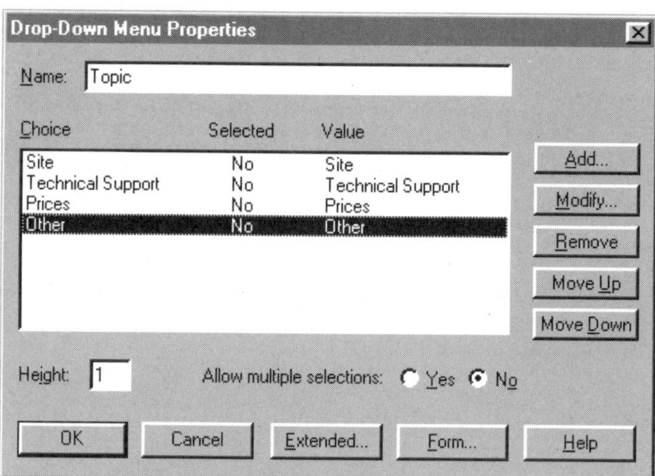

7. You can click the following buttons in the dialog box to perform some additional functions:

   Modify To modify any of the elements in the list, select the element and click Modify. You'll see the Add Choice dialog box for that element.

   Remove To remove any element from the list, select the element and click Remove.

   Move Up To move an element up in the list, select the element and click Move Up. (The elements will appear in the drop-down menu in the order they appear in this list.)

   Move Down To move an element down in the list, select the element and click Move Down.

   In addition, you can enter the height of the menu in the Height text box. Keep the height at 1 for now. The height of the menu determines how many of its elements appear before the user clicks on the menu to activate the drop-down menu.

   Finally, select the No option to disallow multiple selections. Clicking Yes allows the user to select more than one element from the list. This is useful in many situations, such as when offering the user choices of receiving information about various products you might list in the drop-down box.

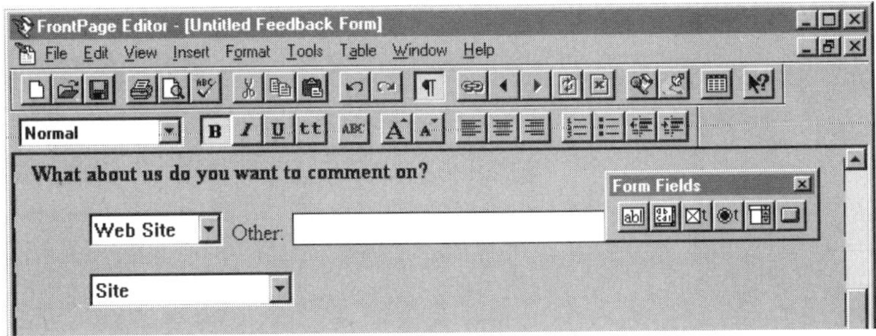

8. When you finish entering the information, click OK.

You've created a four-element list on a drop-down menu. You can create all drop-down menus in the same fashion.

Creating a one-line text box Next we'll create a one-line text box that appears next to the drop-down menu, for users to enter an element if they chose (Other) from the drop-down menu.

1. Position the cursor next to the drop-down menu you just created. Press the Spacebar to create a little space between the drop-down menu and the text box. Type *OTHER:*, and then press the Spacebar one more time.
2. Click the One-Line Text Box toolbar button. You'll see the Text Box Properties dialog box:

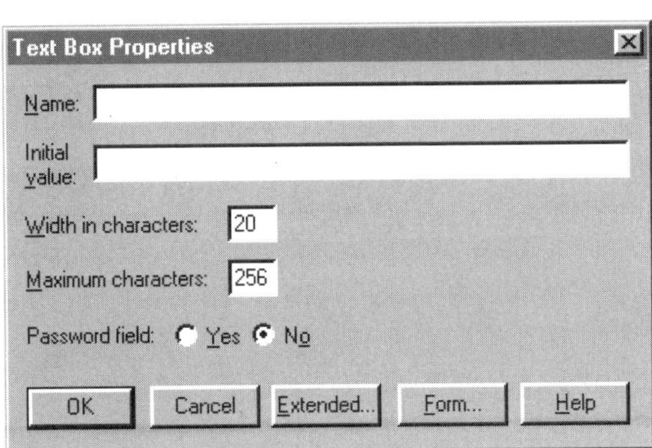

3. In the Name text box, enter *IfOther*. You'll use this name later on when configuring the confirmation page.
4. Do not enter anything in the Initial Value text box. In this instance, because the text box will be used to enter additional elements by the user, there's no need to add an initial value. If you do enter an initial value, it appears in the text box when the user first views the form. The user can change the text if desired.
5. Type *25* in the Width In Characters text box. This sets the initial width of the text box to a rather wide 25 characters, giving it a user-friendly look. If you want to reset the size later, you can click and drag the text box's **size handles** in the Editor.
6. Leave the value 256 in the Maximum Characters text box. This sets the maximum number of characters the user can enter to 256.
7. Select No in the Password Field section to specify that the text box will not be used as a password field in this instance.
8. Click OK after you finish entering information in the Text Box Properties dialog box.

You've just created a one-line text box for a user to enter additional topics that he or she wants to comment on.

Creating a scrolling text box Next we'll create a scrolling text box, directly below the present one on the Feedback Form.

1. Position the cursor next to the present scrolling text box, below the line "Enter your comments in the space provided below:" Press Enter twice to create two blank lines.

2. With the cursor on the second blank line you just created, click the Scrolling Text Box toolbar button.

   You'll see the Scrolling Text Box Properties dialog box:

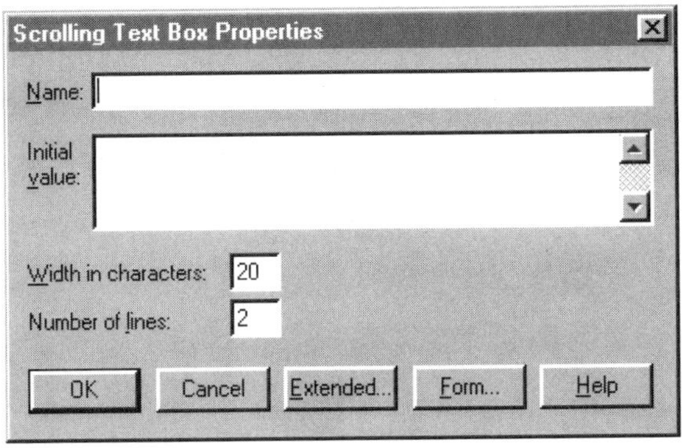

3. In the Name text box, enter *UserComments.* You'll use this name later on when configuring the confirmation page.

4. Do not enter anything in the Initial Value text box. In this instance, because the scrolling text box will be used to enter additional elements by the user, there's no need to add an initial value.

5. Type *50* in the Width In Characters text box. This sets the initial width of the text box to a wide 50 characters, giving it a user-friendly look and feel. If you want to reset the size later, you can click and drag the text box's size handles in the Editor.

6. Type *5* in the Number Of Lines text box. This sets the height of the scrolling text box in number of lines, and five is a good number to start with. Because the text box is scrollable, a user can enter more than five lines of text if he or she wishes, and it's often unnecessary to initially set the text box for more than five lines.

7. Click OK after you finish entering information in the Scrolling Text Box Properties dialog box.

The scrollable text box appears on the screen, directly below the one supplied with the Feedback Form template.

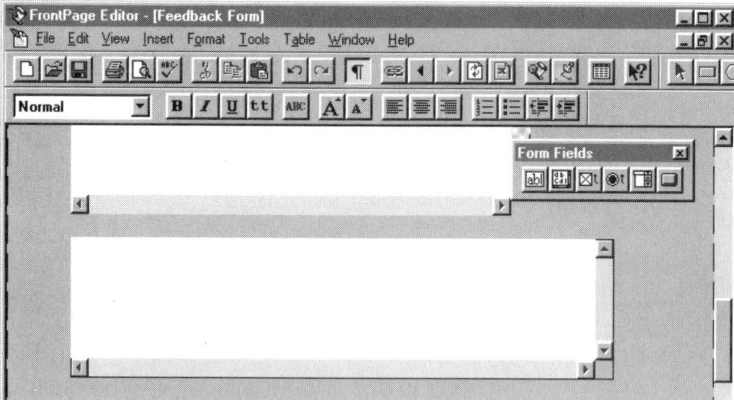

Creating a check box Next we'll create a check box below the present check box at the bottom of the Feedback Form. The check box will allow the user to indicate that he or she wants more information sent via e-mail.

1. Position your cursor at the end of the line that reads "Please contact me as soon as possible regarding this matter." Press Enter twice to create two blank lines.

2. With the cursor on the second blank line you just created, click the Check Box toolbar button.

   You'll see the Check Box Properties dialog box:

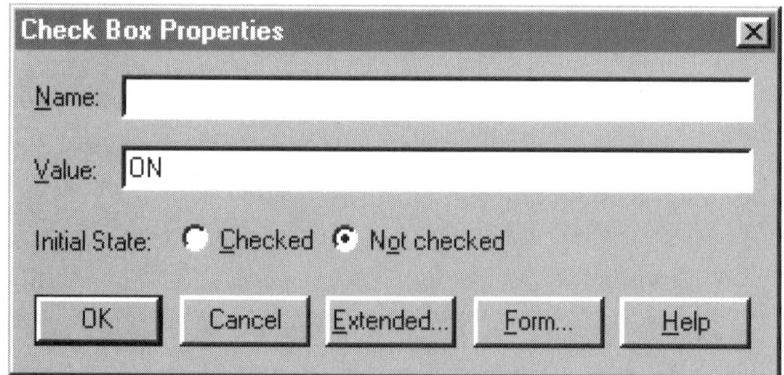

3. In the Name text box, enter *RequestInfo*. You'll use this name later on when configuring the confirmation page.

4. In the Value text box, enter the same value, *RequestInfo*. You'll see this value later when you're reviewing the information the user has sent to you with the Feedback Form. When you see this value, you'll know that the user wants more information sent.
5. In the Initial State section, select the Not Checked option. The check box will be deselected (unchecked) when the user sees it in a browser. In instances like this, it's wise to leave check boxes deselected so that you'll know for certain whether a user actually wants information sent.
6. Click OK after you finish entering information in the Check Box Properties dialog box. The check box appears on your page in the Editor.
7. Press the Spacebar to create a little space between the check box and the text label you're about to add. Then type the following sentence: *Please send me more information via e-mail.*

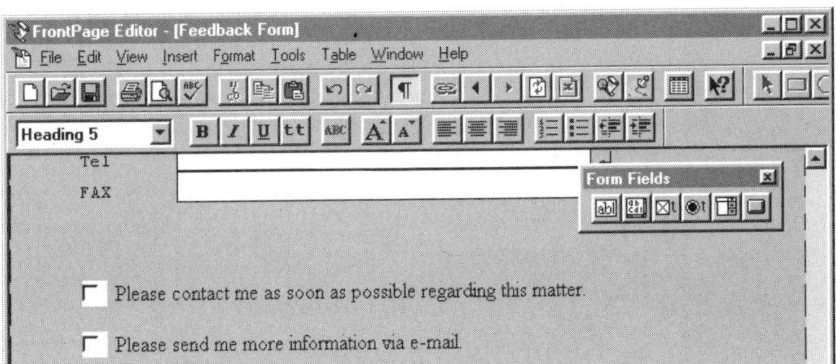

You've just created a simple check box and labeled it for users to indicate they want more information from you. You can create all your check boxes in FrontPage in the same way.

Creating a push button Next we'll create a push button (command button) for users to click when they finish entering information on the form and are ready to send it to you.

1. Position your cursor after the push button labeled *Clear Form* at the bottom of the screen, and then press Enter twice to create two blank lines.

2. With the cursor on the second blank line, click the Push Button toolbar button.

   You'll see the Push Button Properties dialog box:

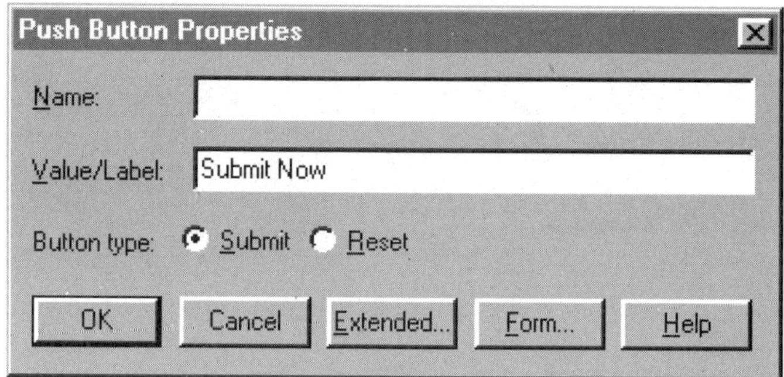

3. Do not enter anything in the Name text box.

   If you supply your own handler by using a CGI script, you can enter a name here and process the form based on the name. But for the purposes of this exercise, do not add a name now.

4. In the Value/Label text box, enter the text that will appear on the push button, *Submit Now.*

5. In the Button Type section, select the Submit option. This allows the button to submit all information a user has entered in the form to the handler on the web server. Selecting the Reset option turns the button into one that resets the form to its initial state when a user clicks the button in a browser.

6. Click OK after you finish entering information in the Push Button Properties dialog box. The check box appears on your page in the Editor.

Your form now has three push buttons at the bottom.

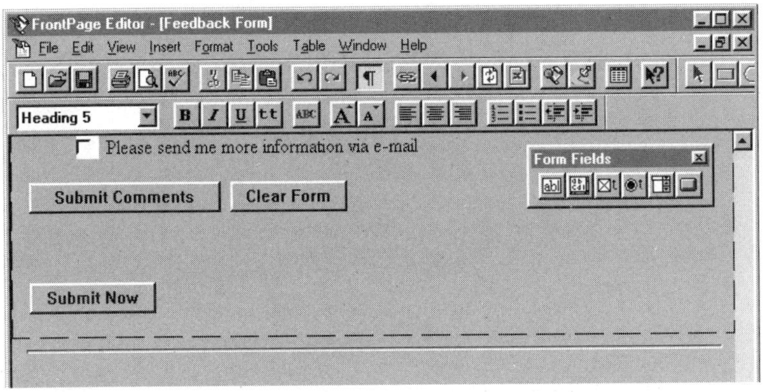

Creating a Confirmation Page

A confirmation page presents information back to a user who has submitted it, so the user can confirm that the information is correct and can make changes if any information is incorrect. It's not necessary to use a confirmation page in FrontPage, but it is a customary gesture that can add a professional touch to your site.

If your intranet site contains an information form for employees to complete, it's wise to supply a confirmation page so that the user can confirm that the information he or she entered is correct. Of course, the user is expected to input the information correctly on the form, but mistakes always happen, and the confirmation page can help them catch many mistakes before they become permanent.

You can make any page into a confirmation page—a page becomes a confirmation page when you denote it as such in a Form Properties dialog box for any form. (You'll learn more about this in "Specifying Form Settings" later in this chapter.) You use Confirmation Field bots to present the information on the confirmation page for the user to review.

Let's step through the process of creating a confirmation page. For this example, we'll use the form fields we created in the previous section. First we'll start the easy way: by using a template to create a confirmation page for us.

1. In the Editor, create a new page using the Confirmation Form template. Choose New from the File menu, select Confirmation Form from the list of wizards and templates in the New Page dialog box, and click OK.
2. When the page appears in the editor, save it; title it *Confirmation Form* and give it the page URL *confirmation.htm*. We'll refer to this page from now on as the Confirmation Form.

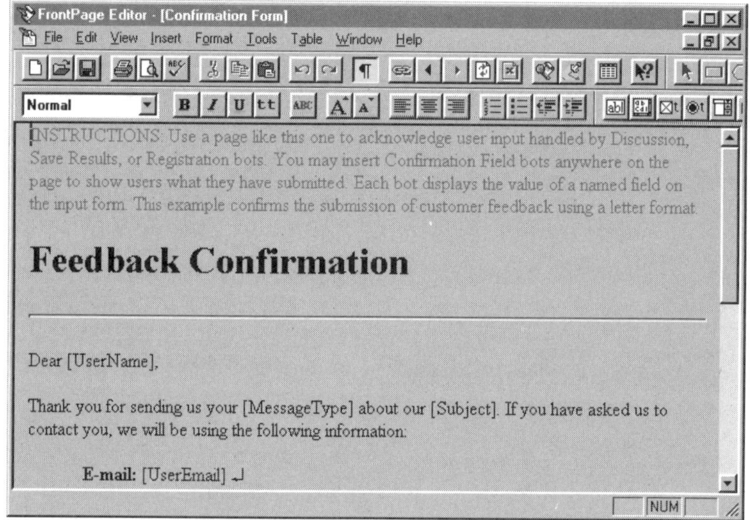

You'll see that the Confirmation Form is a template that's ready for you to customize. It's designed to be used with the Feedback Form template, and it includes many of the form field names used in that template. These names appear in brackets; they're actually individual Confirmation Field bots.

If you move your cursor over one of these bots, such as the bot labeled *[UserName]*, you'll see that the cursor turns into the cute little bot cursor. The value of the UserName field will replace the string *[UserName]* when the Confirmation Form appears to a user in a browser; whatever name the user entered will appear there. All Confirmation Field bots on the Confirmation Form work in the same manner.

The Confirmation Form also includes some introductory and conclusion sentences that you can use; you can change any of this information if you want to.

Inserting a Confirmation Field bot on the form When you know what information you want to present to the user for confirmation, you're ready to insert Confirmation Field bots on the page. Using the fields you created earlier, here's how you can do it:

1. First, replace the bot labeled *[MessageType]* with the one you created called *[CommentType]*. Position your cursor to the right of the [MessageType] Confirmation Field bot and press the Backspace key. This is an easy way to delete any bot on a page.
2. Next, insert a bot for the form field called *[CommentType]*. From the Insert menu, choose Bot. In the Insert Bot dialog box, select Confirmation Field, and then click OK.

   The Confirmation Field Bot Properties dialog box appears:

   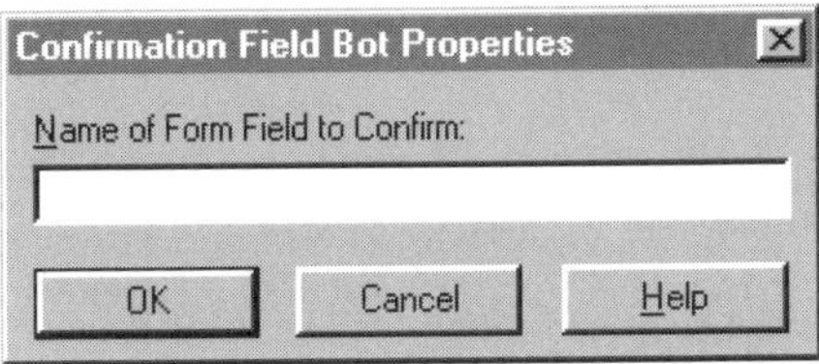

3. Enter the name of the form field whose information you want presented; in this case, enter *CommentType*. Then click OK.

   You'll see that the Confirmation Field bot labeled *[CommentType]* has been inserted in the middle of the sentence. This example only shows how you can replace a bot, but of course you can create original sentences and insert bots in the same fashion for presenting form field information on a Confirmation Form.

   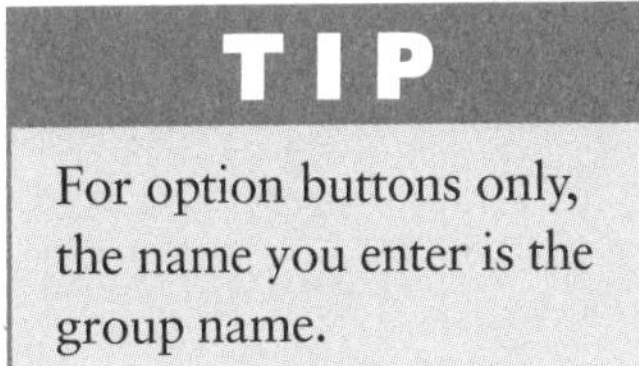

   TIP

   For option buttons only, the name you enter is the group name.

   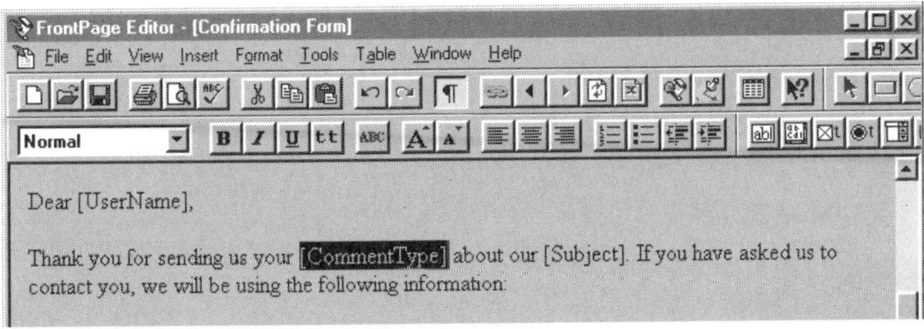

4. Using the same process, you can create original sentences or replace existing bots for the other form fields you created earlier. Among these fields are the drop-down menu named *Topic,* a one-line text box named *IfOther,* a scrolling text box named *UserComments,* and a check box named *RequestInfo.*

It's a good idea to include a link at the end of the Confirmation Form that returns the user back to the Feedback Form if he or she needs to change any information. It is also wise to include other navigational links on this page, such as links to the site's home page, a Table of Contents page, or the major sections of the site, so the page doesn't seem like a dead end to the user.

Specifying Form Settings

Here's where it all comes together. You create forms by assembling a collection of form fields on one page, and you can present the information back to the user for confirmation on another page using a Confirmation Form. But in order for the two pages to work together, you must specify this relationship in the Forms Properties dialog box. You'll also specify the type of handler you want to use on the web server for collecting and saving the information a user inputs in a form.

FrontPage includes two forms in addition to the traditional data-collection form we've discussed so far: the discussion form and the registration form. Their handlers are specified in the Forms Properties dialog box. If you create a site using the Discussion Web Wizard, you're actually creating a form for users to "fill out" as the site is in use. When a user submits a message to the discussion group, the Discussion Bot handler saves the information on the server so it can be accessed by others in the forum. You'll learn more about using discussion and registration forms later in this chapter.

Assigning a Form Handler

A *handler* is an application on a web server that communicates between the server and the user in relation to a form. Handlers can send messages to the user (via Confirmation Pages, for example), and they store the information that's sent from a form to the web server by a user. You assign and configure a form's handler in the Form Properties dialog box. Here's how:

1. You can open the Form Properties dialog box for the form you're assigning the handler to in one of two ways: You can right-click on any open space of the form, and then choose Form Properties from the pop-up menu; or, if you're already in the Properties dialog box for any of the form fields, you can click on the Form button to reach the Form Properties dialog box.

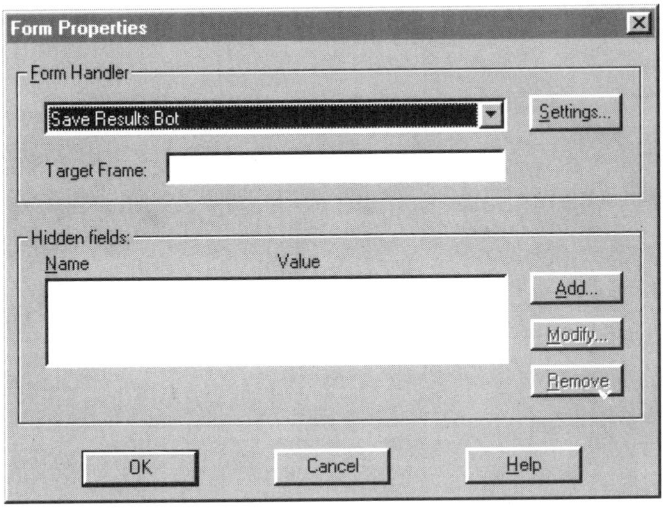

2. From the drop-down list box in the Form Handler section, select a handler. You have four choices:

   Save Results Bot A form bot that collects information from a form and stores it in the format of your choice. Stored information is appended to other information in the file you specify. Use this bot for standard data-collection forms.

   Registration Bot A form bot that allows users to register themselves for access to a service. This bot adds the user to the service's authentication database, and then collects other information from the form and stores it on the web server in the file and format you specify. Use this bot to allow users to automatically register for a service offered on your web site.

Discussion Bot A form bot that allows users to participate in an online discussion. FrontPage has greatly enhanced online discussions, allowing basic discussion group administration abilities. The Discussion bot gathers information from a form, formats it into an HTML page, stores the page on the web server, and adds the page to a Table of Contents and a text index. The bot can also gather other information from the form and store it on the web server.

Custom CGI Script A custom script that you supply; in terms of forms, these are scripts on a web server that store and manipulate the information gathered from a form. Custom CGI scripts can be written to add functionality to your web site beyond what FrontPage's bots can offer. For example, a company might want to program a CGI script that allows a user to access corporate database information via the site.

3. After you select a handler, click the Settings button to the right of the drop-down list box to configure it.
4. Each handler has its own Settings dialog box. Configure each handler accordingly, and then click OK to close the settings dialog box. Then click OK to close the Form Properties dialog box. The following sections show how to configure the form handlers.

Configuring a Save Results Bot

TIP

You can use the Save Results bot as the handler for pages created with the Feedback Form and Confirmation Form templates.

You configure a Save Results bot in the Settings For Saving Results Of Form dialog box, which you can reach in the fashion described in steps 2 and 3 above.

The Results tab of the Settings For Saving Results Of Form dialog box is shown on the facing page.

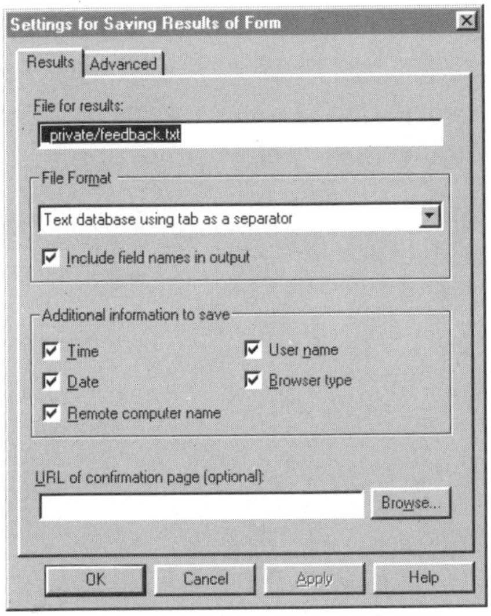

To configure the Save Results bot, do the following:

- Enter the name and location of the file you want the results saved to. The location can either be within or outside the current web site. If it's in the current web site, you might enter *_private/feedback.txt.* The results will be saved to the file called FEEDBACK.TXT in the _private directory in the directory for your web site.

  If a results file does not exist at the time the first results are saved, FrontPage creates the file.

- Select the file format of the results file from the drop-down list in the File Format section. You have numerous choices:

  HTML Formats the file in HTML using normal text with line endings.

  HTML Definition List Formats the file using a **definition** list to format name-value pairs.

  HTML Bulleted List Formats the file using a bulleted list for name-value pairs.

  Formatted Text Within HTML Formats the file in HTML using formatted text with line endings.

  Formatted Text Formats the file with formatted text, an easy-to-read format.

Text Database Using Comma As A Separator Formats the file in a text format with commas used to separate values. Use this format if you want to manipulate the information in a database or similar application.

Text Database Using Tab As A Separator Formats the file in the same way as above, but using tabs instead of commas to separate values.

Text Database Using Space As A Separator Formats the file in the same way as above, but using spaces instead of commas to separate values.

- Select the Include Field Names In Output check box to save the field name along with the field value in the results file.
- Select the check boxes in the Additional Information To Save section to include the corresponding information in the results file.
- If you've created a confirmation page for users to confirm the information they've entered, type its **page URL** in the URL Of Confirmation Page text box. This page will be displayed by the browser whenever the form is submitted to the web server.

  If you do not specify a confirmation page here, the Save Results bot will create and maintain one automatically.

  You can configure advanced settings on the Advanced tab:

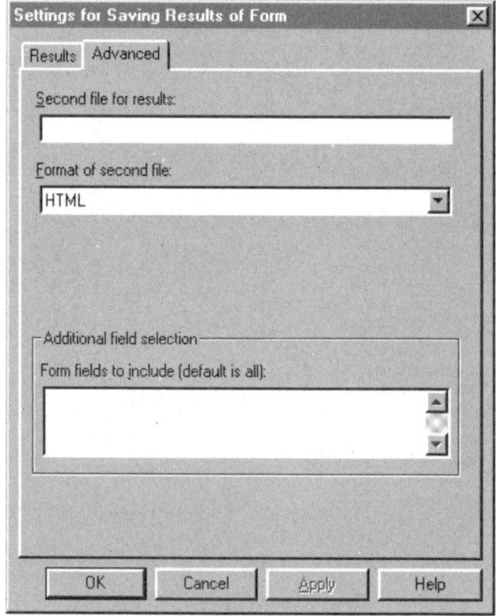

- If you wish, specify a second results file in the Second File For Results text box. Enter the location and the filename. You can use a second file if you want to use results files for more than one purpose, such as manipulating one in a database and printing the other out for your review. If you enter a name for a file that does not exist, FrontPage creates the file the first time the form is submitted.
- Select a format for the second results file in the Format Of Second File drop-down list box.
- In the Additional Field Selection section, you can specify the order in which form fields should be written to the results file. Separate multiple entries with commas. If you specify fields in this section, it's a good idea *not* to specify the use of a confirmation file on the Results tab—FrontPage will present these fields in a confirmation file of its own.

After you finish entering all the information you need to configure the bot, click OK to close the Settings For Saving Results Of Form dialog box.

Configuring a Discussion Bot

You configure a Discussion bot in the Settings For Discussion Form Handler dialog box, which you can reach in the following way:

> **TIP**
>
> You can create a discussion web site using the Discussion Wizard. For more information, see Chapter 4.

1. Open the Form Properties dialog box for the discussion form.
2. Select Discussion Bot from the drop-down list box in the Form Handler section, and then click Settings.

   The Settings For Discussion Form Handler dialog box appears. The Discussion tab is shown on the next page.

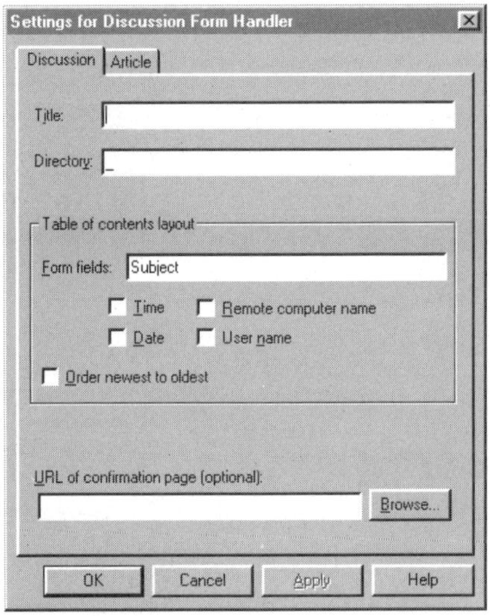

On the Discussion tab, enter the following information:

- Name the discussion group in the Title text box. The name will appear on pages containing articles.
- Enter the name of the discussion directory in the Directory text box. If you used the Discussion Web Wizard to create your discussion web site, the directory you specified in the wizard will appear as the default. The directory name must be eight or fewer characters, one of which is a beginning underscore (_).
- In the Form Fields text box in the Table Of Contents Layout section, enter the names of the form field(s) you want displayed in the Table of Contents in the discussion group. If you enter multiple names, you must separate them with blank spaces.
- Select the appropriate check boxes if you want to display the time and/or date the article was submitted, the remote computer name the article came from, and the user name of the article's author.
- To place the most recently submitted articles first in the Table of Contents, select the Order Newest To Oldest check box.
- If you wish to display a confirmation page when users submit messages to the discussion group, specify its page URL in the URL Of Confirmation Page text box.

Click the Browse button to find the page among a list of pages in the site open in the Explorer.

You specify the layout of each article in the discussion group on the Article tab:

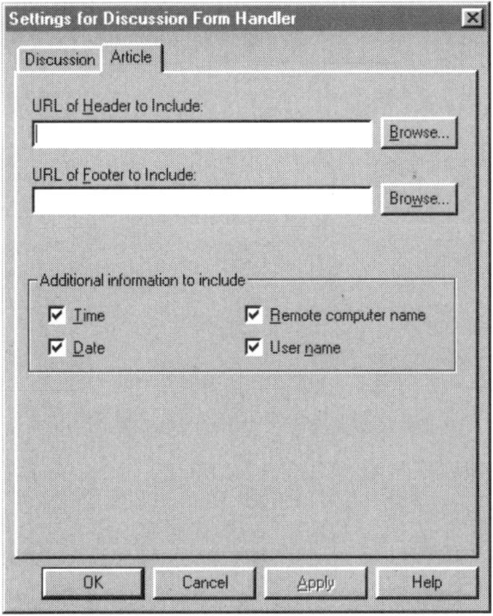

- To use a page as a header or footer of each article, you can specify the page in the URL Of Header To Include text box or the URL Of Footer To Include text box.
- In the Additional Information To Include section, select the appropriate check boxes if you want to include the time and/or date the article was submitted, the remote computer name the article came from, the user name of the article's author, or some combination.

After you finish entering all the information you need to configure the bot, click OK to close the Settings For Discussion Form Handler dialog box.

Configuring a Registration Bot

You configure a Registration bot in the Settings For Registration Form Handler dialog box, which you reach the following way:

1. Open the Form Properties dialog box for the registration form. You can create your own form to use as a registration form, or you can use the User Registration template for this purpose. The registration form must be located in the **root web** site.

2. Select Registration Bot from the drop-down list box in the Form Handler section, and then click Settings.

   The Settings for Registration Form Handler dialog box appears, with three tabs. The first one is the Registration tab.

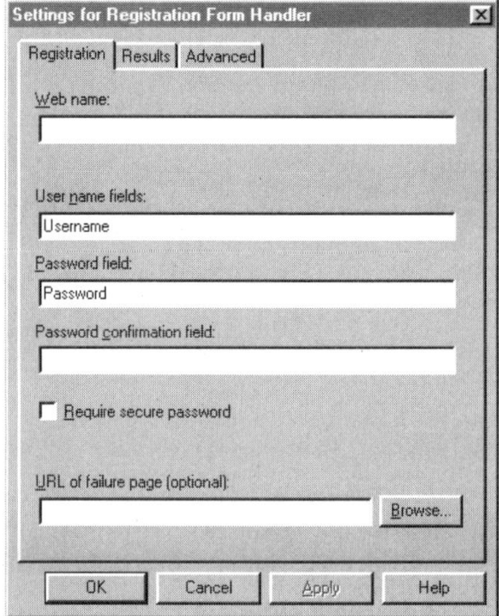

   To configure the Registration Bot, do the following:

- In the Web Name text box, enter the name of the web site you're allowing the user to register for.
- In the User Name Fields text box, enter the name(s) of the field or fields on the form that the user inputs his or her name into. The user name is constructed from the contents of these fields.
- In the Password Field text box, enter the name of the field for the user's password. This field must be a one-line text box with the Password Field option set to Yes.
- In the Password Confirmation Field text box, enter the name of the field for the user's confirmation password.
- If you want to require that the user supply a secure password (which consists of six or more characters and does not partially match the user name), select the Require Secure Password check box.
- You can also supply a failure page, which notifies the user that a registration attempt failed. Supply the page

URL for this page in the text box at the bottom of the dialog box. Supplying this page is optional, but it's a good idea to include a page like this in your site.

The Settings For Registration Form Handler dialog box also includes Results and Advanced tabs. These are configured exactly the same as described above in "Configuring a Save Results Bot."

Configuring a Custom CGI Handler

You can also configure settings for a custom CGI handler if you decide to use one in your web site.

You configure a custom CGI handler in the Settings For Custom Form Handler dialog box, which you can reach in the following way:

1. Open the Form Properties dialog box for the form.
2. Select custom CGI Script from the drop-down list box in the Form Handler section, and then click Settings.

   The Settings For Custom Form Handler dialog box appears:

   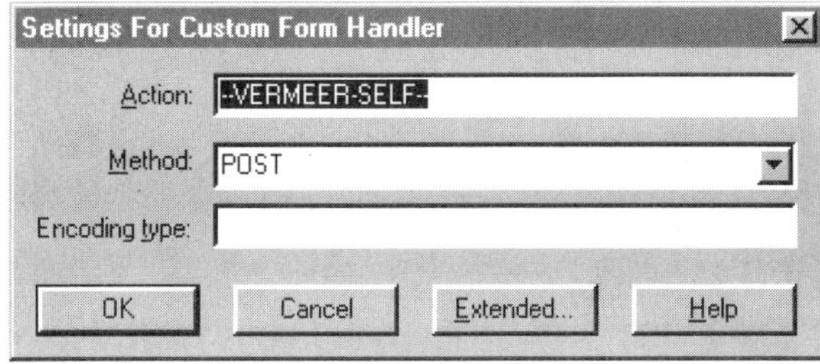

   To configure the custom CGI handler, do the following:

- In the Action field, enter the **absolute URL** of the CGI form handler.
- Use the Method drop-down list box to select a method of submitting information to the handler—Post or Get. The Post method passes the name-value form field pair directly to the form handler as input, and the Get method encodes the form's name-value pairs and assigns the information to a server variable, QUERY_STRING.

- In the Encoding Type text box, enter the standard used to encode the form data that's passed to the handler. The default encoding method is *application/x-www-form-urlencoded;* leave this field blank to use the default.
- To add extended HTML attributes that are not supported in FrontPage, click the Extended button.

Coming Up

You've now explored the big, amazing world of FrontPage bots and forms. This ends Part 3; in Part 4 you'll be introduced to FrontPage's server-related offerings, including the Personal Web Server and the FrontPage Server Extensions.

PART 4

The Server End

Chapter 9
Web Servers

FrontPage Knows Servers

All the wonderful web sites you'll design and create with FrontPage won't do you a lick of good if you don't keep them on a web server. Sure, you can always develop individual HTML pages, link them together, and view them in a browser, but if you want someone else to see your site, you have to put it on a server. Furthermore, your site must be on a server in order for you to use the Explorer to work with it. (The Editor can work with individual HTML pages separate from a server.)

In simple terms, a web server is a computer that stores and manipulates sites. The **server** is run by server software, which communicates between the server and the **client** (the machine on which a browser is being used to view a site). The web server market is growing large and competitive; many versions of web servers are on the commercial and shareware market today, meeting various needs and running on different platforms.

This chapter discusses how FrontPage interacts with the numerous web servers; it does not discuss the pros and cons of the servers themselves. There is much information to be had concerning the advantages and disadvantages of major web servers, particularly in Internet-related periodicals and on the server manufacturers' World Wide Web sites.

Once you make a choice of a web server to use with FrontPage (perhaps you already have a server up and running), chances are that FrontPage will interact with it smoothly.

FrontPage supports the most popular shareware and commercial web servers in use today, via software programs known as the FrontPage Server Extensions, which are discussed later in this chapter. (You'll also find a list of the web servers that FrontPage supports later in the chapter.) The Server Extensions are the go-between from the FrontPage client to the web server, helping both parties communicate behind the scenes.

If you're lucky, you might not need to buy a web server at all; FrontPage comes complete with its own server, called the Personal Web Server.

The Personal Web Server

The Personal Web Server is a 32-bit server application supplied with FrontPage; it is designed to work directly with FrontPage-created web sites. The Personal Web Server is best used as a low-volume server; its ideal uses are for testing sites and for acting as the main server for a low-volume intranet at a small company or organization.

Here's about all you'll ever see of the Personal Web Server—this is the window that's normally minimized when the Explorer is running. When you launch the Explorer, FrontPage launches the Personal Web Server simultaneously.

Many FrontPage web-site developers create their sites locally, on a network or even on a single computer, and test them with the Personal Web Server before moving the site to a higher-volume server within their company. The Personal Web Server can help you test all aspects of a FrontPage site, including links to the Internet and the World Wide Web, the use of FrontPage's **bots** and forms, and any other content that requires communication between the client and server.

The Personal Web Server is based on National Center for Supercomputing Application (NCSA) standards, and it fully supports the Hypertext Transfer Protocol (HTTP) and Common Gateway Interface (CGI) standards. It's compatible with existing **CGI** scripts, so you don't need to be concerned with writing new scripts if you decide to use the Personal Web Server.

The Personal Web Server doesn't need to be configured; it's configured automatically when you install FrontPage, along with its specific set of Server Extensions. You can run the Personal Web Server on a local machine or on a machine connected to a network. If you create and edit sites using the Personal Web Server on a local machine, you can often expect the communication between the FrontPage client and the Personal Web Server (for example, when opening or saving a web site) to be slower than when you run the Personal Web Server over a network.

> **TIP**
>
> FrontPage stores the Personal Web Server configuration files in the FPServer\Conf directory, and automatically backs up the files and stores them in the same directory.

The FrontPage Server Extensions

Suppose for a second that you're stranded in Russia, but you only speak a wee bit of Russian. Could you survive? Probably. Could you communicate? Sure, a little bit. But could you communicate *well?* Probably not. You'd need a translator to make sure you come across the way you want to.

The FrontPage Server Extensions perform this kind of translation duty between your FrontPage site and a web server. Each set of Server Extensions is a software program that lives on the web server and intervenes whenever communication takes place between your site and the server. In this way, FrontPage can communicate with a large number of web servers on the market today.

The FrontPage Server Extensions are a good bargain today for a number of specific reasons:

- They're free.
- They make uploading a site to a web server fast and easy with FrontPage. Without the Server Extensions, you'd have to upload your FrontPage site to the web server via the FTP protocol or via the Microsoft FrontPage Publishing Wizard. (See "The FrontPage Publishing Wizard" later in this chapter.)
- They make sure that FrontPage's bots work as they're intended to work. For example, if you use a Search bot in your FrontPage site, the Server Extensions ensure that the bot will perform as it's supposed to. Without the Server Extensions installed, the bot won't work.

Web servers and platforms As of this writing, FrontPage Server Extensions are available for the following web servers. The list will undoubtedly grow in the coming months:

Commercial web servers:

- Microsoft Internet Information Server
- Netscape communication and commerce servers
- Open Market Web Server
- O'Reilly WebSite

Noncommercial web servers:

- NCSA
- Apache
- CERN

Platforms:

- Microsoft Windows 95
- Microsoft Windows NT Workstation and Windows NT Server
- UNIX (including Solaris, SunOS, HP/UX, IRIX, and BSDi)

Where to get 'em You can download the FrontPage Server Extensions from the FrontPage section of Microsoft's web site at http://www.microsoft.com/frontpage. Look for a link to the FrontPage Server Extensions section on that page, and then follow the directions to download the Server Extensions you need.

Installing the Server Extensions Follow the specific instructions accompanying the Server Extensions to install them on your web server. To implement their use within FrontPage, see the next section.

Server Administration

You can perform most everyday server management tasks in the Explorer. For example, you can change parameters and other settings for your sites; change passwords; enable and disable administrative, author, and end-user access and authoring privileges to the site; and configure **proxy servers** via commands on the Explorer's menus. Most of these commands have to do with site-specific tasks. Chapter 3 contains detailed information on using these commands.

Tasks that deal with aspects of the web servers, such as setting and changing a server type, configuring Server Extensions, changing the port a server is on, and so on, must be performed elsewhere, outside of the FrontPage client. You can perform these and other tasks quickly and easily in a program called the FrontPage Server Administrator.

The Server Administrator

The FrontPage Server Administrator is a program that helps you carry out numerous tasks related to installing, uninstalling, and configuring various elements of the web servers you use with FrontPage. If you use the Personal Web Server, it will be installed and configured when you install FrontPage. Its Server Extensions will also be installed and configured at the same time. However, if you decide to use FrontPage with any other web server, you must first install the web server, and then use the Server Administrator to link the server with FrontPage by configuring a port and installing the Server Extensions for that web server.

FrontPage comes with two flavors of the Server Administrator: a Windows version and a command-line version. Both are found in the Program Files\Microsoft FrontPage\bin directory on the drive or server that FrontPage is installed on. The Windows version is FPSRVWIN.EXE, and the command-line version is FPSRVADM.EXE. You can launch either application by double-clicking it in the Windows 95 Explorer.

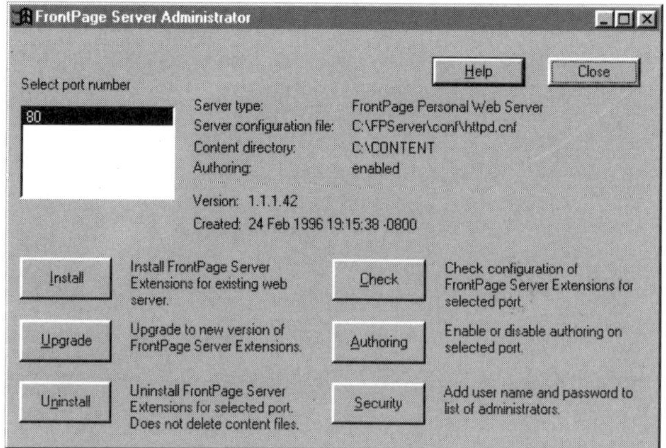

The Windows version of the Server Administrator.

Below are step-by-step procedures for tasks you can perform with the Windows version of the Server Administrator. Explicit directions for using the command-line version can be found in FrontPage's online help under the topic "FrontPage Server Administrator—Command Line Version."

Here's what you can do with the Server Administrator:

Install FrontPage Server Extensions To install a set of FrontPage Server Extensions for an existing web server, you must first install the web server—and it's a good idea to test it using a browser to ensure that it works properly. After you're sure it's working properly, do the following:

1. Launch the Server Administrator.
2. Click the Install button. In the Configure Server Type dialog box, from the drop-down list box select the web server you want to use with the FrontPage Server Extensions, and then click OK.
3. The Server Configuration dialog box appears. You'll be prompted to enter some information, depending on the server you're installing the Server Extensions for.

Personal Web Server Enter the full directory and name of the main server configuration file, HTTPD.CNF. By default it's c:\FrontPage Webs\Server\conf\httpd.cnf, but if you specified a different program directory at installation, you will need to adjust this.

Netscape servers Enter the port number for the server you're installing the Server Extensions for. Server configuration information is kept in the Windows NT or Windows 95 registry, in a different area for each port.

WebSite If you are using the multi-homing feature of WebSite, enter the fully qualified domain name for the server host you are installing.

TIP

FrontPage supports multi-homing for all web servers that offer this feature. Multi-homing is the ability of a single web server to host sites for multiple domain names; for example, the domains *www.malina.com* and *www.don.com* might actually reside on a single server.

Enter the specific information, and then click OK to close the Server Configuration dialog box.

4. In the FrontPage Server Administrator dialog box, click Close.

Uninstall FrontPage Server Extensions Uninstalling Server Extensions removes the _vti_bin directory that holds the Server Extension executable files, as well as the _vti_txt directory containing the site's text index. It also removes the section for the selected port from the FRONTPG.INI file in your Windows directory. It does not remove content files, such as HTML files or image files.

To uninstall Server Extensions for a particular port, do the following:

1. Shut down the server.
2. Launch the Server Administrator.
3. From the Select Port Number list box, select the port for the Server Extensions you want to uninstall.
4. Click Uninstall. A Server Administrator dialog box appears, asking you to confirm the uninstall operation.

5. Click OK.
6. In the FrontPage Server Administrator dialog box, click Close.

Change a server's port number To change a server's port number, you must first uninstall the Server Extensions on that port, change the port number, and then reinstall the Server Extensions.

To change the port number of a web server that already has the Server Extensions running, do the following:

1. Shut down the server.
2. Launch the Server Administrator.
3. In the Select Port Number list box, select the port number you want to change.
4. Click Uninstall to remove the Server Extensions from the port, and click OK to confirm your action.
5. Change the server's port number according to the directions supplied with the web server. For example, you can change the port number for the Personal Web Server in the Port line of the HTTPD.CNF file.
6. Click Install in the Server Administrator to reinstall the Server Extensions for the new port. Enter any required information in the Server Configuration dialog box, and then click OK.
7. Restart the server.
8. In the FrontPage Server Administrator dialog box, click Close.

Add or change an administrator's user name and password There are two ways to change administrator user names and passwords in FrontPage. If you have a site open in the Explorer, you can use the Web Permissions command on the Tools menu to change this information for that site only. With the Server Administrator, however, you don't have to have a site open in the Explorer, and in fact you can change administrator names and passwords for any site on any web server you have access to. Simply follow the steps on the facing page.

1. Launch the Server Administrator.
2. Click Security. You'll see the Administrator Name And Password dialog box:

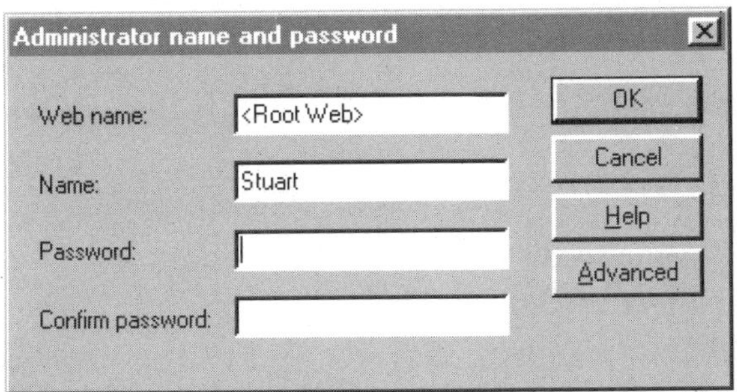

3. Enter the name of the site in the Web Name text box.
4. Enter the administrator's name and password in the next two text boxes, and then confirm the password in the last text box. If the name is already registered, the password will be changed to the password you enter.
5. If you want to restrict administrative operations based on **IP addresses**, click the Advanced button to reach the Internet Address Restriction dialog box. Administrative operations will be limited to machines whose IP addresses fall within the restrictions you specify. For example, if you specify *200.130.*.**, only machines with IP addresses that begin with *200.130* will be allowed to perform administrative operations to the site. After you enter this information, click OK.
6. Click OK to close the Administrator Name And Password dialog box.
7. In the FrontPage Server Administrator dialog box, click Close.

Enable or disable authoring on a selected port Disabling authoring on a port means you disable authoring for every site accessible by FrontPage on that port. So, if you want all your FrontPage sites on a particular port to be untouchable by those who top out at author-level access, you can do the following:

1. Launch the Server Administrator.
2. From the Select Port Number list box, select the port on which you want to enable or disable authoring.

3. Click the Authoring button. The Enable/Disable Authoring dialog box appears, indicating whether authoring is currently enabled or disabled on the port.
4. Click OK to enable or disable authoring for the port. A Server Administrator dialog box appears, indicating that the operation was successful. Click OK.
5. In the Server Administrator dialog box, click Close.

Upgrade older FrontPage web sites when you install a new version of FrontPage When you install a new version of FrontPage, you must upgrade sites created in the older version. This copies the necessary files from the FrontPage installation area to the content directories in the sites. Content files or image files in the sites will not be changed.

Here's how to upgrade those old sites:

1. Launch the Server Administrator.
2. Click the Upgrade button.
3. You'll see a Server Administrator dialog box telling you of the impending operation. Click OK. The Server Administrator upgrades the old files and returns you to the Server Administrator dialog box.
4. Click Close to close the dialog box.

Internet Service Providers

You can always choose to forgo the potential headaches of running your own web server and let someone else take the aspirin for a change. **Internet Service Providers** (ISPs), also called web hosts, are companies that house your site on their server and provide you with a variety of services—often for a very low fee when compared with the cost of hospitalization for those suffering nervous breakdowns when their web servers go on the fritz three times in the same week.

Most ISPs charge periodic fees (often monthly, biannually, or annually) to house your site; these fees generally increase with the size of your site. Some ISPs also charge according to the number of hits your site receives, or to the bandwidth of information transferred between your site and those who view it.

The advantages of using the services of an ISP include not having to worry about maintaining a web server in-house, and faster user access to your site. ISPs often have the fastest connections available on the Internet. In addition, you avoid the expense and hassle of having to install a **firewall** server to protect your company's computing resources if your site is on the World Wide Web.

The disadvantages are relatively few; among them is the fact that you're not the one in control. Also, nearly all business owners dream of having business go so well that their sites must expand to meet the growing consumer need for information; if these dreams come true for you, it might be easier (and ultimately less expensive) to manage a large site in-house instead of over a distance.

Microsoft is in the process of forging agreements with many of the major ISPs to ensure that they include the FrontPage Server Extensions as part of their service offerings. That way, it'll be easier to upload your FrontPage site to their servers, and you'll be ensured of keeping FrontPage-specific functionality (such as that of FrontPage's bots) in your site.

As an ISP, AT&T is acting in this capacity already; look for news on other ISPs entering the picture soon. To find out more about ISPs and FrontPage, see the FrontPage section of Microsoft's web site at http://www.microsoft.com/msoffice/frontpage. If you're an ISP in search of more information, that's also the place to go. You'll find a link to the section "Internet Service Provider Information" on that page.

The FrontPage Publishing Wizard

Many smaller ISPs might not offer the FrontPage Server Extensions for some time. In the past, this made it difficult to move an entire FrontPage site to one of these web servers, because you'd have to do it manually instead of using the Copy Web command in the Explorer. To upload a site to an ISP's server, you had to "FTP" it—meaning you had to use the **FTP** protocol to transfer your file from your computer to the server. This process involved several steps, because you'd have to move several directories to the server—including content directories, image directories, and more.

But now you can manually transfer a FrontPage site to a server that does not support the FrontPage Server Extensions in a few easy steps. If you'd rather stay with your current ISP even though it doesn't offer the Server Extensions, you can use the FrontPage Publishing Wizard to move your site there.

The FrontPage Publishing Wizard allows you to perform one-button publishing of a site to an ISP's server. You can download the FrontPage Publishing Wizard from the FrontPage section of Microsoft's World Wide Web site for free. See the FrontPage home page at http://www.microsoft.com/msoffice/frontpage for more information.

Keep in mind, however, that if you post your FrontPage web site to a server that does not have the FrontPage Server Extensions installed, you'll lose some FrontPage-specific functionality, such as that of the FrontPage bots. The site will still work, but without that functionality.

Appendix Installing FrontPage

So you're ready to take the big step and install FrontPage version 1.1. It's not such a big step, really—compared with installing other applications, the FrontPage installation takes very little time on most computers, and it's incredibly easy. This appendix will step you through your installation of FrontPage version 1.1, whether you're installing it for the first time or installing it over version 1.0.

Before you install FrontPage, however, you should read the file FPREADME.TXT, which is on the first FrontPage disk. It contains specific information on known problems with FrontPage, additional tips on running and troubleshooting FrontPage, a description of the FrontPage TCP/IP Test utility (which you can use to learn your host name, IP address, and other network-related information), and technical-support information and contacts.

System Requirements

To use FrontPage, you need the following:

- Microsoft Windows 95 or Microsoft Windows NT version 3.51 or later
- Personal computer with a 486 processor or faster
- 8 MB of memory required; 16 MB of memory recommended if you're using the Personal Web Server
- 20 MB of available hard disk space

- VGA or higher-resolution video adapter (SVGA 256-color recommended)
- Microsoft Mouse or compatible pointing device
- Winsock 1.1-compliant TCP/IP or later; if you have Windows 95 or Windows NT with TCP/IP installed, you have the base software required.

Installation

You can install FrontPage version 1.1 on a machine that does not already have FrontPage 1.0 installed, or you can install it over version 1.0. See below for tips on installing over version 1.0. The installation process is the same in either case:

1. Exit all Windows-based applications on your machine.
2. Insert the first installation disk, FrontPage 1.1 Disk 1, in your floppy drive.
3. Launch SETUP.EXE from Disk 1. In Windows NT, you can do this by opening a window to your 3.5-inch floppy drive and double-clicking SETUP.EXE. In Windows 95, open the drive in the Explorer and double-click SETUP.EXE.
4. You'll see the Welcome screen in the InstallShield Setup Wizard, urging you to close all programs before continuing. Click Next.
5. In the Destination Path screen, Setup tells you the directory it will install FrontPage in. The Windows 95 default directory is c:\Program Files\Microsoft FrontPage, and the Windows NT default directory is c:\Microsoft FrontPage.

   If you want to install FrontPage in another directory, click the Browse button to locate it, and then click OK to return to the Destination Path screen. Click Next to continue.

> **TIP**
>
> If you want to quit Setup before it installs FrontPage, click Cancel in any screen. No files will be copied to your hard drive.

6. In the Setup Type screen, you're asked to choose between a typical and custom installation. Here are the differences:

   Typical installation Setup installs the FrontPage client, Personal Web Server, and the FrontPage Server Extensions for the Personal Web Server.

   Custom installation You select the combination of the FrontPage client, Personal Web Server, and/or the Server Extensions that Setup installs, and locations for each. In a network setting, you can choose a custom setup if you only want to install the FrontPage client on a local machine. You can link the client to a server after installation by using the FrontPage Server Administrator. (See Chapter 9 for details.)

> **TIP**
>
> Web sites created in FrontPage 1.0 are fully compatible with version 1.1. If you're installing over version 1.0, you can install any of these elements over those in 1.0 and still use your old web sites.

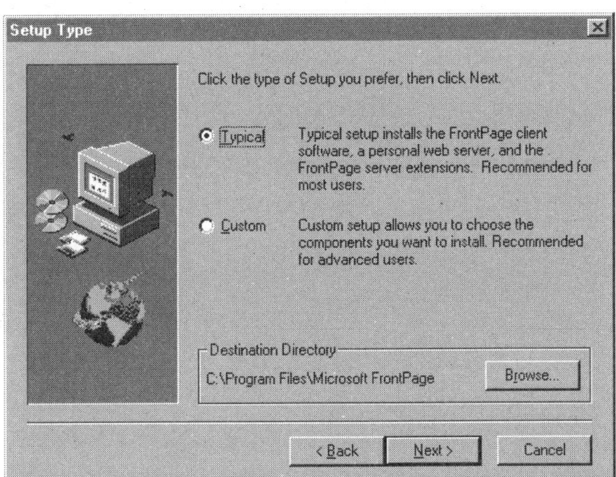

   Select either the Typical or Custom option, and then click Next. If you select Typical, skip to step 7. If you select Custom, proceed to step 6a.

6a. If you selected a custom installation, the Select Components screen (shown on the next page) allows you to select which portions of FrontPage to install. Select any combination of the Client Software, Personal Web Server, and Server Extensions check boxes, and then click Next.

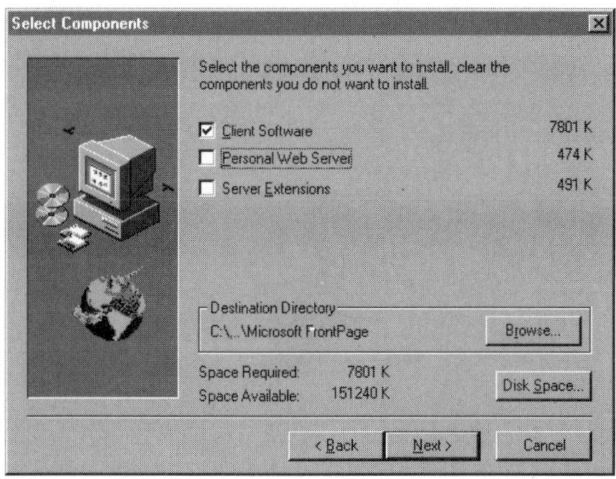

7. Next you're asked to specify where you want the Personal Web Server installed. This is also the location that FrontPage will use to store any sites that you create. If you selected a custom installation and did not choose to install the Personal Web Server, you will not see this screen.

   The Default directory is c:\FrontPage Webs. If you want to install the Personal Web Server in a different directory, click Browse, select the directory, and then click OK. Click Next to continue.

8. Next, in the Select Program Folder screen, you specify where you want the FrontPage program icons to go. Setup will create a Microsoft FrontPage program folder to hold the icons; if you want to put them somewhere else, select a different folder in the Existing Folders list box. Click Next to continue.

9. Now you're just about done—you'll see the Start Copying Files screen, where you can confirm the information you entered in the wizard. Verify everything in the Current Settings list box.

   If you want to change any information you've entered in the wizard, click the Back button until you reach the appropriate screen(s). Make the necessary changes, and then click Next until you once again reach the Start Copying Files screen. Click Next to have Setup begin copying files to your hard disk.

10. Insert each of the remaining five installation disks as Setup prompts you.

11. As Setup nears completion, it presents the Administrator Setup For Personal Web Server dialog box (if you chose to install the Personal Web Server). Enter the name and password you wish to use, and then confirm the password by entering it again. Then click OK.

> **TIP**
>
> You can change your user name and password later if you wish, either in the FrontPage Explorer (using the Permissions command; see Chapter 3) or by using the Server Administrator (see Chapter 9).

12. When Setup finishes, you'll see the Setup Complete screen, which is the final wizard screen. You can start using FrontPage immediately by selecting the Start The FrontPage Explorer Now check box. Click Finish to complete your FrontPage installation.

Installing over version 1.0 If you're installing version 1.1 over version 1.0, you can upgrade the client and install the new Personal Web Server in a different directory. Then, you can evaluate the new Personal Web Server while still using the older version.

Do not install the new version 1.1 client in the same directory as the version 1.0 client. If you choose to use the default directory to install the client in the version 1.1 Setup wizard, you won't need to be concerned with this.

After you install version 1.1, if you don't want to use the version 1.0 Personal Web Server any longer, you can delete the following items from your hard drive:

- The c:\vermeer directory
- In Windows NT 3.51, the Vermeer program group
- In Windows 95, the Vermeer folder
- The files c:\Windows\vermeer.ini, c:\vermeer.log, and c:\vermeer.out
- The following five files in the c:\Windows\System directory: vt10wel.dll, vt10tl.dll, vt10txt.dll, vt10utl.dll, and vt10htp.dll. These are large files; their removal will free up lots of space on your hard drive.

Uninstalling FrontPage

If by some freak of nature you contract "mad cow disease" and decide you want to uninstall FrontPage, here's all you have to do:

In Windows 95 In the Control Panel, double-click the Add/Remove Programs icon, select Microsoft FrontPage from the list box, and click Add/Remove. Windows 95 asks you to confirm the removal. Click Yes to uninstall.

In Windows NT 3.51 Click the Uninstall Microsoft FrontPage icon in the Microsoft FrontPage program group.

Glossary

Absolute URL A URL that is complete, with a protocol, host name, directory name, and file name, such as http://www.acme.com/welcome.html.

Active link A link that is currently selected in a web browser.

Active page The page currently being edited. The active page is indicated by a title bar background if the window is maximized and by a title background if the page is minimized.

Address A paragraph style usually used to enter Internet addresses on the page. Address paragraphs are usually displayed in italics.

Annotation bot The Annotation bot inserts text on a page that can be viewed from the FrontPage Editor but not from a web browser. Use an Annotation bot to insert place-holder text or notes to yourself as you create your web pages. Annotation text is displayed in purple and retains the character-size and other attributes of the current paragraph style.

Article A single entry in a discussion group. An article can optionally be a reply to a previous article.

Authentication database A server-specific database that matches user names to passwords.

Base URL A base URL is a URL that is used to convert relative URL's on the page into absolute URLs. A base URL should include a document name part, such as http://sample.com/subdir/sample.htm, or a trailing slash, such as http://sample.com/subdir/.

Bit depth The number of bits used to represent each color of an image per pixel. (A bit is a binary digit—either a 0 or a 1.) The greater the bit depth, the more bits used to represent a color, which means more colors that an image can support.

BMP A file format for images created by Microsoft and IBM. Some BMP images are compressed using RLE-type compression.

Bookmark A named set of one or more characters in a paragraph that can be the target of a link.

Bot A dynamic object on a web page that is evaluated and executed when the author saves the page to the server or, in some cases, when the reader links to the page.

Bot cursor The robot-like cursor that appears when you move the FrontPage cursor over an area of the page containing a bot.

Browser See **Web browser**.

Bulleted list The paragraph style that presents an unordered list of items.

Cell padding The space between the contents and inside edges of cells in a table.

Cell spacing The amount of space placed between cells in a table. The border width around a cell is determined by the table's cell spacing.

Cell The basic component of a table. In a table, the intersection of a row and column forms one cell.

CERN image map dispatcher The program htimage.exe, which handles server-side clickable image maps when the image map style is "CERN".

CGI Common Gateway Interface. A standard for programs on a server that run in response to input from a web page.

Change style window A window on the FrontPage Editor's toolbar in which the user can choose the format of currently selected paragraphs.

Check box A form field that presents the reader with a selection that can be chosen by clicking on a box. When the box is selected, it is displayed with a check mark or X.

Child web Any web other than the root web on a given web server.

Clickable image An image containing one or more invisible regions containing hypertext links. When the reader places the cursor over an image containing links, the cursor indicates the presence of links by changing appearance, typically to a pointing hand.

Client A machine that uses resources located on a server. The FrontPage client software consists of the Explorer, the Editor, and the To Do List. These access information from web sites located on a web server (such as the Personal Web Server).

Client-side image map A clickable image that encodes the destination URL of each hotspot directly in the image map. Client-side image maps do not require processing from your server to resolve the destination of a link based on cursor coordinates.

Clipboard A temporary storage area for cut or copied items.

Column The cells arranged vertically in a table.

Configuration variable Information about a page or web that is stored with the page or web. FrontPage includes standard web configuration and page configuration variables. Authors can also define their own web configuration variables. Configuration variables can be displayed at runtime using form results bots or substitution bots.

Confirmation Field bot The Confirmation Field bot is replaced with the contents of a form field. It is useful on a form confirmation page, where it can echo the user's name or any other data entered into a field.

Confirmation page A web page that is displayed when a form is submitted. You specify a form's confirmation page in the form handler's dialog box. More than one form can use the same confirmation page. The link between a confirmation page and the page containing the form is shown in the FrontPage Explorer, but it is not shown in the outline of the web generated by the Table of Contents bot. If you do not specify a confirmation, FrontPage form handling bots will generate one by default.

Current web The web currently opened in the FrontPage Explorer.

Custom dictionary A dictionary of words built up by the spelling checker that, although not in the standard dictionary, should be accepted by the spelling checker as correct. The custom dictionary is in the file *dict.u* in the frontpag\bin directory. You can edit this file with a text editor. Each author has a unique custom dictionary.

D

Date bot The Date bot is replaced with the date the page was last modified by the author or by another bot.

Default URL On a clickable image, the URL that is used when the user clicks outside of any hotspots on the image.

Definition The second of a pair of paragraphs formatted as a dictionary entry. The first paragraph is the term, and the second paragraph is the definition.

Definition list A list of terms and corresponding definitions.

Design Wizard The FrontPage program that guides the author through the basic steps that create a web of a common type, such as Corporate Information.

Discussion bot A form bot that allows users to participate in an online discussion. The Discussion bot collects information from a form, formats it into an HTML page, and adds the page to a table of contents and to a text index. In addition, the Discussion bot gathers information from the form and stores it in one of a selection of formats.

Discussion group A web that supports interactive discussion of topics by users. Users submit topics by entering text in a form, search the group using a search form, and access articles using a table of contents.

Discussion group directory A directory of a web containing the results of a discussion group. The name of a discussion group directory must begin with an underscore character, as in: _discussion. Discussion group directories are not visible from the FrontPage Explorer. However, they can be searched by a Search bot.

Domain name The unique name that identifies an Internet site. A domain name has two or more parts, separated by periods, as in—my.domain.name.

Drop-down menu field A form field that presents a list of selections in drop-down menu style. A set of drop-down menu form fields can be configured so that one item can be selected at a time or so that many items can be selected.

Editor An interactive program that can create and modify files of a particular type. For example, the FrontPage Editor is an HTML editor.

Emphasis text The HTML character style used for mild emphasis. This style is usually displayed as italic.

EPS Encapsulated PostScript image format. These files are primarily used on PostScript printers.

Extended attribute An HTML attribute not directly supported in FrontPage that can be entered as a name/value pair from the selected object's properties dialog box.

External link A link to any page that is not part of the current web.

File A named collection of information that is stored on a disk. Also, an Internet protocol that refers to files on the local disk.

File type The format of a file, usually indicated by its filename extension. Editors usually work on a limited set of file types.

Firewall A method of protecting one network from another network. A firewall blocks unwanted access to the protected network while giving the protected network access to networks outside of the firewall.

Follow link cursor The cursor displayed by the FrontPage Editor during a Follow Link command.

Form A set of data entry fields that get processed on the server when the user submits the data. Data is submitted by clicking on a button or, in some cases, by clicking on an image. A form's boundaries are invisible to the user. The FrontPage Editor optionally displays them as dotted lines.

Form bot A FrontPage bot that supplies runtime processing of a form. FrontPage supplies a form discussion, registration and save results bot.

Form field An item on a page into which the reader can supply information either by typing text or by selecting a field.

Form handler A program on a server that runs when a user submits a form. A FrontPage form is associated with a handler in the Form Properties dialog box.

Formatted text A mono-spaced paragraph style in which white space (space characters, TABS, etc.) is displayed as entered in the FrontPage Editor. This style is useful for tables and programming code samples.

Formatting toolbar The FrontPage Editor toolbar that contains commands that reformat selected paragraphs or text.

Forms toolbar The forms toolbar contains commands that create parts of forms.

Frame A single element of a frame set; a named scrollable region in which pages can be displayed.

Frame set A web page that defines a set of named scrollable regions in which other web pages can be displayed.

FrontPage Editor A FrontPage program for creating, editing, and testing web pages.

FrontPage Explorer The FrontPage program that lets the author view the structure of a web and operate on an entire web.

FrontPage Server Extensions The FrontPage Server Extensions are programs and scripts that support FrontPage and extend the functionality of the Personal Web Server. The FrontPage Server Extensions are available for popular Windows NT and Unix web servers.

FTP The Internet File Transfer Protocol. An ftp URL points to a file that is available for access across the Internet.

GIF Graphics Interchange Format. A method of encoding images. This method compresses its data using the LZW compression technique.

Gopher The Internet directory-based document retrieval protocol.

Heading One of six paragraph types that are displayed in large, bold typefaces. The size of a heading is related to its level: Heading 1 is the largest, Heading 2, the next largest, and so on. Use headings to name pages and sections of pages.

Hidden directory A directory in a web with a name beginning with an underscore character, as in: _hide. By default, pages and files in hidden directories cannot be viewed from the FrontPage Explorer.

Hidden field A field on a form that is not visible to the user. Each hidden field is implemented as a name-value pair. When the form is submitted, its hidden fields are passed to the form-handler along with name-value pairs from each form field.

Home page The home page is the starting point in a web. It is the page that is retrieved and displayed by default when you visit a web.

Hotspot A graphically defined area in an image that contains a hypertext link. Hotspots can overlap.

Htimage.exe The CERN image map dispatcher. This program handles server-side clickable image maps when the image map style is "CERN".

HTML HyperText Markup Language. The industry-standard language for describing the contents and layout of a web page. The FrontPage Page Editor reads and writes HTML documents.

HTML attribute A name/value pair used within an HTML tag to assign additional properties to the object being defined.

HTML Markup bot The HTML Markup bot is replaced with any arbitrary text you supply when you create the bot. This text is substituted for the bot when the page is saved to the server as HTML. Use this bot to add non-standard HTML commands to a page.

HTML tag An element of an HTML page that identifies an HTML object's type, format, structure, and hypertext links.

Http The Internet protocol that allows web clients to retrieve information from web hosts.

Hypertext Text, usually presented in a color different than the text surrounding it, that is linked to places within or outside the web site.

Image A graphic in GIF or JPEG file format that can be inserted on a page. FrontPage lets you import images in the following formats and insert them as GIF or JPEG: GIF, JPEG, BMP (Windows and OS/2), WMF, TIFF, MAC, MSP, PCD, RAS, WPG, EPS, PCX, and WMF.

Image form field A form field that displays an image in a form. By clicking on the image, the user submits the form.

Image toolbar The FrontPage Editor toolbar that contains commands that operate images.

Imagemap.exe The NCSA image map dispatcher. This program handles server-side clickable image maps when the image map style is "NCSA".

Include bot The Include bot is replaced with the contents of another page in the web.

Insert Link dialog box The FrontPage Editor dialog box in which you bind a hypertext link to the selected graphic or text.

Interlaced image A GIF image that is displayed full-sized at low resolution while it is being loaded, and is displayed at higher resolutions until it finally attains a normal appearance when it is fully loaded.

Internal link A link to any page or other file that is in the current web.

Internal web A collection of webs created within an organization and accessible only to members of that organization.

Internet A global network comprising thousands of smaller computer networks that began in the late 1960s as a U.S. government communications project. Mainly used by government and research institutions until the late 1980s, its popularity grew with the spawning of the World Wide Web.

Internet Service Provider (ISP) Also known as an Internet access provider. ISPs are gateways to the Internet for businesses and individuals, often providing access to a range of Internet services such as the World Wide Web, e-mail, and Internet newsgroups.

Intranet See **Internal web.**

IP address An IP (Internet Protocol) address is a standard way of identifying a computer that is connected to a network. The IP address is four numbers separated by periods, and each number is less than 256, for example, 192.200.44.69.

IP address mask The IP (Internet Protocol) address mask defines a range of IP addresses so that only those users whose IP addresses fall within the range are allowed access to an Internet service. To mask a portion of the IP address, replace it with the asterisk wild card character (*). For example, 192.200.*.* represents every computer with an IP mask that begins with 192.200.

JPEG Joint Photographic Expert Group. A 24-bit per pixel color image format with excellent compression for most kinds of images.

Local area network (LAN) A group of computers and other devices, such as printers, that are interconnected in a limited area such that any device can interact with any other on the network. LANs are often geographically limited, such as to a single building or department within an organization.

Line A horizontal graphic element on a page.

Line break A special character that forces a new line on the page without creating a new paragraph.

Link A jump from a web page to another page or anchor in the current web, or to a resource on the World Wide Web.

Link View A view in the FrontPage Explorer that displays pages as icons, and graphically shows the links to a page with a line.

List A group of paragraphs formatted to indicate membership in a set or in a sequence of steps. You can create numbered lists, bulleted lists, menus, directories or definitions.

MAC The Macintosh Paint files image format.

Mailto The Internet protocol that is used to send electronic mail.

Menu list A list of short paragraph entries formatted with little white space between items.

Meta tag An HTML tag that must appear in the <head> portion of the document. Meta tags supply information about the document, and do not effect the display of the document. A standard meta tag, "generator," is used to supply the type of editor that created the HTML page.

MIME type A method used by web browsers to associate files of a certain type with helper applications that can display files of that type. Based on the Internet multi-media mail standard: Multi-purpose Internet Mail Extensions.

MSP Microsoft Paint image format.

Name-value pair The name of a form field along with the value of the field at the time the form is submitted. Each field in a form can have one or more name-value pairs, and the form itself can have one or more name-value pairs.

NCSA image map dispatcher The program imagemap.exe, which handles server-side clickable image maps when the image map style is "NCSA".

Nested list A list that is contained inside a member of another list. Nesting is indicated by indentation in most web browsers.

News The Internet protocol for retrieving files from an Internet news information service.

Normal text The default paragraph style of the FrontPage Editor, intended for use in text paragraphs.

Numbered list The paragraph style that presents an ordered list of items.

One-line text box A labeled, single line form field in which users can type text.

Outline View A view in the FrontPage Explorer that displays the pages and links in your web in a hierarchical form, starting with the home page.

Page A single document on a web containing one or more topics that can be linked to from other pages. Topics contain text, images, and hypertext links to other pages or to other Internet services. Because documents on the World Wide Web are not paginated, a page can span many windows-full of information.

Page title A string representing the page. The title is displayed in the FrontPage Explorer and is used by many FrontPage Editor and FrontPage Explorer commands. When you edit a page, its title appears in the title bar of the FrontPage Editor window. Most web browsers display a page's title in the title bar of their browse window.

Page URL A page's name relative to the web containing the page. Page URLs are useful for creating links within a particular web.

Paragraph style A label for a FrontPage Editor paragraph-type. Paragraph style specifies the type of font to use in the paragraph, along with the font's size, and other attributes. Paragraph style also specifies whether or not to use bullets and numbering, and controls indentation and line spacing.

PCD Kodak PhotoCD file image format.

PCX A file format created by Zsoft that compresses its image data with RLE-type compression.

Pixel The smallest element that can be presented on a computer screen or printed on paper. A computer screen consists of thousands of consecutively placed pixels. The higher the resolution of a computer monitor, the more pixels it can "paint" on the screen.

Port One of the input/output channels of a computer. In the World Wide Web, port usually refers to the port number a server is running on. A single computer can have many web servers running on it, each on a different port. The default port is 80.

Properties The values that characterize an item, such as the title and URL of a web, the file name and path of a file, or the name and initial value of a form field.

Protocol A method of accessing a document or service over the Internet, such as ftp, for File Transfer Protocol, or http, for HyperText Transfer Protocol.

Proxy server A server that acts as a firewall, mediating traffic between a protected network and the Internet.

Push button A form field that lets the user submit the form or that resets the form to its initial state.

Radio button A form field that presents the reader with a selection that can be chosen by clicking on a button. Radio buttons are presented in a list, one of which is always selected. Selecting a new member of the list deselects the currently selected item. A form can contain more than one independent set of radio buttons.

RAS Sun raster image file format.

Registered user A user with a recorded name and password. You can register a user with a Registration bot.

Registration bot A form bot that allows users to automatically register themselves for access to a service. The Registration bot adds the user to the service's authentication database, then optionally gathers information from the form and stores it in one of a selection of formats.

Relative URL The URL of a page or image with respect to another page containing a link to that page or image in the same web. For example, the relative URL of the page http://www.acme.com/target/hello.html with respect to the page http://www.acme.com/source/hello.html is .../target/hello.html.

Resource An area of Internet functionality identified by a protocol, such as ftp, gopher, file, or http.

Root web The web that is provided by the server by default. To access the root web, you supply the URL of the server without specifying a web-name. FrontPage is installed with a default web named <root web>.

Row The cells arranged horizontally in a table.

RTF Rich Text Format. A method of encoding text formatting and document structure using the ASCII character set. By convention, RTF files have a .rtf extension.

Save Results bot A form bot that gathers information from a form and stores it in one of a selection of formats. When a user submits the form, the Save Results bot appends the form information to a specified file in a specified format.

Scheduled Image bot The Scheduled Image bot is replaced by an image during a specified time period. When the time period has expired, the image is no longer displayed.

Scheduled Include bot The Scheduled Include bot is replaced with the contents of a file during a specified time period. When the time period has expired, the contents of the file are no longer displayed.

Scrolling text box A labeled, multi-line form field in which users can type text.

Search bot The Search bot creates a form that provides full text-searching capability in your web at runtime. When the user submits a form containing words to locate, the Search bot returns a list of all pages in your web containing matches for the words.

Selection bar An unmarked column along the left edge of the FrontPage Editor window that is used to select text with the mouse.

Server A computer that runs processes shared by users (clients), or software processes that serve client processes. In the World Wide Web, the server is the computer that runs the web-server program that responds to http protocol requests by providing web pages.

Server-side image map A clickable image that passes the coordinates of the cursor in an image map to a handler routine on the server. Server-side image maps require processing from your server to compute the target URL of the link based on the run-time cursor coordinates.

Size handle A black rectangle displayed on a selected form field or hotspot. When you select a size handle, the cursor becomes a bi-directional arrow. Click and drag a size handle to reshape the field or hotspot.

Special character A character not in the standard 7-bit ASCII character set, such as the copyright mark (©). In FrontPage, you add special characters using the Insert menu.

Standard toolbar The FrontPage Editor toolbar contains the most commonly used editing and file menu commands, along with commands that create and test links and commands that start the other major FrontPage components.

Status bar The area at the bottom of the FrontPage Editor or FrontPage Explorer that displays information about the currently selected command or about an operation in progress.

Strong text The HTML character style used for strong emphasis. This style is usually displayed as bold.

Substitution bot The Substitution bot is replaced by the value of a selected page configuration or web configuration variable.

Summary View A view in the FrontPage Explorer that lists all the pages and other files in a web. This list can be sorted by the categories available in the view.

Table of Contents bot The Table of Contents bot creates an outline of your web, with links to each page. The Table of Contents bot updates this outline each time the web's contents changes.

Table One or more rows of cells used to organize the layout of a page or arrange data systematically. In a table, the intersection of a row and column forms one cell, in which you can type text or insert images, forms, or WebBots.

Tag selection A method of selecting a group of objects on a page. Use tag selection to select the members of a list, an entire form, or a bot. To tag select a set of objects, move the cursor to the left of the objects until the cursor becomes the tag-selection cursor and then double-click.

Task An item on a to do list representing one of the actions you need to perform to complete a web. Some tasks are automatically generated by wizards. You can also add your own tasks to the list.

Template A set of designed formats for text and images on which pages and webs can be based. After a page or web is created using a template, you can modify the page or web.

Term The first of a pair of paragraphs formatted as a dictionary entry. The second paragraph is the definition.

TIFF Tagged Image File Format. A tag-based image format. TIFF is designed to promote universal interchanges of digital images.

Timestamp bot A Timestamp bot is replaced by the date and time the page was last edited or automatically updated.

To Do List The FrontPage program that maintains a list of the tasks required to complete a web. To complete a task on the list, click on it; the program required to do the task starts up with the correct file opened.

Toolbar The tool bar is a set of buttons bound to commonly used FrontPage Editor or FrontPage Explorer commands to provide quick access.

Transparency The process of making a color in a GIF image not appear, thus allowing whatever is underneath the image (i.e., in the image's background) to show through.

Typewriter font The text style that emulates fixed pitch typewritten text. Every character in this font is the same width. Typewriter font is useful for computer code examples and for presenting sample input from the user. Formatted text paragraphs always use the typewriter font.

U

Undo Command The Undo command reverses the effect of the last change to a page.

URL Uniform Resource Locator. A string that supplies the address of a resource on the network and the method by which it can be accessed. URLs can be of various protocols. An HTTP URL links to a web page. Other commonly used URLs include Gopher, which links to an Internet Gopher directory, and FTP, which links to a file on an FTP server.

V

Visited link A link on a page that has been selected. Visited links are usually displayed at runtime in a unique color.

W

Web browser A program that retrieves web pages over the World Wide Web and displays the pages as hypertext, with embedded images.

Web name The name of the web. A web name corresponds to a directory name on a web server and is subject to the length, character restrictions, and case sensitivity of that server.

Web title A descriptive name for a web. The web title is displayed in the title bar of the Front Page Explorer window when the web is open. A web title must start with a letter and can have a maximum of 31 characters.

Web A home page and all its associated pages, files, and images.

Webmaster The person at an organization in charge of running that organization's intranet or Internet resources.

Wide area network (WAN) A group of computers and other devices that are interconnected over geographically separated areas.

Wizard A wizard creates pages and webs for you by asking questions about the features you would like to include on those pages and webs. After a page or web is created using a wizard, you can modify the page or web.

WMF Windows MetaFile. A collection of device-independent functions that represent an image. Commonly used to pass images on the Windows clipboard.

World Wide Web A distributed Internet hypertext application that uses the http protocol to retrieve text and other data.

WPG WordPerfect raster-image file format.

WYSIWYG What You See Is What You Get. An editing style in which the file being created is displayed as it will appear to the end-user.

INDEX

Page numbers in italics refer to figures.

F

J

K

L

M

N

O

P

R

S

Kerry A. Lehto has been working with personal computers since the Commodore Vic-20 days in the early '80s. His work history intertwines various interests, including writing and editing in computing, archaeology, and journalism. He also has taught English grammar, coauthored a corporate archaeological style guide, and worked "Grasshopper Patrol" in Wyoming for the USDA. From his home in Kirkland, Washington, he writes for Microsoft's World Wide Web site and offers Internet consulting and business writing seminars through his business, KL Communications. He has a BA in Journalism from the University of Wyoming (go Pokes) and an MA in Journalism from the University of Oregon (go Ducks). When not putting out fires in his automobiles, he plays lots of 9-ball, delves into past-life research, and heads to the Cascades and the Olympic Mountains whenever he can in his green CJ-7.

W. Brett Polonsky has more than 10 years of experience in award-winning graphic design and art direction. He contributed hands-on work to the design and layout of the first two books in Microsoft Press's Ultimate series, the *Ultimate MS-DOS* and *Ultimate Microsoft Office* books. Self-taught in computers, he learned to compute on early Macintoshes and Pagemaker 1.0, and has climbed the ladder to high-end HTML authoring and Web publishing. He currently contracts as a producer in Microsoft's Web Applications Group, creating intranets, Internet sites, and multimedia titles. He lives with his wife, Janell, and his two children, Gage and Emma, in Kirkland, Washington. When not busy with work or family life, he enjoys breaking an occasional 9-ball rack.

Together, the authors offer FrontPage training courses and intranet consulting via their newly formed enterprise, the Kerrett Media Group (KMG).

The manuscript for this book was prepared and submitted to Microsoft Press in electronic form. Galleys were prepared using Microsoft Word for Windows 95. Pages were composed using Pagemaker 5.0 for Windows, with text type in Sabon and display type in Syntax. Composed pages were delivered to the printer as electronic prepress files.

Cover Graphic Designer
Greg Erickson

Cover Illustrator
Scott Baker

Interior Graphic Design & Photography
Polonsky Design

Illustrator
David Holter

Layout Artist
W. Brett Polonsky

Proofreader
Tami Beaumont

Indexer
Leslie Leland Frank

All-Around Great Guy
Kerry A. Lehto